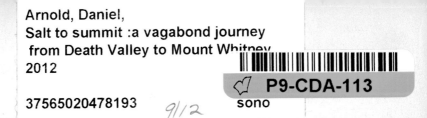

SALT TO SUMMIT

A Vagabond Journey *from*
Death Valley to Mount Whitney

DANIEL ARNOLD

COUNTERPOINT / BERKELEY

To Ashley and Sage

ISBN: 978-1-58243-750-7

Map by Courtney Laird

The following photographs are used courtesy of County of Inyo, Eastern California Museum: Page 116, UNK 498f-Shorty Harris, Death Valley; Page 152, KERR 8a—George Hansen; Page 216, RAM 2824—Alabama Gates Occupation, 1924. On Page 207, the photograph of Mary Austin and Wallace Austin, 1891, is reproduced by permission of the Huntington Library, San Marino, California. All photographs are by Daniel Arnold unless otherwise noted

Interior design by Neuwirth & Associates, Inc.
Cover design by Michel Vrana

COUNTERPOINT
1919 Fifth Street
Berkeley, CA 94710

www.counterpointpress.com

Distributed by Publishers Group West

10 9 8 7 6 5 4 3 2 1

CONTENTS

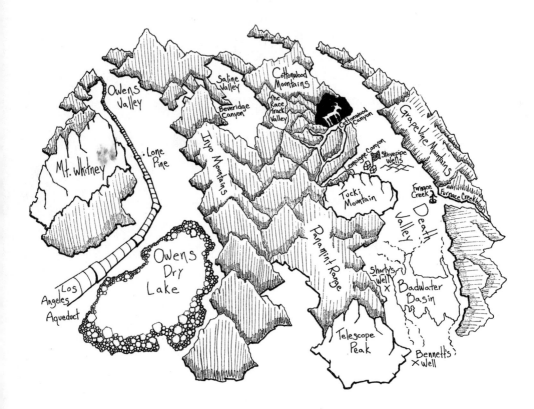

SALT
TO
SUMMIT

Badwater Basin, Day 1

CLIMB YOUR MOUNTAIN FROM THE BOTTOM

Badwater Basin, the sink in the center of Death Valley, is 282 feet below sea level. It is a vast salt pan, the lowest and hottest place in the Western Hemisphere. Getting pinched between the salt and the sun there feels like hanging out in a jerking oven. It's the apocalypse as written by a banana slug.

Due west and a little north, Mount Whitney rises 14,505 feet above sea level. The top edge of the granite crest that cuts California lengthwise into western farm valleys and eastern deserts, its summit is the highest point in the contiguous United States. The upper mountain, a 2,000-foot-high arrowhead of bare granite and snow, points straight up. The blue-gray stone looks unreal from down in the orange and brown below. Eighty air miles separates the summit from the salt.

It wasn't long after I began climbing mountains as a teenager that I first heard of this convergence of mountain and desert. I remember thinking, this must be the perfect way to climb a mountain. Start at the very bottom, and end at the very top. What more could a mountaineer want? The first person to whom I ever mentioned the idea was a graying, wooly-bearded geology professor who had spent some time in the desert. He looked at me in a fatherly way and said something like, "If you think the Sierra is badass, just wait till you're in the desert ranges." Which I took to mean, *Kid, you won't even get far enough to get yourself into trouble.* In the desert, that isn't very far at all.

So I spent years wandering around Death Valley, climbing its canyons and peaks, crossing its dunes and salt flats. The Big Project continued to rattle around in the back of my mind. I came to know Death Valley well and to appreciate the land separating the salt and the mountain as more than just the distance in between. This is the most rugged part of the basin and range, where the peaks and troughs crest highest and dip lowest. The land has personality: reticent, unforgiving, but also a bewitching storyteller when you listen to it, full of magic and beauty and tragedy. I began to see the salt and the summit as the ornaments on either side of the central character: the desert.

The juxtaposition of Badwater and Whitney was noticed in gold rush times, as soon as the first surveyors began to circulate the freakish elevations they had calculated. Josiah Whitney, the geologist enshrined by name on the mountain, gloated enthusiastically over the geographic wonders of California. Newspapers across the border in Nevada criticized the surveying work done, though their complaints focused more on the immodesty of one state claiming both the highest and the lowest points in the country for itself. Years later, when the road connecting Badwater with the Owens Valley was completed, John Crowley, a Catholic priest and booster of all things Eastern Californian, organized an elaborate ceremony involving wagons, cars, an Indian runner, and an airplane relaying a gourd of snowmelt down to the brine at Badwater. Norman Clyde, famous Sierra mountaineer, also took notice of the desert and claimed an odd kind of speed record for himself by starting a stopwatch atop Mount Whitney, racing down the eleven-mile Whitney Trail, jumping into a friend's car at Whitney Portal, and driving to the dunes at Stovepipe Wells in just over seven hours. Now, each July, the Badwater Ultramarathon is run in the opposite direction, and the cars carry only the gallons of Cytomax and kilos of food consumed by the runners along the way.

The thread of asphalt linking Badwater Basin to Mount Whitney is the fastest way to get from one to the other. It's also the least interesting. The road avoids entire mountain ranges and dodges immense canyons. By its very nature, it smooths over the jagged edges of the land—the exact edges I most wanted to get under my skin. I wanted to cross the desert mountains and crawl through the bottom of those canyons, so I planned a different route.

Roads and trails were out. I would avoid anything designed to make travel easy or fast. And I would go at a time of year when the desert would burn and the mountain would freeze. I chose April, hoping for triple-digit temperatures at Badwater and deep snow on Whitney. I wanted to be hot, to be cold, to rub my nose in the largest uninterrupted wildness I could find. I expected the crossing to take two or three weeks. In that time, I imagined, I'd pass through all four seasons. This is the story of a journey through extremes, walking across land that magnifies heat, climbing wind-haunted mountains, wandering canyons where geologic time is laid bare.

Though I traveled alone and off-trail, I had the company of an eccentric group of local ghosts. Long before air-conditioning blunted the summer and fast cars offered instant escape, a handful of inspired lunatics tried to make this country home. This place is undeniably hostile to life, and yet it worked powerfully on the imaginations of certain dreamers, vagabonds, and misfits. More than a story of passing through, this is also a story of trying to stay, of people drawn to the harshest landscape in the American West and held here when the desert got into their blood.

Out in the arid country, the land speaks. Voices leak from the dunes and mining camps, the creosotes and mountains. The more I listen, the more I want to hear. Beware the sun and wide-open distances, guard your water and your sanity, lose yourself in the rocks and canyons, and you'll find the words in the silence.

Chapter 1

HITCHHIKING
IS CARBON NEUTRAL

All told, I have had little travel in my life which has yielded so much profit on the exertion as the old Mojave stage. I understand that the road is well furnished now with gas stations and hot-dog stands, and the trip can be made in a few hours without incident. Which seems on the whole a pity.

—Mary Hunter Austin, *Earth Horizon*, 1932

I began on the corner of Torrance Boulevard and the Pacific Coast Highway, a convergence of a dozen lanes heavy with midday traffic. I had grown out my beard as sunblock. My pants were old favorites, stitched and patched and faded to the color of the desert itself. I carried a gigantic backpack stuffed with empty two-liter soda bottles that I would fill with water when I reached Furnace Creek. The driver of the Torrance 3 let me on without a second glance—I was not the strangest thing floating around the Los Angeles County mass-transit system.

The bus bumped us all along past strip malls and concrete. At the corner of Torrance and Hawthorne, as I waited for a second bus, a kid with a skateboard and baggy corduroy shorts looked me up and down. "Been traveling long?" he asked, at last. I should have said *yes* or *all my life*, but instead I tried to explain that I lived just down the road. "Uh-huh," he said. He seemed dubious but willing to believe that I might be speaking in some kind of interesting code.

Today's highways run straight dead sprints across the desert, slowing only through parade lines of neon-bright food and gas marts. For most people, the Mojave slips by unrecognized—a whisper of air-conditioning, a blur of orange outside the glass. When Mary Austin rolled along the rutted tracks of the sage country, she had time to talk to fellow travelers and study the character of the strange, parched land to which she had come by accident and stayed for fifteen years. Though the modern asphalt web would disappoint her, the stagecoaches still do exist in a form she might find passably entertaining. From my tiny apartment near the ocean, it took me two city buses to cross Los Angeles, a commuter train to escape over the San Gabriel Mountains to Lancaster, and two county buses to curve around the western edge of the Mojave through towns like Inyokern and Olancha.

I have a feeling Austin would have much to say about Lancaster. She knew this patch of ground in the 1880s, when she was a young woman and it was wide open and called the Antelope Valley for a reason. Now Lancaster has filled the space with the kind of ragged-edged crossroads city that fascinated Austin, though I imagine its hungry sprawl would horrify her, too. Lancaster peters out into flat space, the Mojave beginning right where the concrete ends; the light is orange-yellow and flat as the ground, the wind hits the train station with a will to knock it down. But Los Angeles is just over the hill. The local kids waiting for the Bakersfield bus could just as easily have been standing on a corner in Torrance, draped in their plated gold, baseball caps and ear-cigarettes turned backward, elaborate portraits of the Virgin silk-screened on their shirts.

I'd like to have had Mary Austin with me, to see her in action extracting stories from the other passengers. She had an insatiable need for other people's experiences and would go to any length to unearth a tale. Fortunately for her, she was the kind of listener to whom people felt compelled to spill their souls, no matter the contents. Shepherds, priests, Paiutes, mining stiffs and wandering prospectors, spouses (usually wives) abandoned for one sort of desert fever or another—she talked to all of them, and all of them talked to Mary, along with the coyotes, quail, and elf owls, too. She sifted the grains she was given, tossed the dross, hoarded the glints of color, and fused them into the rich composites of people and places with which she filled her books.

Out by Ridgecrest, a little sun-blasted city which to me has always looked in imminent danger of being swallowed whole by the Mojave, I met a woman who climbed mountains in the Sierra in the 1950s and 1960s and had had a passing acquaintance with Norman Clyde. A man from Riverside told me about life as a GI in Germany during the Cuban Missile Crisis, when it seemed the world might end in fire on any given afternoon. As a kid, he chummed with a half-tame raven his brother named Black Bart. Mary Austin would have liked this part of his story. She wrote affectionately about a raven in a Shoshone camp—the bird could practically speak and was treated as another kind of child.

Mary Austin liked nothing better than a long stagecoach ride because on the stage, with nothing to do but talk and watch the world lurch by, the stories came for free. And when the other passengers were dull, or asleep, or too fleshy or tubercular, there was always the driver up on the box in the wind and dust, and he was invariably a salty fountain of happenings and lore. In a car, the drive would have taken me four hours. By bus and train, it took eleven. I didn't mind. Sometimes when I drive to the Sierra, I arrive feeling like my brain hasn't left Los Angeles. There is something octopus-like about the concrete, the immense, curving arms of the overpasses. The city's grip loosens slowly. Puttering on the bus through the desert outskirts allows time for the asphalt to thin and the land to open wide. The creosotes multiply to the horizon and the first Joshua trees shake their jester hats in the wind. There's time for me to come up for air.

No buses run through Death Valley proper. The closest I could get on public wheels was the town of Lone Pine, just under the Sierra Crest, in sight of Mount Whitney. It was the end of March, and the mountain was shaggy with ice and snow. The driver let me off, I walked a few hundred feet down two-lane Highway 136, planted myself under the sign that read FURNACE CREEK 102, and stuck out my thumb.

At the end of the nineteenth century, Mary Austin made her home in the Owens Valley, here in Lone Pine, and north a few miles in Independence and Bishop—farming towns, limited to the water in the creeks spilling off the east side of the mountains. Rain was an anomaly that couldn't be counted on. More prominently, at least to Austin, these places were also mining towns in decline, forever teetering on the edge of the global silver market. A few points up, and the mines turned a profit, the workers were paid, the streets were lively. A few points down, and the ore cost more to pull out of the ground than it was worth, and the wives and children left at home went hungry. California was fifty years old as a state, but this was its far corner. Paiutes lived in a camp above Lone Pine. Down in town, Mexican holdouts tended white adobe houses and gardens full of peppers. Each September, they celebrated Mexico's independence from Spain, just as they had before the Bear Flag Revolt turned California over to America.

The Owens Valley towns are the western edge of Austin's gritty, beautiful, half-real, half-mythic Land of Little Rain, her name for the place and her most famous book. The region extends east and south through Death Valley with only one definite border: the mountain wall to the west, where the dry country begins. The Sierra Nevada reaches so high that its peaks catch all the moisture rolling off the Pacific. By the time clouds float over the crest, they are spent shells worth nothing but a momentary shade patch before they shrivel in the sun and vanish. The Sierra also marks the beginning of the basin and range. The Owens Valley is not a true valley—not made by the passage of water and ice—but rather a basin made by the movement of continents. The land stretched, the mountain ranges pulled apart, and deep troughs opened between them. Standing under the Furnace Creek road sign at the bottom of the Owens basin, I could look west at summits fourteen thousand feet high on the Sierra Crest, or east at summits eleven thousand feet high on the Inyo Crest. East of the Inyos were more desert mountains—the Cottonwoods, the Panamints—and beyond them, Death Valley and the salt.

I don't have much luck as a hitchhiker. Something about the dark beard and big shoulders, I guess. To be fair, I'm not 100 percent sure I'd pick myself up. I tried to be friendly—I smiled and waved and pointed at my backpack, hoping to suggest that roadside serial killers don't go for the Gregory brand. Some people smiled and waved back, which I had a hard time interpreting. Most looked uncomfortable, as if eye contact alone might infect them from the roadside. None so much as slowed except for a pleasant man with a sun-lined face who was only going up the road to Keeler but stopped anyway to chat a moment and wish me luck.

An hour passed, then two. Two immense Vs of geese ribboned across the sky, headed north again. The sun disappeared behind the Sierra, turning the crest into a ragged silhouette, painting the Inyos crimson and purple. I began to eye the buggy, mucky pastures behind the roadside barbed wire. They looked uninviting, and getting more so as it looked increasingly likely that I'd be bedding down among the cow pies.

I didn't care. I was free and happy. No car to feed, no water caches to worry over, no schedule to keep. I was as self-contained as I could hope to be, and my plan was scratch-paper simple. (It was H.W. Tilman, as far as I know, who first suggested that the ideal expedition could be organized in a minute on the back of an envelope.) I had cracked open the door on a new adventure, and I hadn't needed to burn a thousand dollars or gallons of gas to get here.

A dented white pickup materialized out of the dusk and stopped on the shoulder. The driver, a chiseled guy with straight blond hair to his shoulders, jumped out to ask if I needed a ride. Aidan, it turned out, was a climbing guide who'd worked in South America, piloted bush planes in Alaska, done first ascents in China. He told me stories from his recent efforts in East Tibet—blizzards, unstable snow, fragile cornices—and we compared notes on ridge traverses in the Sierra. He was driving straight through Death Valley on his way to Red Rocks outside Las Vegas. We talked mountains and climbers, gossiping like two old hens about the latest successes and divorces within the climbing tribe. He was enthusiastic about my project, and I told him he would be welcome to join me; but there was a woman, also a guide, in Salt Lake City, and he might or might not be falling in love with her, and he had to go find out.

Mary Austin would have been proud of us. We passed the news like a couple of Shoshones or Death Valley miners. The farmers who worked the Owens Valley didn't much interest Austin. Her Land of Little Rain was peopled with nomads. She felt a kinship of circumstance with shepherds and miners who had no fixed place. Her notion of a stable home had crumbled into the Owens dust when she was all but abandoned by a husband who had proved incompetent in all the ways that mattered. Besides, wanderers told the best stories. In her desert writing, tales ricochet back and forth faster than the drifters who tell them. On the vagabond network, legends became living truths.

Aidan drove us up out of the Owens Valley, through the gap between the Inyo and Argus Ranges, past the Darwin Plateau, down into Panamint Valley. He had spent some time in the desert himself. He remembered hearing years ago about a pair who crossed Badwater Basin and deployed snowshoes for the salt marsh on the western edge. This piece of news didn't thrill me. In my last days at home, I had obsessed over the Badwater salt marsh. Its dimensions changed with each new story I heard. Sometimes the whim of the desert produced a narrow strip of mud, sometimes a quarter mile of hip-high muck and neck-high brine. It changed from season to season and, as best I could figure, from week to week. In the end, I decided to bring an extra pair of boots for the marsh—the rattiest I had—to avoid spending the next four days walking around in mud bricks. And I decided to stop worrying about it. But snowshoes! I had images of being mired like a mastodon and preserved for the benefit of future archaeologists. Salt Man Discovered! I asked if Aidan had an inner tube I could borrow to keep my gear afloat. He suggested I try the solo alpinist's glacier-crossing trick and walk in the middle of an aluminum ladder, but he didn't have one of those either.

It was a new-moon night, so it felt black and late when Aidan dropped me off at the Furnace Creek ranger station and the water spigot. The mountains to the east and west were invisible except where their jagged tops cut sharp outlines against the heavy dust of stars. I pulled out my bottles—twenty-one liters in all—and queued them next to the faucet, where I filled them one by one.

Knowing that I would begin with forty-six pounds of water alone made me pare everything else back. For extra clothes I had a long-sleeved T-shirt, a second pair of socks, and a wind shell—no jacket. I had a bivy sack—a nylon envelope that fits around a sleeping bag—instead of a tent. I planned on using rocks instead of toilet paper. Still, I needed food, and my camera bag weighed five pounds, and there were the extra boots, and somehow I had ended up with three books: a wildflower guide because it was the middle of the spring bloom and two novels. Add in the bits and pieces—compass, map, toothbrush, notebook, seventy-foot length of cord for lowering my pack into the canyons—and I had something like eighty-five pounds riding my back as I left the spigot. Stumbling around in the dark, feeling like a newly saddled donkey, I nicknamed my backpack "the goblin." I imagined a flabby toad creature with its arms around my neck and its feet wrapped around my waist, spurs dug into my hips, grunting, *Onward! Onward!*

Badwater still waited twenty miles down the road. I had one more round of hitchhiking and it wasn't going to happen until morning. It felt like the middle of the night, though I had no idea what time it really was. I hadn't brought a watch. I wasn't worried about the ounces; I just didn't want to know the hour or even the day beyond what the sun could tell me. There was a campground at Furnace Creek, but it was filled with RVs and wood smoke—a peculiar odor on an eighty-plus-degree night. I staggered out into the desert and found a convenient sand-bottomed ditch to stretch out in.

I was tired and wired all at once. The sky glowed pale, and the desert buzzed in my ears. I tossed around on my patch of sand, hearing noises that were probably just my mind creaking as it uncoiled. Mary Austin tells the story of a miner who, at the end of sixty years of prospecting, makes one last little strike and decides to quit the Death Valley country and move to the city for an easier life. He returned to the desert in two months, explaining to Austin that every time he walked out the door in the city, there was a house "right bung up against" his eyes. More than anything else, the desert offers space. Vast, uncorked, drown-if-you-don't-breathe-it-in *space*.

▲

My eyes popped open at the first hint of light. The air was five-in-the-morning cool and felt light and clean. A number of years back, on a February morning at five thousand feet in the Grapevine Mountains north of Death Valley, I watched water in my bottle turn to ice in the twenty minutes between first light and sunrise. Now the early-morning decline simply allowed a moment of relief—like a quick, cold shower—before the sun revved up the day.

I stuffed my sleeping bag into my pack and got the goblin up and mounted on my back. We tottered down the road together to the end of the Furnace Creek enclave, where the goblin took a seat and I resumed my roadside vigil from the night before. I spent an hour on the receiving end of a lot of downright hostile looks from middle-aged guys with neck wattles and wives done up shiny like the cars they drove. True enough, it's a long way to anywhere from the side of the road south of Furnace Creek—a committing place to pick up a hitcher.

The sun topped the Funeral Mountains and set about igniting the day. Stones made the ground, billions of jagged, desert-varnished chunks all jigged together in the top layer. There is sand in Death

Valley, and there is salt, but mostly this place is built of rock: dry stone mountains shedding their bodies piece by piece into the basins below. Along the road, miraculous yellow sunflowers on foot-high stems sprouted from between the stones—miraculous because they apparently needed neither dirt nor rain. The flower fields stretched down toward the salt and up toward the mountains, an immense multitude of little suns looking back up at the big sun above. Close by, I watched a three-inch green caterpillar with black tiger stripes and a spike like a rose thorn sticking out of its rear rip into one of the flowers, massive mandibles slicing and chewing. It hardly seemed fair to grow straight out of stone in the middle of the desert only to be devoured by a dinosaur caterpillar with the soul of a chipper-shredder, but Death Valley is a hard place.

The campground stirred to life. A few people walked along the road admiring the sunflowers. I made a point of talking to every one of them as they passed by. One friendly man with a white walrus moustache asked me where I was going. When I told him Badwater Basin, he said, "Why? There's nothing there!" The more I thought about it, the more I liked his way of summing up the place. "Sure," I said. "It's the deepest pile of nothing on this side of the planet." Put this way, the idea seemed to grow on him, too. An hour later, he was back with two friends in an enormous pickup to offer me a ride.

We sped down the last bit of road, moving fast according to the odometer, but slow relative to the desert. One of the driver's friends said he couldn't judge distance here. Five miles to a bend in the road would turn out to be twenty; then he'd get tricked the other way and a far distant hill would come right up alongside the truck in just a few minutes. The same thing happens to me. There's nothing to pin a scale line to, no visual guides in the basins below the mountains. In other landscapes, lakes and hills and zones of flora along the way provide natural mileposts. Here you can spend the better part of a day walking straight toward your destination in the company of the same rocks, creosotes, and sunflowers you started out with.

At the Badwater pullout—a wide spot in the road with an outhouse built like a bomb shelter and some interpretive signs—a middle-aged woman with short, curly hair and perfect posture asked if I had been the hitchhiker at Furnace Creek. She was terribly sorry she hadn't picked me up, but her backseats were folded down. She waved one hand at a great hulk of silver Lexus and I noted that yes, indeed, her rear seats *were* folded down. I asked her if she would put a letter in the mail for me instead. In my notebook I had ten prestamped postcards all addressed to my wife. I had gotten this notion from the original Sierra mountaineers, who spent summers in the mountains and communicated with their families by passing mail along to anyone they encountered. I was curious to see if the same idea would work a hundred years later or whether my postcards would end up wrapped around chewing gum wads and forgotten. I wrote Ashley a quick note saying I'd made it to Badwater and passed the card to the woman, who handled it as if it were a precious artifact. I felt pretty confident Ashley would get that letter.

Meanwhile, the sun ratcheted higher into the sky. The morning had melted into dragon breath. I could practically feel the air crackle as it rubbed past me. My pupils shrank to pinholes against the glare off Badwater, and the light still seemed to hit the back of my skull. The people at the pullout returned to their wheeled refrigerators and rolled away. But I was done for a time with the world of concrete and machines. I picked up the goblin and stepped out onto the salt.

Chapter 2

——

DEATH VALLEY

I thought of the bounteous stock of bread and beans upon
my father's table, to say nothing about all the other good
things, and here was I, the oldest son, away out in the center
of the Great American Desert, with an empty stomach and a
dry and parched throat.

—William Lewis Manly, *Death Valley in '49*, 1894

Salt-walking below sea level on a hot day in Death Valley feels like
wandering through a fever dream. The sun has incinerated the
surface of this place—burned off the plants, boiled off the water,
stripped it down until what's left is an abstraction of a landscape. I
was an ant on the bottom of a stone box: a floor of salt, two walls
of rock, and a lid of hot, heavy sun. In a half hour, the near shore,
where I had begun, fuzzed out, leaving only a line between white
and brown an indeterminate distance away. The far shore looked
the same, a distant line that could have been one, five, or fifteen
miles off. I walked, but the horizon never budged. My eyes told
me that I might as well be standing still.

The author on the salt.

Beyond the edge of Badwater, the surface of the salt cracked into hexagons and pentagons. The edges looked furry with salt hair. Salt water percolates up through the cracks between the plates. When it evaporates, fresh particles of salt get left behind. As the plates expand and press against each other, their outer edges curl, making saucers, hundreds of thousands of them. Between the saucers, threads of fresh salt grow out sideways.

I took a break after an hour and sat by the goblin in a five-foot saucer of salt. This seemed wrong. Salt is supposed to come on saucers; serving up lightly broiled human on crockery made of salt sounded like something from down the rabbit hole. If I quieted my breathing, I could hear the salt flex in the sun. *Creak. Pop.* Eerie sounds, almost musical. I looked back the way I'd come and tried, at first, to figure out how far I'd walked, but then gave up and stared at the mountains instead.

Death Valley isn't just low; it's deep. To the west, the Panamints top out at the summit of Telescope Peak, 11,300 feet above the salt; to the east, the Black Mountains gain 6,600 feet. The Grand Canyon, averaging about a mile deep, would rattle around in Badwater Basin like a walnut in its shell. There are no foothills here. The mountains jump straight off the basin floor, steep and bare. The geology is a carnival show of colors and species of stone. The Black Mountains alone sport hundred-million-year-old granite, billion-year-old gneiss, and garish, million-year-old mixes of sedimentary and volcanic rock colored green, orange, tan, and pink.

The salt sits uneasily in the mind. Legends of all kinds crop up in old stories: thin crusts over ponds of alkali dust, like bad ice on a lake; pickled bodies trapped under blocks of clear salt; poison gases leaking up from below. Back on my feet, I lurched from saucer to saucer. I couldn't shake the feeling that I was too deep to be breathing regular air. Unruly corners of my brain wondered if I was underwater. Maybe I was drowning. A psychological trick, maybe, but the atmosphere felt thick down there. And I couldn't help noticing that I was walking on the bottom of what was once a gigantic lake.

Fifteen thousand years ago, I'd have been under something like three hundred feet of water; a few hundred thousand years ago, the water might have been twice that deep. Strandlines and remnant beaches on the sides of the Panamints and Black Mountains suggest ghostly shores. The ice age cycle poured rivers off the eastern Sierra that overran the Land of Little Rain. A string of lakes in presently dry basins ended in Death Valley, where the water had nowhere left to go. Even now, water survives the trip to Badwater.

It arrives underground, flowing through sand and gravel below the outwardly dry riverbed of the Amargosa. It trickles through pores below the skin of the Panamints, licking salts off the rocks along the way. Water oozes around in the mud below the surface of Badwater until it's burned off by the sun, leaving behind the minerals it carted through the desert. The salt flats trace perfect outlines of a wet landscape. Creeks, shorelines, even deltas are all easy to see from above and made of glittering white.

In the middle of Badwater, I floundered through a square mile of upheaval where sheets of salt crust buckled up like pressure ridges in pack ice. Telescope Peak filled the sky. The vertical difference between the top and me was just a few hundred feet shy of the basecamp-to-summit rise of Mount Everest. Snow capped the Telescope's last thousand feet. The view looked scrambled, like something from a hall of mirrors. Salt below, snow above—two strips of white with an 11,000-foot wall of bare desert in between. I've been up there. One November, I climbed from the western edge of Badwater to the Telescope's top with an old friend. On the mountain, we worked through zones of rock and flora: cottonwoods and grapevine in blue dolomite, prickly pear and sage between quartz monzonite boulders, loose shale and the inverted tree line of pinyon pine and juniper. Coming down in the dark by headlamp, we passed under the spectral green eyeshine of a mountain lion watching us from a ledge.

Badwater's far shore shimmered into view. One moment it was vague and tomorrow-ish, and the next I could see rocks and individual mesquites. The west side is the "wet" side of the basin. All throughout the spring, the snow on Telescope Peak melts and leaks down through the underground capillaries, and where it collects in Badwater, it smooths out the salt. The saucers faded away and other shapes appeared. I crossed long sections of corduroy

Upheaval in the salt.

ridges. Salt peas, like pellets of snow, crunched underfoot. Fumaroles and blowholes punctured plates of salt. I imagined steaming water vapor burping up from below. Long crystals of clear salt filled cracks in dry mud. The mud turned liquid, and I sank laces deep, then ankle deep, but just as my boots disappeared and the mire began crawling up my shins, I found enough resistance to support me (and the goblin). We squelched forward. The goblin hissed in my ear not to drop him. I told the flabby whiner that if we went in, we'd go in together.

The salt ebbed into a strip of soft alkali soil, like a sponge underfoot. Shin-high pickleweeds clumped up every five feet. Not much else can handle the soapy soil at the edge, where salt meets desert, and pickleweed, at least in Death Valley, grows only here in the alkali margins. It has evolved to populate this one narrow zone, and then it's gone. The tiny pickles, which are really the plant's leaves rolled up into warty, drought-busting cylinders, are reputed to be nutritious. I found them briny and gelatinous and didn't stop to graze.

Mesquites crowded the rocky soil at the edge of the alkali, their dilemma visible from their position on the desert chessboard. Water pools underground at the bottom of the basin, and mesquites are thirsty plants—but they can't live on salt the way pickleweed can. They gather as close to the water as they can get without crossing the alkali line. Mesquites have immense root systems, blind fingers groping through the flesh of the desert. Their taproots can grow a hundred feet long. As with so much in the desert, we only see the visible tuft, while the real work goes on out of sight, away from the sun. Those roots must have been finding something good at the edge of Badwater because the local mesquites were electric green, almost glowing.

I stopped and tried to wriggle deep enough under a mesquite to get something between me and the sun. Trucked in fresh and juicy from the Pacific, I already felt cooked. On the salt, there had been nowhere to hide—the sun pressed down on me from above and rebounded off the endless white to dazzle me from below. The only shelter I'd had all day was my own hat. I was ready to lie down in some shade and rest my back and brain.

I squirmed around and cozied up with the mesquite thorns. I still couldn't escape. The mesquite stood fifteen feet high, solid green—you'd think it would have a cool hollow somewhere under its branches. But the sun came right through the spindly wood and feathery leaves, as if they were specifically designed to make heat and light miss. Which, of course, they were. Plants in the desert desiccate just like animals, and they answer with spines and cylinders and skinny leaves with less grip for wind and sun.

Possibly it was hotter under the mesquite than out on the desert. It felt that way. Temperatures here tend to increase the closer a thermometer moves to the ground. The Death Valley record at head height, in the shade, is 134 degrees Fahrenheit, but ground temperatures have been measured as high as 200 degrees. Lying down to rest may be the worst thing to do. At least if I were walking, I'd have something to distract myself from the uncomfortable sensation of my brain floating away. So I got myself upright again and walked uphill through sand and rock. A huge water mirage, like a paused tidal wave, hovered over the salt to the south. I emerged near Shorty's Well, which might still be a well if you had a shovel and six hours to kill, but for all practical purposes it is a giant sandbox filled with mesquites.

Several springs and old wells leak out of Badwater's perimeter, though it's hard to know which trickles the desert will reclaim in any given season. Several miles south of Shorty's Well is Bennett's Well, where the Bennett and Arcane families waited and starved for nearly a month in January and February 1850. They were the stragglers of the mass westward migration of 1849. Fifty thousand forty-niners crossed to California overland that year. A few hundred of them arrived in Salt Lake City too late in the summer to cross the Sierra Nevada near Lake Tahoe. Instead of attempting the already infamous Donner Pass up north, they pointed their wagons south down the Old Spanish Trail, which was nothing more than a horse track through the Mojave with bad feed and long, dry stretches leading eventually to the little town of Los Angeles. Only one wagon had ever made the crossing by that route, but the emigrants had dreams of gold and nightmares about Mormons, whom they considered suspicious and vengeful. The Bennetts and Arcanes joined a large train of over a hundred wagons that moved out of Salt Lake City in early autumn.

A map surfaced in the wagon train with a tale to tell of a shortcut. In the nineteenth century, these maps floated around the West like bad genies. This one offered already-weary pioneers a savings of five hundred miles off the Spanish Trail. Speculation ran wild through the train—no one could talk of anything else. At night, the men lit bonfires and gave speeches, a singularly futile exercise since none of them knew anything about the country and all they had to debate were a few lines on a piece of paper owned by a man who had never traveled the route in question. The Reverend J.W. Brier, heading to California with his wife and three children, gave the shortcut his impassioned benediction. Maybe he fancied himself Moses and dreamed of being led through the desert by a pillar of fire. Captain Hunt, the man the pioneers had hired to lead them down the Spanish Trail and the only man among them familiar with the land, advised that the shortcut would more likely lead right to hell.

At the cutoff the map described, the train divided. Some waited until the last minute to decide whether to pull their oxen left or right. At first, a large majority chose the shortcut, but a few days of uncertainty and untracked wilderness cooled their enthusiasm, and most turned back around to rejoin the Spanish Trail. Emigrants in twenty-seven wagons remained to pursue the route so clear on the map and in their minds. That the lines on the map bore no resemblance at all to the land was almost beside the point. They put their faith in what *ought* to be—in their understanding of lines created by men or God or purblind hope—but not in the land.

Green growing things shriveled away as they pressed further west. They could feel the land becoming dry, sparse, burnt. Lake mirages in empty basins tricked them over and over. Water eluded them. They had no native desert sense. Occasionally they would intercept an Indian and try to extract directions to Owens Lake from their captive. This was a preposterous question. The lake was still several hundred miles away and blockaded by desert mountains. The hijacked Indian would generally provide a vague gesture and then run away at the first opportunity—an eminently sane response to the appearance of scores of pale people dragging carts directly toward the most barren place on the continent.

They passed through what is now southern Nevada. What began as an almost soldierly train with divisions and marching orders became a ragged band of half-starved individuals pushing forward because they did not think they could make it back. They split apart into smaller units and spread out so that their animals might have some chance of finding feed. And they split apart so that they would feel less moral obligation to strangers. The families—the Bennetts, Arcanes, and Briers—were shunned because it was expected that the women and children might start to die. The single men did not want to be torn between their sympathies and their lives. All of them began to abandon their belongings: tools, furniture, objects of value hauled nine-tenths of the distance across the continent, now worse than useless.

In small groups they funneled through a gap between the Black and Funeral Ranges and rolled down into Death Valley. Down below sea level, the Jayhawkers, an outfit of mostly young Illinoisans, slaughtered their remaining oxen and burned their wagons to smoke the meat. Their camp was dismal: lost and frightened men, fires burning all day and night, ox carcasses that were little more than bags of bones. The men fashioned backpacks and rawhide moccasins and hoped to escape over the mountains to the west on foot. One speculated that they had found the very place where God turned Lot's wife into a pillar of salt. The Bugsmashers—a group from Georgia and Mississippi—also left

Death Valley on foot. The Bennetts and Arcanes clung to their wagons for the sake of their children. The two families crossed the bottom of the valley and turned south, looking for a wagon pass through the Panamints. They followed a wide canyon wash high up above Badwater, but their oxen stalled out on the steep upgrade. Cliffs blocked the way through the next canyon south. The disappointment nearly undid them—they had truly believed they were about to cross the mountains and descend into a fertile land of fruit trees and gold. There was no grass or water in sight, and they had to retreat back to the springs at the edge of Badwater.

I left Shorty's Well and walked uphill, trading mesquites for creosotes where the land began to climb up off the valley floor. I crossed a dirt road, put it out of sight behind me, then turned north and passed through yellow-blooming creosote and open desert. The first whites may have seen a blasted barrens, but in fact I was walking through an ancient pharmacopoeia. Shoshones used creosote as a cure-all. Pulverized leaves acted as an antibiotic for open wounds, and bitter teas made of boiled stems and leaves treated colds, stomach distempers, tuberculosis, and cancer (though the lignans in creosote also appear to be toxic to the kidneys). Creosotes look arranged: the plants stand at a regimented distance, here roughly fifteen feet apart. But the pattern amounts to nothing up close, the way impressionistic paintings become smudges at a few inches. I felt hypnotized by the silent crowd. Their method is all about water. Each plant drains exactly the amount of desert it needs to live. Its roots choke out any encroachers.

Under the creosotes stretched fields of stones, mostly loose and jagged. I don't usually feel sorry for rocks, but in Death Valley they look tortured, and they are, by the wind and sun and salt. I saw boulders with cavernous holes on their upwind faces gouged out by sand-laden wind. I saw dismantled boulders. Salt crystals invade their seams and pry them apart from the inside. Most of the exposed rock faces were tanned shiny brown and black, a chemical varnish involving clay, iron and manganese oxides, and heat. I was feeling salt-weathered and desert-varnished myself, and loose rocks kept willfully rolling out from under my feet, leaving me stumbling around while the goblin dug in its spurs.

The surface rocks are so sharp they might as well be made of razors and crushed glass. The Bennetts had to cut moccasins for their surviving oxen from the hides of the dead ones. Steep-walled channels cut the ground. Rolling a wagon through here must have been a nightmare. And for what? To reach California with your grandma's armoire and your father's tools? Men on horses could cross the continent in a few months. Oxcarts took double or triple the time. So why not sell the furniture and make the crossing unencumbered but for a little gold in your saddlebags? The risks run by chaining yourself to a cart in the middle of the American West hardly seem worth the heirlooms.

William Lewis Manly was the one man among the forty-niners in the desert who had no particular attachments to physical objects. He was twenty-nine and had spent the better part of the previous ten years traveling the Midwestern wilderness with what he could carry on his back. Born in Vermont in 1820, Manly rode the wave front of western migration. His journey across America reads like a cross section of the continent. As a young boy, he moved with his family to Michigan. At the time, Michigan was considered the far west. They broke a farm out of the wilderness, where they were almost entirely independent, down to the wool and flax for their clothes. My favorite story of Manly's young life happened just before he left home to seek his fortune at the age of nineteen. He'd been preparing timbers for the new Michigan Central Railroad, and when he was ready to depart, he took his savings to the company store to outfit himself. You might've expected him to buy a horse or a new gun. Instead he bought "three nice whitewood boards, eighteen inches wide." From those three boards, he built himself a boat. And a traveling chest. And he and a friend piloted their craft two hundred miles down the Grand River to Lake Michigan. From the woods and his parents, he had learned self-sufficiency and a careless confidence with whatever materials were at hand. In the Wisconsin Territory, Manly had a varied career: lead miner, fur trapper, wood chopper, hunter. Ten years later, perspectives had changed. Michigan was no longer the far west, and gold had debuted in California. Manly's friend, Asabel Bennett, was taking his family to the new west, and he invited Manly to join them.

Manly became separated from the Bennetts at the beginning of the crossing and ended up leading a crew of six teamsters through an improbable series of adventures, including running several hundred miles of the Green River in dugout canoes they made with hatchets after flipping their first boat in a bad rapid. It was plain dumb luck that crossed Manly's path with the Bennetts' just outside Salt Lake City after months apart. Reunited with his people, Manly gave all his money to the teamsters who had stuck with him, reasoning that they had the greater need. Growing up in a household in which money was an oddity used only to pay taxes, Manly never seemed to acquire much attachment to the stuff. He continued west with his rifle, the buckskins he had made for himself in Wisconsin (and worn every day since), and the two hickory shirts and two years' worth of ammunition he had packed away in Bennett's wagon.

Manly and the Bennetts traveled south from Salt Lake with the larger train, then took the cutoff at the beginning of November and stuck to it. A month slipped by with nothing but more sunburnt land on the horizon. They talked of food. The families had all come from prosperous farms where they piled their dining tables high with good things. Now they watched their children shrink inside their clothes and reminisced about beans and bread. Stories of plenty told by starving men and women haunted Manly. It was one thing for him—an unattached adventurer—to be there, but he found deeply unsettling the desire that caused mothers and fathers to leave their farms and carry their children across the continent for the sake of the yellow metal.

Manly ranged the hills while the wagons crawled through the low places. He was a virtuoso with a rifle, probably the best light-skinned hunter in the district, but he found nothing. There simply were no meaty creatures anywhere to kill. He wrote that a hunter could carry a vest-pocketful of powder for a month here and never use it all. Sometimes he would be up on the hills and buttes for two or three days before he returned to the wagons to share what he had seen. Most of that time, he spent searching the distance for hill-joints where they might find water. At night, on his own, he would brood in the dark. Every day, the land ahead looked worse and worse. His people looked hollow-eyed. He struggled to see a future in which they survived. Instinct urged him to escape while he remained strong. But he felt soul-sick when he seriously considered abandoning his friends and their children. Each time he put self-preservation aside, he felt better for it.

When they arrived in Death Valley, Manly raced ahead to learn what he could of the terrain. On Christmas Day, he caught up with the Briers and camped with them in the Furnace Creek Wash. They had just slaughtered another of their oxen. The meat was little more than slime. They ended up boiling the hooves and hide in hope of eking a few extra calories from the animal. Manly was surprised to hear Brier giving his children an earnest lecture on the value of early education. The desert was stripping them all down to their essential characteristics. It revealed the Reverend James Brier as a brittle, didactic visionary with no practical inclination for survival in the wilderness. The Briers were kept in motion not by their Moses, but by Juliet Brier, a small, competent woman who apparently could stay alive and active on nothing but coffee.

Manly continued deeper into the valley, where he found the Jayhawkers burning their wagons. He watched them divide their jerky and the last of their flour and rice, which they measured out a spoonful at a time. He talked to them about the route they intended to take over the mountains and concluded that the families with their wagons had no hope of following. On the way back to his people, he crossed ways with Mr. Fish, a middle-aged Indianan who had decided to leave the wagons and push forward on foot. Noticing that Fish carried a long, handsome whiplash wrapped around his waist, Manly asked the man why he carried something so useless. Fish supposed he might be able to trade it for food later. The way Manly told this story, it's clear he thought the man kept those yards of expensive leatherwork only because he could not bear to leave them behind.

From the elevation I had gained on Badwater, I could see the features of the salt and the tilt of the Black Mountains and the Furnace Creek Wash, down which the emigrants all tumbled one after the next in their disordered groups. After spreading out across the desert, they arrived within a few days of each other, as if the low point of the continent had some kind of strange gravity. The valley had probably never seen a white face before, and just like that, it had a hundred of them wandering around it like so many ghosts.

I stopped for the day nowhere in particular among the creosotes and stone fields. I had no definite destination. One patch of desert was as good to sleep on as any other. Metallica's "Wherever

I May Roam" had stalked through my brain all afternoon: I put my head down on a rock padded with my extra shirt, and suddenly I was home. The sun hung low and hot above the Panamints. Half-dazed, I read through the last of the heat, trying to distract myself from the gallons of water sitting cool and smug inside the goblin. After sundown, I could have a drink. In the meantime, I fantasized about a Slurpee in a bucket.

The pioneers had no sense of scale. No place they had ever seen before—not the Rockies, certainly not the Appalachians—threw its mountains so high, so abruptly. They were looking at Telescope Peak and the Panamint Range, but they thought it was the Sierra Nevada. All the way across the continent, the Sierra had shadowed their future, and here was this massive, snow-capped mountain sailing miles above their heads. So they saw the mountains their map and their own preconceived notions told them to see. When the Bennetts and the Arcanes and the other few wagons and teamsters that had fallen into their orbit turned south through Death Valley to search for a wagon pass, they thought they were looking for Walker Pass through the southern Sierra. They imagined that the farming community of Tulare, with all the greens and blues the name had acquired, waited just over the crest. In reality, it was a hundred miles and three mountain ranges away.

Denied in the canyons, remanded to the edge of Badwater, Manly must have felt he had come to the end of the world. He once called a green, table-flat prairie ringed by oaks in Wisconsin the most beautiful place on earth. Here everything was the opposite. The plants assumed nightmarish shapes, useless to whites or oxen. Black, orange, and tan mountains clawed the sky. Nothing covered the bones of the earth but crushed rock and salt. His premonitions seemed bound to come true. They were stuck in a funnel of desert with their wagons and their children and no escape.

Telescope Peak.

The sun dropped behind the Panamints. A ten-mile shadow took me and my neighbor creosotes. The land sighed in relief, an almost audible exhale. The sudden shade made me shiver even though it must still have been well into the eighties. I drank some water now that I wouldn't sweat it right back out. An hour passed, and the planets appeared, and then the stars and galaxies, until the whole sky turned to silver dust.

▲

The forty-niners were probably the first whites in Death Valley, but to give them much distinction as explorers would be silly. Native

Americans had lived in the valley on and off for at least several thousand years. Shoshone families lived there year-round for much of the second millennium. They were nomads of temperature. With eleven thousand vertical feet between Badwater and the summit of Telescope Peak, and a change of about four degrees Fahrenheit for each thousand feet of elevation, they had something close to a 50-degree temperature range over a distance of ten miles. A 125-degree day torching Badwater? The Shoshones were high on the mountain collecting pine nuts in crisp, light, 80-degree air. Telescope Peak buried in snow? They were down on the valley floor working mesquite bean flour into cakes of bread. In between, there were wild grapes hidden in Hanaupah Canyon, prickly pear joints to roast, desert crucifers with leaves like cabbage.

George Hansen, a Shoshone whose first name was foisted on him years later by a prospector who hired him as a guide, and whose last name was assigned to him by the Bureau of Indian Affairs, was a boy of about ten in 1849, when the pioneers came stumbling through. One night, he and his father crept down from the Panamint side to watch the Jayhawkers burn their wagons. As an old man, he recalled the flames and shouting men and others who vomited from eating ox flesh that had putrefied while still attached to the living animal. They approached the whites in total stealth, as if trailing bighorn sheep. Hansen and the other Shoshones knew the whites were sick and in trouble, but they also feared these strange interlopers with their guns and wheels and ribby, bawling cattle.

The Shoshones maintained silence and cover. Most of the whites thought the place empty—they didn't know they were being watched. The desert had eyes too secret for their own. George Hansen saw the Jayhawkers walk up the valley and cross the Panamints to the north. He saw the Bennetts and Arcanes roll their wagons south, watched them attempt to cross the mountains and wind up back at the edge of Badwater. If he had crept close to them, as he had the Jayhawkers, he would have heard a tense discussion of the future.

Asabel Bennett was bewildered in the most literal sense of the word. The map and his concept of the West had led him so far into trouble he no longer knew what direction to try next. None of his former prosperity or zeal for Western gold could lever him and his family out of the desert. So he asked his friend, Lewis Manly, to go on foot to find the route to western California and return with food while the families waited at the spring, where they would at least have water. Manly was willing, and one of the teamsters of the Green River party, John Rogers, agreed to go, too. Despite the danger and responsibility, Manly must have felt some relief to be asked. He would at last be able to move at his own speed without feeling any guilt over leaving the others. Some of the emigrants at the spring were reluctant to stop and wait. They didn't question Manly's good intentions, but couldn't help thinking that any man lucky enough to escape such a place would be a fool to come back. Arcane slaughtered an ox to give the "boys" provisions. So emaciated were the cattle that seven-eighths of the flesh of the entire ox fit into Manly and Rogers's knapsacks. They agreed to be back in two weeks.

Manly and Rogers left the next morning with a gun apiece, one blanket for the two of them, and canteens made by strapping powder cans together with strips of cloth. They each had a knife, a hat, and a knapsack filled with half-dried, half-putrefied ox meat. In a sense, for all his life, Manly had been cultivated for this one task. He knew how to travel the world with a knife and a gun. But he also had an inborn reverence for duty and family. His need to save Sarah Bennett, Abigail Arcane, and their little ones meant he understood, in a way that many of his fellows did not, that life continued on the frontier only through them.

Manly and Rogers scrambled up the wash where the oxen stalled and up into the canyon above. Crossing the crest of the Panamints, they saw the true Sierra Nevada for the first time, still seventy miles away, though Manly thought it looked more like two hundred. The sudden appearance of the mountain wall in its full winter white killed any lingering hope that Tulare might be just over the hill. The desert ran right up to the Sierra and even farther to the south and southwest, where a flat plain stretched beyond the horizon. They descended another canyon on the west side of the Panamints. At night, they slept "spoon fashion," as Manly put it, under their single blanket. The air seemed to siphon the juice right from their blood. Down in the Panamint Valley, they found a clear-running creek and ran to it to bury their heads in the flow, only to find it salty as brine. Past the salt creek, they found the body of Mr. Fish, fancy whiplash still wrapped around his waist.

They crossed a low range of black hills and found tracks that turned out to belong to the Jayhawkers. They spotted a pond in the center of an otherwise dry lake bed, but the water was alkali and colored like wine, a painful reversal of the storied miracle that only left them thirstier than before. They chewed bullets to keep saliva flowing. The next day, in the predawn, Rogers discovered thin panes of night-frozen dew. They each ate a mouthful of ice, then collected all the rest they could find, which was just enough to fill their kettle. Manly credited the find with saving their lives.

The two men curved south through the Mojave and caught up with straggling Jayhawkers and Bugsmashers. Nightmarish juxtapositions filled Manly and Rogers' days. They wandered through a vast emptiness, but continually ran into other half-starved men dragging their own selves through the desert. They might share a night and talk balefully of the pleasure of food, but in the morning, they scattered again, each small group searching for the leak of water that would sustain them for one more day. Manly wrote of the panicky feeling of mornings when they left camp unsure whether they would ever taste water again. On one night, some older men approached Manly with a list of names and addresses and asked him to contact their families and tell them what had happened in the desert.

Ten days and 250 miles after leaving the edge of Badwater, Manly and Rogers crested the San Gabriel Mountains and looked down on oaks, a thousand acres of grass meadow, and hundreds of fat cattle. "If ever a poor mortal escapes from this world," Manly wrote, "and joys of a happy heaven are opened up to him, the change cannot be much more than this."

They were foreigners in this paradise. With no Spanish between them, they couldn't tell their story or even ask for help. It took them days to organize supplies for the families. By the time they were outfitted with three horses, some flour, beans, dried meat, and wheat, and a skinny, one-eyed mule, the agreed-upon two weeks had nearly passed.

Back on the Mojave, one of the horses died en route, and the other two had to be left to perish because they balked in the canyons. When Manly and Rogers recrossed the Panamints, they had only the beans, flour, and meat, and the little mule. Anxiety wore them down. The families might already have given up and left and could be wandering, lost and starving. Or they might be dead next to their spring. Manly worried that Indians might have discovered and murdered them—as if George Hansen and his relatives hadn't known right where they were all along. The two rescuers descended the Panamints and tracked north through the valley toward Badwater. They found Richard Culverwell lying faceup on the valley floor. He was supposed to have been in the camp with the families. His body seemed to confirm all their fears. The wagons came in sight, but they were empty and dismantled. Manly fired a shot in the air—and the Bennetts, Arcanes, and all their children came rolling out from below the wagons, where they had taken shelter from the sun.

Twenty-six days had passed since Manly and Rogers left. The Bennetts and Arcanes were the only ones still at the spring. All the others had quit the camp in small groups as the days of idleness and worry multiplied—Culverwell had been among the last to leave, only a few days before. If any of the family members felt that one mule and some beans and grain were a little less than they had hoped for, they kept the opinion to themselves. Sarah Bennett wrapped her arms around Manly, cried, and said, "Good boys . . . God bless you forever! Such boys should never die!" At least now, Manly and Rogers could prepare the families for what was to come and could steer them to the water holes along the way. After the weeping and hugs and stories, the little group of wanderers planned its exodus. The Bennetts and Arcanes gave up the idea of keeping their wagons and made canvas holsters for the babies, which they strapped to the oxen. Abigail Arcane, resigned to carrying only the clothes on her back, chose her finest dress from the wagon, tacked extra-long ribbons to her hat, and dressed her boy Charlie in his best suit. Manly reported that she looked fairylike fluttering through the desert.

Two days later, they crested the Panamints—four men, two women, four children, eleven oxen, a dog, and the mule. The last of the forty-niners. At the crest, Manly took Bennett and Arcane to the outlook where they could see in both directions, back over the desert they had crossed and forward to the Sierra Nevada.

The families leave Death Valley on foot.
Illustration from William Lewis Manly's *Death Valley in '49*

Bennett and Arcane were flabbergasted by the land, and particularly the mountains, which stood ten times higher than what they had expected. They took their hats off and looked back, and one of them said, "Good-bye, Death Valley." Manly didn't record which of them fixed the place with its white name. Whichever one of them said it, you can be sure he had "Yea though I walk through the Valley of the Shadow of Death" in mind. Maybe we all walk through the valley of the shadow, but for the emigrants in Death Valley, it must have felt very real and close. They descended the western Panamints, leaving the Shoshone some strange souvenirs and a few more years of peace and quiet.

▲

My eyes opened as the stars began to fade and a blue line appeared to the east above the Black Mountains. Waking up in the desert happens to me with the suddenness of a lifted curtain. A few minutes later, the sun touched the Panamints. Don't blink: The soft colors of morning live only a moment. The light hardened from rose to flat in the time it took me to get upright and brush my teeth.

I pulled on my boots and repacked the goblin. I had consumed twelve pounds of water and food the first day, but the difference on my back was less of a relief than I had hoped. The air looked like noon but felt like night, still fresh and cool. I walked through more fields of sunflowers and stones, the stems of the flowers threading up through the rocks underfoot. I saw rock daisies and notched-leaf phacelia, which hung purple bells from fronds that looked strangely succulent, almost fernlike. Nothing moved.

I continued north up Death Valley, leaving Manly and the families behind. To my right, the land sank into the salt. To my left, huge canyons curved down the eastern face of the Panamints, spewing massive alluvial fans from their mouths. One, about five miles wide, an undulating pile of rock rubble that could bury Lancaster, took me most of the morning to cross. In the middle of the fan, I found three pine trunks, about eight feet long and three feet thick. The nearest trees were eleven miles away and seven thousand feet above my head. And that's the paradox of the place. The labors of water were everywhere, but there was no living water in sight. Periodic flash floods have washed the millions of yards of stone rubble down through the canyons and out into the valley. Riverbeds snaking and branching through the debris looked so fresh and clean-cut, the water could have been turned off just yesterday. But decades might have passed since surface water cut those channels. Nothing else comes along to stir up the rocks, so the land stays just as the water left it. The pine trunks were polished smooth in transport, so obviously water-worn that it was easy to imagine them rolling and tumbling down muddy, fast-moving currents.

I crossed another dirt road running up the big fan through the rocks and creosotes. Looking so much out of place that it might as well have been a forty-niner's oxcart, a Subaru was parked at a wide spot in the track. I tucked a postcard to Ashley under one

Gravel ghost.

windshield wiper. I considered plunking down my mud-crusted spare boots on the hood as well, with the hope that the driver would take them off my back and transport them to a dumpster, but I decided I might be pushing my luck, so they stayed tied to the goblin.

The temperature spiked. Flowers multiplied underfoot. The beds of old water tracks were filled with gravel ghost, the most perfectly named of all desert flowers. Around my knees, bright, white, many-petaled heads bobbed in the wind, apparently unattached until I looked closely and found thin gray stems.

I walked down the far side of the big fan, back below sea level and to the edge of the alkali. The air shimmered with rising heat. It was the view from inside a boiling pot. I found a mesquite that actually did have some shade and stretched out below it before I even realized I had decided to stop. Earlier in the morning, I had stuck my foot through the underground tunnel of some desert burrower. It wouldn't have mattered, except the goblin decided to go one way and I another. The goblin won, and I ended up sprawled in the rocks with a gaping rip through the knee of my pants. I had a needle taped to a water bottle and some loose thread, so I sat under the mesquite in my underwear and stitched up the tear.

Every time I try to hide out under a mesquite, I think of John LeMoigne. Old John made the Death Valley region his home for thirty-five years before a hot August day in 1918 or 1919, when his body was found under a mesquite with no one around but his two burros, also dead. I've often wondered about his state of mind at the end. Did he think he had found shelter, that he would ride out the heat and be back on his feet in an hour? Or did he know he was in trouble?

In a sense, the forty-niners who strayed into the desert were lucky. They arrived in Death Valley in January. In any other season, they would have become the desert version of the Donner Party. Culverwell died. Fish and his partner Ischam died. Depending on which story you read, a couple of Jayhawkers were also killed by heat or bullets or Indians. But most of the emigrants—and all three families—made it through. Their survival didn't keep the sensationalists of the next fifty years from telling stories about hundreds of emigrants perishing in flames and eaten by reptiles in the bottom of the pit. Writers, at least, felt an urgent need for symmetrical spectacles: one lot of pioneers starving and consuming each other in the snows of Tahoe, the other lot leaving their bones in the sand. What symmetry does exist comes from the mountains, the Sierra Nevada. The wall of peaks forced the emigrants north or south, up over Donner Pass or down through the desert.

From under my mesquite, I could see the tops of the Grapevine Mountains at the far northern end of Death Valley. Haze or dust puffed up above their summits. The air felt like a pair of hands wringing the water out of me. I had two problems—a cracked throat and a heavy pack. Two problems with the same solution. I cheated, just a little, mentally reapportioning the water I carried until I'd stolen enough from future days to justify an extra half-liter for today.

I put my pants on and the goblin on my back. I saw more of the dinosaur caterpillars with the tail thorns. They waddled piti-lessly from flower to flower, munching and munching with those giant mandibles. I walked the edge of the alkali line. On one side, pickleweed grew from soft, white soil with a consistency like stale bread if I stepped on it. On the other, desert holly grew out of hard alluvial stones. Zebra-tail lizards sprinted away from me, the most skittish rising on their hind legs to run. Zebra-tails go up-right at full speed, and then they become barely distinguishable blurs of gray and black, like tricks of the eye. To my right, the white flats threw back the sun. The glare off the ground seemed collected and magnified, a continuous bomb blast of light.

The air began to move fast to the south, feeling massive, like an ocean tide. A sound in the wind—a repeated clank like rocks striking—made me think of borax teams. Had I been here on the alkali line in the 1880s, I could have watched the twice-weekly run. Eighteen mules, two horses, two wagons, and a water tank all chained together to haul borax out of the salt. Each wagon had seven-foot-diameter wheels and a payload of ten tons. They began just a few miles from where I was stirring up the zebra-tails. The wagons went south past Badwater, then up through Wingate Pass and over the desert to the rails at Mojave. They were nineteenth-century semitrucks, 150 feet long from the nose of the lead mule to the tank towed behind the ten-foot-tall wagons. I have seen pictures but never quite been able to imagine those enormous contraptions, half mule, half machine, heaving through this empty place. It's easier for me to hear them, the chuckle of the wheels and chains, the bawling of the skinner damning his mules with every blue word in the book.

The sun began to fall down toward the Panamints. The air turned hazy and orange. The wind picked up. I noticed, belatedly, that I could no longer see the sky. The dust storm I had watched puff up above the Grapevine Mountains from under my mesquite had traveled fifty miles down-valley. I was about to be consumed.

I left the alkali line behind for the last time and pushed uphill, up the contours of another fan. The air thickened from orange to brown to gray. Across the valley to the east, the Funeral Mountains turned to ghosts and then disappeared. The wind swung down on me, pushing me backward, blowing the air out of my mouth and packing my teeth with grit. The Panamints, which were practically on top of me, faded away. The air rasped against the stones, a vibration I could both hear and feel.

Caterpillars swarmed over the rocks and flowers. The biggest had grown so fat they could barely stay upright. Their legs were overwhelmed by their shiny green and black bodies, like putting a Winnebago on the chassis of a Honda. They hurried toward the next flowers, flopping over on their sides and stumbling up again, mandibles grasping in anticipation. I could practically hear the flowers screaming. In the roaring wind and gloom, it was the attack of the vegetarian zombies.

I couldn't see the sun at all, but eventually the light dimmed down toward dark and I stopped for the night in a patch of gravel in the middle of the storm. The creosotes shook and bent in the wind. Dust found its way behind my eyes and down my throat. The caterpillars squirmed all around me. In the half-light, with the white wind blowing, the desert looked wintry—except that the air still felt exhaled from a furnace. I drank my stolen half-liter of water as slowly as I could and had to force the bottle away from my lips when the time came. I could have drunk an extra gallon and still been parched. My skin and joints felt crackly. Like an infection, the desert had gotten back into my blood. A wind gust threw sand in my face. I went to sleep under the roar.

Chapter 3

TUCKI MOUNTAIN

These men will build ditches for water, an' reservoirs an' towns an' cities, an' cross the desert with railroads. An' they'll grow rich and proud. They'll think they've conquered it . . . a thousand years might pass with fruitfulness in control of man. But all that is only a few grains of time . . . the desert works ceaselessly and with infinite patience. The sun burns . . . the mountains wear down atom by atom, to be the sands of the desert. An' the winds . . . they blow the sand an' sift an' seep an' bury.

—Zane Grey, *Wanderer of the Wasteland*, 1923

The curtain lifted on a new desert and a new me. The mountains were back on all sides. Overhead the sky turned pale blue, with just enough leftover dust to make the air powdery. The wind had relaxed into a quiet ebb and flow, like breathing. I had gone to sleep pinched with thirst, and I woke up comfortable. My body had let go of its expectations. I could feel myself drying out, my blood running thicker, my skin pulling tighter. Instead of fighting the desert—struggling to keep the dry out and the moist in—my body had come to terms.

I had options on the map ahead. I could go west, up the Black-water Wash, to check out the former bedlam mining camp of Skidoo. Or further north through Death Valley on the alkali line. The one seemed repetitious; the other, crowded. I knew there would be SUVs and roads up around Skidoo. That was a kind of bedlam I could skip. But I was antsy to get up off the valley floor. Between the two, to the northwest, stood huge, hulking Tucki Mountain—ten miles wide and seven thousand feet over my head. I hadn't ever heard of someone going right over the top of Tucki, up one side and down the other. There were beautiful canyons up there—I had prowled around their lower narrows—and hints of bighorn sheep even higher. On the other side of Tucki, at the little park service outpost of Stovepipe Wells, I'd fill my food bag and water bottles.

I passed the Blackwater Wash and walked through fields of strange stones. Red, orange, tan, green, black, shot with crystal dikes and mineral doodles. Some had been cut clean through, like loaves put in a bread slicer. The wind had stripped and sharp-ened other rocks until their layers stood out like stacked knives. Desert pavement clanked and resettled under my feet. The creo-sotes could barely manage here. Instead of squeezing against each other's water domains, they stood far apart, lonely outposts of growth. Giant reefs of black basalt pushed up through the Tucki Wash. I turned west, away from the salt, and passed between the reefs while the rust-red cliffs and contorted folds of Tucki filled the sky above.

The goblin—down around sixty pounds and still purging—felt manageable for the first time. My legs recalled their desert timing, and my feet wasted less energy rolling loose rocks. I thought of the Shoshones migrating up and down the Panamints, of prospec-tors waking each morning to break rocks and going to sleep at night on other rocks. Their bodies must have become rock, too,

Sliced stone in the Blackwater Wash

muscle and skin hardly distinguishable from the raw earth they wrestled every day. We play a lot of games now and produce remarkable athletes, swimmers, and runners with bodies tuned like racing engines. But for bare physical toughness, give me a lifetime of living, sleeping, and eating off the desert. George Hansen still lived in the Panamints in his late nineties. Whites who survived the mines and heat and alcohol seemed to greet old age with a clawed hand wrapped around its neck. They shambled across the desert, their dried-out hides filled with nothing but muscle and gristle, cursing their luck and swinging their pickaxes right up until the moment the desert claimed them.

The land curved up toward Tucki. The valley floor tilted into view below. For the first time since stepping out on the salt, I

Morning shadows and dust wreathe the Black and Funeral Mountains.

could actually see the whole outline of the alkali. It had been a white blur of visual noise, depthless, semi-infinite, but now it settled out flat. Shorelines wound through coves of sand. Solid white creeks bent through the rocks and found inlets. Beyond the salt, mesquites drilled the sand for water. Above the mesquites, the creosote bloc monopolized the alluvial fans, and above them, the soft, young stone of the Black Mountains—twisted with spires, ridges, folds—was wreathed in dust and long shadows.

The dust kept the morning cool even as the sun pumped itself up brighter and hotter. I planned on sleeping somewhere near Tucki's summit, hidden from me now behind buttresses like shoulders heaved into the sky. Shedding four degrees Fahrenheit per thousand feet, if I walked fast enough up the seven thousand feet of mountain ahead, I might keep the same temperature all day long.

I like the idea of heading up or down the mountain with the changing temperature. The white model for living in the West requires barricades and power plants. Frigidaires for summer, furnaces for winter. We like to plant our homes on a fixed square of dirt and then defend the space inside against the seasons as they pass. By moving with the seasons, the Shoshones regularized their climate without the infrastructure—no insulated boxes crusting the ground like so many barnacles, no hydroelectric dams or sooty air. Their legs did a little work, and the thermoclines did the rest.

I don't mean to glorify the lives of the Death Valley Shoshones too much. There was nothing easy about living in Death Valley. The small family clans and their broad dispersal suggest the amount of food that could be gleaned from the desert. When wild mesquite beans are a staple, hunger can't ever be that far off. They also ate bunch-grass seeds, Joshua tree buds, pack rats, and chuckwallas (a common fat-bodied lizard—the chicken equivalent of desert eating). Rabbits provided meat and fur for blankets. A mountain sheep meant feast times. They had strange legends and dreams filled with shape-shifting animals—small wonder if they were half-starved all the time and living on potent desert plants. The stars bloomed and multiplied in the evenings, and the Panamint Shoshones were incredible storytellers. The whole history of The People, which is how they referred to themselves, unfolded over and over again each night. Children hovered around the stories, absorbing what they could. Women wove baskets of coiled willow and black devil's claw, stylized with butterflies or lizards, works of beauty and genius that could hold water and sometimes took months to finish.

Like many other Native American groups, the Death Valley Shoshones were called Digger Indians by some of the first whites who passed through. The name was loaded with scorn, meant to show the inferiority of a people who slept and scratched in the dirt. Digging in the desert for food was a savage lifestyle. Digging in the desert for metal to give to men in cities in exchange for food—*that* was industrious, the American dream. The irony would be more humorous if the superiority complex of the whites hadn't killed so many Shoshones. The only real difference I've been able to find between the daily business of the Indians and the prospectors is that the Shoshones had more time to stare at the mountains and the prospectors drank more whisky. At least both got to watch the stars at night, which is more than can be said for the guy in the city on the receiving end of all that desert metal.

The individual lives ended by conflict between whites and Shoshones are tragedies; the loss of the original Western culture might be worse. We can't all migrate up and down the Panamints, but it would be to our benefit if we understood how to work with the seasons, how to live in the West without climate control. We'd help ourselves by developing a desert mind-set, the old-American tradition of commonsense minimalism.

I entered a broad basin filled with blooming creosote. Every plant glowed yellow. The air felt thick with heat and plant oils. I could practically hear the flowers humming to their pollinators. A prairie falcon cruised by overhead. The Tucki Wash poured past me, seeming to braid and roll like a river, except for being made of orange stones sprouted with yellow and green creosote. A big river, too, a mile wide and seven miles long, and it ran right up into the arms of the mountain. As I pulled closer to Tucki Mountain, it swelled up and began to swallow me, blocking out the west and a quarter of the sky, and wrapping the walls of the canyon around me to the north and south.

A river made of stone has a kind of implacability that is not entirely comforting. There is something eerily *patient* about the big red curves of the mountains here, the heavy stillness. Mortality and frailty feel more inescapable in Death Valley than anywhere else I travel. Our timescales are comically disconnected. The desert, with its billion-year-old rocks, won't twitch during the time it takes me to finish my little dance. Here, I am the mayfly who lives for a day. Even the creosotes—scraggly little shrubs—are ancient. Creosotes clone themselves. New shoots grow up from the root crown even as inner stems die. Creosote rings twelve thousand years old have been found, a passage of time equivalent to the entire human presence in Death Valley.

The endurance of the desert was much on the mind of Zane Grey, famous writer of Western melodramas. In the early twentieth century, Grey was a macho Danielle Steel, banging out a best seller a year. His tales of riders and outlaws and lonesome, lawless towns in Utah, Arizona, and California sold millions of copies. Which means that, at a rough guess, more people have seen the desert as he presented it than with their own eyes. I find his books bizarre and fascinating. He force-fed his characters romantic lard by the tubful. But every so often, while chewing through the fat, I'm stung by a sharp line of thought—a cactus spine hiding in the greasy pâté.

Grey jabbed me this way with a miner named Dismukes, who talks of the age of the desert and the projects of men. Dismukes imagines engineers lifting the Colorado River from its banks and spilling the water over the desert, making it bloom. He laughs at the idea—not because he disbelieves in it as a possibility, but because of the hubris it requires, the presumption of control. Dismukes prophesizes. He makes the land immense and the men tiny.

Time stretches out ahead and behind them. Their scratchings on the surface get blown away on a breath of wind. It's a beautiful image of geologic *momentum*. Dismukes's men throw up temporary interruptions to the overwhelming work of the earth. Though he doesn't name it, what Grey describes through Dismukes is specifically the Imperial Valley in Southern California, which had been the northwestern corner of the Sonora Desert until irrigation transformed it into America's winter fruit basket. Would Grey give Dismukes the same opinion today? I'm not sure. Our lives are just as short, but the scars we've cut in the ground go deeper than could have been imagined a hundred years back. *Wanderer of the Wasteland*, one of the two novels I carried with me, was one of Grey's favorites. Not shy about his self-importance as a writer, Grey all but wept over the work, calling it "wonderful, beautiful, terrible" in the journal he kept as he wrote it. I brought the book because I wanted to see what Grey made of Death Valley. The heart of the story is set in a canyon right here in the eastern Panamints. The canyon itself is a fiction, but the salt and the Funeral Mountains and the pressure of the sun besiege Grey's characters.

Reading Grey in the desert felt unexpectedly right. The extravagance of his characters and landscapes seemed more purposeful. Early in *Wanderer*, the hero, Adam, educates himself by studying desert animals: snakes, jackrabbits, ants, kangaroo rats, horned lizards. He admires their enlarged eyes, ears, and jaws. He marvels at the hardness of their lives and their relentless defense of their individual niches. Looking at the plants in the Tucki Wash, I thought I saw where Grey's idea of character came from. All the visible organisms have been sharpened, literally, by the sun and wind, by intense competition for water and food. Their individual traits, like those of Grey's characters, become exaggerated by their geography.

Cottontop cactus.

I passed a cottontop cactus anchored to the stones, and it didn't have just a few spines for form's sake—it had a full sheath of wickedly curving, interlocking barbs that covered every inch of its barrel body. Dismukes the miner—short, broad, obdurate, and bristling with antisocial maxims—seemed to stare right back at me. Flowers didn't just poke up through the gravel; their colors looked unearthly. I saw sundrops, like little porcelain cups, radiating shades of lightning yellow far too big for such a small weed. And I couldn't help hearing Adam drawl out to a woman on a borderland farm at the end of the book: "That's the desert's work, Mrs. Blair. On the desert nature makes color, as well as life, more vivid, more intense."

Intensity and stillness. Tiny flashes of impossible color against sky-high waves of red and tan. Contradictions piled one on top of the next. Despite the conspicuous rattle of my own heart, despite the frank eagerness of the flowers, a feeling of monumental calm held the Tucki Wash, an assurance of time turned slowly into land. But the scene looked a little grim, too. The cottontops barricaded themselves behind their weapons. The leaves of the creosotes shimmered with poisonous resins, which, along with making the leaves indigestible to insects, work like Gore-Tex in reverse, allowing water in but not out. Under the quiet patience of age and slow growth, conflict continued. The Death Valley plants hiding behind their sharp points and chemical defenses could hardly be called peaceful.

I had a lot of time to stare at the plants and imagine the pressures that had made them. Walking seven miles in a straight line over a jumble of stones gave my mind more than enough space to wander. The mountain stayed straight ahead of me, and the salt straight behind. Brittlebush exploded from the ground, all green leaves and sunflower heads, pushing its growth in the spring boom, before the long decline to bleached white stems and shriveled leaves of summer. The huge black reefs of rock I had passed through at the bottom of the Tucki Wash dwindled to dark stripes. The creosotes lost their monopoly to spindly ephedra and a profusion of sage and shadscale. The cottontops increased as I gained altitude, first in ones and twos, then in whole families of fat, green barrels dressed head to toe in red-tipped spines.

High up in the Tucki Wash, I passed more contorted rocks. Every time I saw a mass of quartz half-buried, I kicked it over. I was looking for gold. But what would I have done if I had seen any? Packed kilos of quartz on my back over Tucki for a few grains of color? No, it was useless to me, but it would have been a thrill to catch sight of the stuff so many men had hunted. And that's the insanity of gold. Most of the world's gold doesn't do any actual work for us at all. You can't make a building out of it the way you can with iron; you can't get energy out of it like with uranium. A fraction gets turned into rings and necklaces, and the rest simply gets hoarded. No wonder the Shoshones couldn't get the hang of prospecting. They could never quite convince themselves that this rock was in fact superior to all the other rocks.

Above me, the mountain kicked up, all cliffs and canyons, red and brown. Geologically speaking, Tucki is called a turtleback, which describes its shape perfectly but doesn't do much to capture its immense size. The shell of this turtle is twelve miles long and ten miles broad. I was just approaching its shoulder, where the shell jutted out most steeply. Up above that—well, I didn't know what would be up there. I had been all around Tucki, but the rim of the mountain always prevented me from seeing the upper curve of the mountain's back.

My canyon tightened without becoming truly narrow. The bed of the wash tilted down and rocks rolled out from under my feet. Scrappy cliffs of gray and tan rock scabbed the canyon-sides. Dry falls of the same shattered rock interrupted the wash. To my left a canyon branch ran up to a portal of pale blue sky and then fell down into another canyon to the west. I followed the main branch deeper in toward the mountain.

Loose rock crusted the falls. I worried more about the holds keeping attached to the cliffs than my hands staying attached to the holds. I scrabbled up three short falls, generating little cloud-bursts of falling stones, then hit a fourth too high and crumbly to climb. A bypass to the right offered zigzag ledges through bands of orange and gray cliffs a hundred feet high. The ledges sloped out and down and shook off rocks and gravel wherever I touched. I eased myself around corners and up crumbling ladders of stone. The goblin chortled in my ear and tugged me backward into space.

On a crest above the fall, I saw more of the same. Crumbling rock, unstable talus, orange and blue cliffs that looked more than ready to begin their journey down to the salt. But straight above me, up the canyon-side instead of up the canyon wash, I thought I could see the joint where Tucki eased and the lid of the turtleback began. So I plowed right up the canyon wall and came over the rim of the mountain and stepped into another world. Angles vanished. Reds and browns disappeared below me. Everything had been made of sharp, jagged lines. But now the land curved. The back of Tucki *rolled* to the distant summit, big billows of dark green shadscale-covered land-swell. I pushed up to a high knob and had a seat.

Death Valley gaped wide below me. The bottom was deep and far away. This desert was often called a primitive place by Easterners like Manly, people from Vermont or Ohio or Missouri. Here there are no forests or other visible subdivisions and neighborhoods of life. From up above, the creosotes blend with the rocks, the mesquites with the sand. What's left is the bones of the earth, undressed. One immense square notch of salt, sand, and rock, with nothing green or growing to clothe it. Its huge nakedness affected the minds of the Easterners in strange ways, drove them to torrid affairs of love and hate with the desert. Many of them—men and women both, including Mary Austin—described the desert as a voluptuous and implacable woman. "I know well what like she would be," Austin wrote. "Deep-breasted, broad in the hips, tawny . . . full lipped like a sphinx . . . and you could not move her, no, not if you had all the earth to give."

There was still a lot of Tucki between me and the summit. I walked on, up one curve after another. Each wave-crest revealed more big green rollers I hadn't been able to see before. The summit seemed to be walking away from me faster than I was walking toward it.

Shadows spilled away from the sun, drowning the troughs between the billows; dark air pooled below the green waves. I walked up a ridgeline between two amphitheaters, my legs declining with the day's end. The landforms were immense, and I felt very small. The amphitheaters on either side of my ridge were canyon heads, just the very beginnings of the red-brown gorges cutting through Tucki's shell below the rim. Still, they bottomed out five hundred feet below me on one side, a thousand on the other. The summit complex rose up on the opposite side of the larger canyon head. It would have to wait for tomorrow. I stopped at a saddle between two rollers with plenty of flat space to sleep between the shadscales. The wind swung through, and I stayed low. Birdsong floated up in lulls between the gusts. To the east, Death Valley sank into shadow. To the north, Tucki's head slipped from pink to gray-green. To the south, Telescope Peak—five thousand feet higher still—lifted its snow up into the last orange sunset light.

Telescope Peak from Tucki Mountain.

The view reminded me again of Zane Grey. What Adam finds in the canyon in the Panamints in *Wanderer of the Wasteland* are a husband and wife engaged in a bizarre suicide pact. The woman, Magdalene, stares up at Telescope Peak from down in the canyon and says, "I've faced my soul here . . . and I would endure any agony to change that soul, to make it as high and clear and noble as the white cone of the mountain." Under the hyperdrama is a notion I appreciate: Land becomes the language of the mind. Emotions and dreams become attached to places bigger than ourselves. We aspire to mountains. And the desert? Grey looked at Death Valley and got not much farther than death. He put his suicides there and vivisected them with heat and thirst and sinister geologic fantasies. The land is a barely recognizable caricature, a tool Grey used to prod his own notions of guilt and mortality.

All day the light had slipped from one shade to the next on Tucki Mountain. Cedar, rust, iron, lavender, and sage on the mountain's roof, the colors changed with the hour and my angle. Now, as night rushed in from the east, the mountain went dark and the colors lifted into the air. Deep midnight blue filled Death Valley, and above that a razor-sharp line in the sky and a thin layer of opalescent pink.

▲

I woke up cold. When I reached for the bottle I had left out, I found ice around its cap. A gain of six thousand feet had been enough to drop the nighttime temperature below freezing. I put on all my clothes—which meant that I added my wind shell to what I already had on. I hopped around in the shadscale like an idiot for a few minutes, then threw the goblin on my back and ran for the summit.

Twenty minutes of steep land-waves and sunlight stirred up enough body warmth for my muscles to calm down. My brain began to deice itself, too, and my peripheral vision filled back in. I saw my first Mojave fishhook, a little cactus that looks like a miniature cottontop except for the long, blood-crimson hooks reaching out through its clusters of spines. Hundreds of burrows of all sizes tunneled into the ground. Certain districts looked so compromised with entrances and diggings that I wondered what kept the hillsides from slumping down. Rabbits and pocket gophers and maybe gray foxes resided in those holes, curled nose-to-tail and probably wondering what manner of beast was stumping around up above. I saw bighorn tracks and scat. Truth be told, one of the reasons I had wanted to cross Tucki was the hope of seeing a mountain sheep. Though its provenance is murky, *tucki* may have

Morning light, and Death Valley, from Tucki Mountain.

been a Panamint Shoshone name for bighorns. Etymology aside, George Hansen specifically described the mountain as a sheep-hunting ground for him and his family.

The sun and the mountain curved up off their separate horizons. I walked a horseshoe path around the big canyon-head. The mountain rolled on above me, each wave-crest revealing more land-swell. Ascending notes of birdsong tracked the progress of the sun. I topped a curve higher than all the others and had a seat on the summit.

Like the foaming crest of a distant tidal wave, the Sierra Nevada broke up on the western horizon. The cold desert air magnified details. I could see the peaks distinctly: the north face and southern roof of Mount Langley, the sharp points of the Corcoran Spires,

The Sierra Nevada fromTucki Mountain.

the narrow eastern profile of Mount Russell. Mount Whitney looked aloof and jagged. Somehow the mountain looked much farther off than the simple number of air miles between me and it. It seemed to be in, and of, another world. I understood why Manly thought it two hundred miles away. North of the Whitney group, Mount Williamson and the Palisade Crest curled up into the sky. For the first time, I could see the future. The journey took shape right there, salt behind, summit ahead. In between were the rucked-up Cottonwood Mountains, the Saline Valley, the massive black wall of the Inyo Range, the trench of the Owens Valley, then, finally, the Sierra. Everything I could see, the entire Land of Little Rain, stood in the shadow of Mount Whitney. The shadow of death? No, more like the rain shadow of the Sierra.

The mountains make the desert. Wet air rolls in off the Pacific Ocean in foggy masses, but when the prevailing winds push moisture over the peaks, the wet falls right out. The sky can't hold it. The Sierra captures the most rain and snow, but one after the next, the Inyo, Argus, Cottonwood, and Panamint take whatever is left. By the time the wind blows down into Death Valley, the air has been stripped bare. Evaporation rates near the salt are freakish. The sky is a vampire, the aridity often more dangerous than the heat. Stories from the early mining camps tell of wood curling and splitting in the single-digit humidity of summer months, chairs and tables falling to pieces simply through contact with the air.

In wetter times, the mountains made lakes. The snow and rain they collected ran down into the basins, which had no outlets. Owens Lake, at the foot of the Sierra, one of the last ice age lakes to survive until being drained to water Los Angeles, brought birds by the millions. Avocets, phalaropes, ducks, geese, pelicans. When Lake Manly—the name geologists have given the body of water that has occupied Death Valley on and off over the last million years—was full as well, birds must have jammed the sky. Even after Pleistocene Lake Manly disappeared ten thousand years ago, smaller lakes in Death Valley came and went, gathered and evaporated. Indians predating the Shoshones camped by the changing shoreline. Archaeologists still find their traces on long-dry beaches up among the creosotes. A hunter on top of Tucki would have seen clouds of migrating birds on all sides, diving down into the basins, flying over the mountains, headed north or south with the season.

What would Dismukes have to say of that scene? A string of lakes in every basin from here to the Sierra, and ten million ducks

The author on top of Tucki Mountain.

quacking and wheeling above and below. Would he still talk of the patience of the desert? Or just the narrow window of human experience? Even now, every once in a while, the ghost of Lake Manly returns. It happened in 1969 and again in 2005. Wild thunderstorms dropped rain so fast that North America's most ephemeral big puddle shimmered back to life for a few days, a mirage come true, before disappearing into the sky.

I stepped down off the summit. Tucki felt like an island above the salt and sand, the white and orange desert—as unconnected from the land below as Mount Whitney had seemed from Tucki's top. The bighorn tracks increased. Their prints were everywhere, their droppings still soft and rank. I expected to see one at any moment, just over the next green wave. The shadscale rolled down from under my feet and disappeared over the rim of the mountain. Beyond the edge and far below, I looked back down to sea level: yellow-orange sand flats pulsing with light and heat. The mountain hid a 6,000-foot drop just out of sight.

I began to feel oddly unreal. The rabbit burrows and mole holes and bighorn scat all signaled lives in motion. And I saw nothing aside from the wind passing through the sage. There were creatures, apparently, all around me, cycling through their daily habits. Knowing this made my own presence tenuous somehow, a little bit ghostly. I seemed to be traveling a different plane from theirs, sharing only a backdrop. Even when birdsong reached me, I rarely saw the singer, and then only for a moment before it flicked away.

The sun crested, then began to slide west. The green roof of Tucki stretched on in front of me. Coming down off the upper curves of the mountain felt like falling in slow motion. I could feel the tilt of the earth and gravity pulling me where I wanted to go, but I might as well have been trekking through a dream for all the forward progress I made.

When I did reach Tucki's rim, the shadscale gave up all at once. Orange stones and tan cliffs fell away down into an immense canyon-head ribbed with bare ridges of purple-banded gray. The land seemed torn off, the way the mounds of green ended and the canyon began. I passed around the canyon-head and walked ridgelines of loose rock. Bighorns had preceded me here, too. Turds and narrow hoof-paths were scattered in all directions: across shifty scree, atop bare knobs, up cliffs. Their traces said there was nothing they wouldn't climb, nowhere they couldn't go. I decided there had to be a bighorn hiding behind just about every rock. I absolutely expected to turn the corner and see big, shiny-black goat eyes peeping down at me.

I crossed a high divide populated by decrepit old hoodoos crumbling off the edge. A new canyon, much larger than the first, gouged out a mile-broad amphitheater below me, a bowl big enough to offer stadium seating for a few million people, and we could all sit there and watch the wind and the desert colors bleeding from orange to white to purple, only I had it to myself. Miles away and deep in its central gorge, I recognized the geometry of Mosaic Canyon. And I knew what I would find down there at the funnel bottom: trails and cars and a graded road to the canyon mouth. Not the place for me. I contoured on ridgelines around the entire amphitheater, winding around towers, scrambling over pyramids of loose scree, counting invisible sheep.

Over the next divide, a deep, straight canyon climbed up out of a confusion of dark blue cliffs and peaks. It ended at the bottom of another amphitheater, this one shaped more like a cylinder than a bowl. Cliffs tumbled down to the stripe of wash below. Here was the head-branch of Grotto Canyon, my destination. The highest segment of wash hit the well of the amphitheater a thousand feet below me. A rogues' gallery of shattered cliffs and Damoclean stones waited between my toes and the canyon floor. I like to think I get along well with rocks, but the vibe coming up from below was pretty unsociable.

I sat the goblin where it wouldn't roll and went scouting, hoping to find a hidden passage into the canyon or at the very least some rock that didn't crumble under the weight of a glance. But it all appeared the same, a vertical sea of cracked plates and gravel cut through with gully funnels of loose debris. By the time I returned to the goblin, the canyon wall directly below looked as good (or bad) as any other.

Goblin on my back, I plunged down the first hundred feet, trying to find bare rock between curtains of gravel that felt like marbles underfoot. Tall corkscrew pinnacles with caves in their roots twisted up over my head. The rock was orange and brittle and made hollow clacking sounds when I knocked on it. The caves looked open-mouthed and toothy. Though I am always suspicious of what whites write about Indians, I have read that the Death Valley Shoshones hated caves and would sleep outside in thunderstorms rather than inside a rock. Looking at these ragged holes smirking out from under their spires, I understood. At best they looked simply malevolent. At worst they looked like perfect mountain lion dens—and where there are bighorns, there are cats. I'd likely have chosen the thunderstorm myself. Getting soaked in the desert is a temporary condition, after all.

Below the spires, the canyon wall steepened and I began the real climbing with the rock in my face and my fingers spidering around, searching for holds. Cottontop cacti grew out at strange angles from the rock, roots wedged into improbable cracks, bodies curving up toward the sun. Great—if I slipped I'd first be whacked with spiked clubs before rolling over the nearest edge. I gave up on the idea of finding genuinely solid edges for my fingers and settled instead for holds that I thought might at least crumble slowly. Bighorn turds showed up on any ledge wide enough for me to stand upright. I wasn't sure whether to be encouraged by their presence or to figure that the sheep were laughing at me. *Baahaha.*

I stemmed down a tight gully, each foot and hand, left and right, pressing against opposite walls. The veneer rock creaked and broke free. My boots and palms dug down a layer and stuck. Stones clattered out from under me, ricocheting off the cliffs and disappearing into the canyon hundreds of feet below. What kept such rotten stone vertical? Why hadn't it all fallen off long ago? I guess there's only more bad rock under the outermost, and it keeps going down and down.

Just above the canyon floor, the rock transformed. My gully necked down into a tight cleft cut through a plug of smooth, gray dolomite. High above, from the edge of the canyon, I hadn't been able to see inside this slot. All the way down I imagined an unclimbable fall hidden in its belly that would send me right back up the nine hundred feet of vertical kitty litter I had just descended. Sticking my head over the edge, I saw short, blank drops and water-sculpted ripples that pleated the rock, making it look like draped fabric. But I also saw holds. I dug out the length of cord I had brought along for the purpose and lowered the goblin into the shadows. Then I tiptoed down the smooth, cool stone, fingers and boot edges finding chinks in the gray armor. The walls of the slot reached up and seemed to pinch off overhead. I doubted the sun ever touched the bottom.

Stepping down into the perpetual twilight and a bed of soft gravel left by the last flood, I finally found my sheep. Vertebrae, pelvis, femurs, skull with thick, brown horns half-curled. All picked clean except for two shinbones with fur and hooves still attached. For the second time of the day, I had the feeling that the sheep were alive here in a way that I was not—that they fully inhabited the desert, while I sifted through the debris on the surface, the turds and bones they left behind. I have seen bighorns, but never really understood them. They seem to pop into existence—kicking over stones, galloping up ridgelines, not delicate creatures in the slightest—then, *poof*, they vanish again, over the next ridge, night-black eyes following paths I can't make any sense of.

It wasn't the first time I'd found a bighorn carcass in an apparently inaccessible place, either, walled in on four sides by high cliffs and blank drops. Animals fall, just like people, and once there, scavengers can't haul their bodies out to scatter the bones. But that explanation has never fully satisfied me because I've also reached boxed-off holes in Death Valley canyons and found sheep scat and no bones. Which means bighorns can get out of these places, too. (Or they take potshots from above to perplex people like me—I won't trust goats not to play tricks.) I have also heard it suggested that bighorns are drawn to deep narrows at life's end. And this does make sense to me. When the desert is so hot and bright, these cool, calm slots are a natural place to want to lie down.

I did not lie down with the sheep bones, though it was hot out and getting hotter as the sun stoked the afternoon and I shed elevation. I climbed down the exit fall from the bighorn grave, then down more falls, with chutes between them and water grooves cut through the walls and floor. The last fall led to a high-walled gateway of gray stone, which opened out onto orange light and orange rock, the head-branch of Grotto Canyon.

Canyons crack the northern edge of Tucki's shell, just as they do to the southeast, where I had first come up. But where the Tucki Wash stays broad and open, all of the northern canyons squeeze down. I had crawled through Grotto Canyon's lowest slots, so I knew the flavor of what to expect. But I'd never been to its middle or upper reaches. I knew almost nothing about the canyon beyond the first couple of miles. And that was part of the appeal, to unwrap a surprise at every bend.

I crunched through the gravel in the wash, letting gravity pull me forward. The afternoon stretched out, the sun hung heavy in the west, but I knew it wouldn't last, and I had several thousand feet and miles of canyon to descend before I could stop. I was down to my last few liters of water and the odds and ends at the bottom of the food bag.

The wash ran straight ahead, cleaving through Tucki. The canyon parted the earth, and I descended into the mountain. Walls of tan and blue rock massed above me. They stood higher and higher as I burrowed deeper. Cottontops leaned out from the stone, backlit by the sun, looking suicidal except that their size said they had occupied those perches for decades or more. A bright red weed, dead and dry, filled pockets of the wash. When I peeled back its skin, I found a vertebral line of miniature barrels laid end-to-end, a perfect wooden water pipe grown up its stem.

I turned a corner in the canyon and an eighty-foot fall dropped away below my feet. The rock spilled over the edge, straight and holdless, shaped to the image of the water that had made it, the flash floods of each new century shaving the stone. I had a confined, gun-sight view of cliffs to the left and right. I tried the left first, scrambling up a buttress and balancing out along a catwalk ledge. The ledge rounded the cliff face and delivered me to a narrow ridgeline. A second canyon, dark and narrow, cut in from the side, and my ridge became the dividing line between the main channel and tributary, a high, sharp isthmus before the confluence. Straddling the ridgeline, I scuffed along, feeling like a beetle crawling along the business edge of a knife. I palmed the crest and squeezed with my knees because my footholds kept crumbling out from under my boots and flying down the hundred feet to the wash below.

A jagged fin of rock thirty feet high breached the ridge. I got close enough to touch it, just in case the rock revealed miraculous holds, but up close, it was as steep and sharp as I had imagined. Stone sentinel forward, empty air to the left and right, I turned around and shuffled back the way I'd come.

To the right of the fall, a gigantic buttress blocked me in. No ledges crossed its face, so I walked up-canyon looking for a way to pass over its top. I waded up a loose gully crowned with short cliffs. Scrappy softballs of orange and blue rock shifted and rolled underfoot. I gained several hundred more feet before I could look for a way down the other side. When I did cross over, I found rock that broke away underfoot with a dusty rattle, an old man's cough. Brittle crusts passing for stone made me think of osteoporotic bones. But I could see ledges connecting in slashes down the face. I traversed back and forth, changing directions so many times I lost count. I felt like a ball in a pachinko machine, rattling down toward the bottom, hoping luck was with me and I'd land somewhere good. I tried not to think too much about the groans and sputters vibrating up through the stone.

Back down on the wash, I could feel the tilt of the ground and gravity pulling me forward. The canyon narrowed and deepened. The sun dropped below the edge of the mountain. The air and stone turned gray. I watched an immense steel-blue wall come toward me with each step I took, a quarter mile ahead and gaining fast. Another big fall interrupted the wash. Layers alternated down its drop—one hard, the other soft. The soft rock had been stripped away by passing water and time; the hard layer jutted out in yard-thick rectangular stripes. I came partway down a gully to the side and partway down ladder-rung layers made for a giant.

Down below, in the wash again, the big, steel-blue wall unfolded. It lifted its top ridge into the sky and threw its wings out wide. It was a single wrinkle on Tucki's knee, but it blotted out half my world. How was I going to get around it? I had no idea. The canyon ahead *felt* steep, a premonition of gathering angle, of elevation shed fast. The wash turned to run alongside the wall. Layers of red and gray striped the rock from top to bottom, each thickness representing an accumulation of years in an era so distant that earth with its inhabitants might as well have been an alien planet. The gravel ended, and I plunged into a twisting, stone-bottomed narrows. The corridor turned left, pierced the wall, and the bottom dropped out.

I peeped into the air below my feet, feeling downright skittish because the rock was smooth and round and seemed to want to suck me over the edge. The canyon did not go around the red and gray wall—it punched through. It ran down tightly boxed corridors *inside* the wall, where soft layers had been stripped away, then plunged over the hard layers. I could see three huge drops and hints of others hidden inside shadowed passages. The falls and narrows, cliffs and strata, dizzied me. I couldn't capture it all. There was too much upheaval. Too many walls and veils.

I left the goblin in the narrows and climbed a face to the left, edging up on little holds to reach a ledge from which I hoped to see more. I followed this shelf out around the sheer drop of the fall, heels out and face in, but my ledge dwindled and disappeared into a steep slab. I made a few tentative moves out on the slab, but I could feel my boot soles grind and skate, tiny motions that hatched swarms of wings in my belly. The drop was close, and if I began to fall for real, nothing would keep me. I took a look around from the end of the ledge. Steep, bad rock everywhere, the big falls lurking below. Hopeless. I retreated back to the narrows.

I made quick mental calculations. I had two liters of water and, at most, two hours of daylight. If I needed to backtrack all the way up Grotto Canyon, to return to the rim of Tucki and start over down a different canyon, then minutes were precious. If I started now, I would probably still need to work through part of the night. My water situation, I guessed, would mean trouble in the afternoon of the next day. I had until then to get out of the canyons. I felt suddenly, foolishly, thirsty. I was Pavlov's dog in reverse, my salivary glands clamped off by a clap of the canyon's hands.

But I hate unanswered questions. Bad as the canyon looked, my view had been narrow. Damn the dry mouth and the dark. I had to see more. I scrambled up to the right through a long gully filled with decomposing gravel. It topped out on a spur a few hundred feet above the goblin. The spur was a single, solid projection poking through a mountainside of choss. Tucki tumbled past my stance, a suspended avalanche of junk rock that looked much too steep to be stationary. The stone shingles looked poised, like they had all just paused to gather breath before completing the work gravity had set out for them. Down below, the polished inner corridors of the canyon bottom looked even more inaccessible, blocked not only by their own high walls, but also by the gigantic wave of rubble above and below me. I looked down into the canyon, but I saw myself schlepping back up Tucki in the feeble blue fog of my headlamp.

I took one last look around and noticed a crease in the surface of the rubble. A fracture line? No. I looked close. A sheep trail. It ran down-canyon, level with the top of the spur. Just a faint impression of passing hooves, really, not even a continuous line. It contoured around buttresses, ducked below cliffs, went out of view behind a pleat in the canyon wall and reappeared on the other side. Standing on the spur, I lost the thread after a few hundred feet. Half of what I unspooled in my mind was projection and guesswork anyway. The tracks looked audacious, preposterous. They walked right through the middle of the avalanche.

I plunged back down to the goblin and threw it on my shoulders. I had no idea where the sheep would lead me, but if I wanted to find out, now was the time. I churned back up the scree gully, caught a breath on top of the spur, then stepped out into the bighorns' domain. It wasn't a path so much as a line of hoof strikes, and my boots didn't quite fit the prints. There was always some extra rubber hanging over. The outside edge of the tracks crumbled and spat rock shards down the canyon-side. The rocks rolled, then leapt, then dove out of sight. The sheep kept a level contour, but the canyon cut deep into the mountain. The canyon floor dropped five hundred, then a thousand feet to my left, and the rim rose a thousand feet to my right.

I couldn't see more than a dozen steps ahead. Corners and cliffs and the mountain-wide asylum of unstable stones drowned out the little nicks the sheep had left me. My perspective warped into a strange shape, taking in the big, empty space below, the mass of poised rock above, but only a few yards forward. At the end of one set of hoofprints, another dozen would appear, and that was enough. The ribbon they made through the cliffs and stones vanished behind me as soon as it appeared ahead.

I lost their tracks and found myself cliffed out. I backtracked through a puzzle of rock, like a climbing detective looking for signs. I lost the way again and wound up on a treadmill of skittering shingles, with a long way to tumble if I joined the rocks falling away below my feet. When I stuck to the tracks, the way forward unfolded step by step. I have no idea how the sheep chose this way, instinct or process of elimination or a Moses of their own. But clearly they knew where they were going. In places, they leapt gaps cut by slides or incipient tributary canyons. The hoof-marks on either side struck deeper. Looking at the prints, I could see the sheep tense and uncoil, could picture them arched and airborne just long enough to make contact with the far side. I followed along. They zigzagged up solid cliff ledges, where they left no tracks. I worked to think like a sheep, to follow the ledges they would have picked.

Always we made progress down the canyon. We passed over—*high* over—the worst of the narrows. They looked spectacular: dark, secret, tortuous. Familiar parts of Grotto Canyon appeared ahead. The sheep rounded a broad curve in the canyon wall. The view opened up, and I realized that I was going to make it, that the sheep were taking me right where I wanted to go.

The canyon wall broke down. A wide ramp fifteen hundred feet long pushed out into the space below me, where before there'd been nothing but cliffs and drops. The ramp stepped down to a familiar confluence in the lower canyon. The sheep tracks petered out. Maybe that was their way of saying, *on your way now*. Or maybe the bighorns use the ramp, too. Maybe I simply lost their tracks when I no longer needed them. I lumbered down the long prow, feeling clumsy, noticing that it was twilight and my legs had worn out their elastic again. I scooched off ledges and crabbed across slabs, too tired for grace.

I touched down on the wash just as the shadows hardened and night spilled into the canyon. My joints felt loose, my muscles roasted, but the gravel of the canyon floor was smooth and cool. I took off my boots and socks and sunk my toes into the stones.

Once I was down, I was down. Without stirring from my seat, I rolled out my sleeping bag right there in the gravel. I drank all but my final liter of water and ate my last two tortillas, plain, and the dust from the bottom of a bag of pretzels. There was some blankness—I lost a little time, I'm not sure exactly where—but when the bats began swinging close above my head, I perked up enough to lie myself out flat.

I was sure I would simply dive into a deep black pool the moment the back of my head touched down on my shirt bundle, but sleep proved hard to find. My thoughts blew north and south. Elation at the sudden appearance of the narrows, the awesome drop of the falls, the trap, the deliverance of the sheep tracks. Foolishness at having put myself there in the first place. If I had wanted to, I could have found out more about the middle canyon in advance. But I hadn't wanted that. I wanted the uncertainty, the awe, the sudden jolt of thirst. I wanted to be alive and feel big things. At what cost? I tossed and turned on my gravel patch, looking for a comfortable position for my body and a comfortable frame of mind. Dawn came slowly.

Chapter 4

STOVEPIPE WELLS

The point of view is born of the desert herself. When you are there, face to face with the earth and stars and time day after day, you cannot help feeling that your rôle, however gallant and precious, is a very small one. This conviction, instead of driving you to despair as it usually does when you have it inside the walls of houses, releases you unexpectedly from all manner of anxieties. You are frightfully glad to have a rôle at all in so vast and splendid a drama and want to defend it as well as you can, but you do not trouble much over the outcome because the desert mixes up your ideas about what you call living and dying.

—Edna Brush Perkins, *The White Heart of Mojave*, 1922

Sunrise colors streaked the sky. The canyon was gray and still. The gold and pink overhead looked liquid—molten slicks blown over the top of the canyon by a solar wind.

I moved slowly, shaking off the night. Bonanza King dolomite made the walls—hard, gray stone that looked deep, almost purple, a 500-million-year-old marine layer laid down when Death Valley was under the Pacific Ocean. Canyon floods have pulled the

Pygmy cedar in Grotto Canyon.

dolomite into curves and slides. I climbed down dry falls, palming ripples, padding down rock spun into glass. A few pygmy cedars grew out from cracks in the walls, orange trunks bulging up from the rock, opening into fans of crooked limbs and green needles. The canyon walls curved in overhead, making the wash feel almost subterranean.

I slipped through the last narrows and down the last fall. The canyon opened into a wide wash cut through a wider alluvial fan. I was back, back down to sea level, back in the open desert. I walked out into the sun.

Death Valley is a hundred miles long, end-to-end, and for most of that distance, the mountain ranges on either side run tightly parallel to each other. To the south, the Panamints stare across at the Black Mountains. To the north, the Cottonwoods watch the Grapevines. The exception is a wide spot in the middle of the valley, where the western mountains step back off their line by ten miles. This extra belly of flat ground pooches out just north of Tucki Mountain, and it becomes a giant eddy pool for the north-south winds.

The winds come tumbling out of Nevada, pouring straight and fast through the trough between the mountains. They pick up

Grotto Canyon.

sand and dust. Then, halfway down the valley, part of the sky current hits the north face of Tucki and curves westward into the
basin. And as the winds curve and swirl, the sand falls out and
builds dunes.

I walked through creosotes and boulders down from the mouth
of Grotto Canyon. Sand lapped against the bottom edge of the
alluvial fan in long ripples. Standing waves stepped up from there,
crests and troughs building to the high dunes, giant mounds rising
above the rest.

Hips and shoulders of sand curved up to peaks like tented silk.
Mary Austin's tawny desert-woman stands right here. The land is
almost embarrassingly voluptuous. I'm half surprised the RV-ing
armies of Christ and Muhammad haven't complained to the park
service about the indecency. As Austin points out, you couldn't
move those sand piles. They are alive, born of force as much as
sand. The big dunes keep their shapes from decade to decade:
every year, the same lines and curves and peaks—patterns made by
the wind raking the land. The inertia of time and the desert is built
right into them. Behind the dunes, the purple and red Grapevine
Mountains twisted up into the sky.

My stomach whined and made noises like the last cup of
water down a drain. I mentally listed the things I'd like to eat.
Pizza. Blackberry pie. Half a dozen Jonagold apples. I played a
game: What would the forty-niners' food fantasies have been?
Tables spread with mutton and eggs and ice cream? No beef, I
presumed, given their desert diet of rotted ox meat. Cornbread?
Sponge cake? Jackrabbit sushi? The first real meal that Manly and
Rogers ate on the far side of the Mojave was a stew of hawk, quail,
and crow. Manly reported that the quail was delicious, the hawk
pretty fair, but the crow abominable. I guess they weren't hungry
enough yet.

Dunes and the Grapevine Mountains.

The buildings and sun-lit roofs of Stovepipe Wells surfaced a few miles off. They looked like bee boxes set down among the creosotes. Details traveled through the dry morning air as through a lens. I could see the stars and stripes of the flag over the ranger station, which meant it was sometime after eight thirty. My stomach fussed again and said it knew exactly what time it was. I walked on, sand to my right, stones rising to Tucki on my left. Some Jayhawkers and Bugsmashers passed by here, along the edge of the sand, after leaving their burnt wagons by the salt. Others probably went up and over the Tucki and Blackwater Washes. Their routes are hard to pin down. The landmarks they described are unhelpful. Rocks. Sand. Mesquites. The land had no names, and the men were half out of their minds anyway. They merged and dispersed like birds in flight. Along the way, a group of them buried something like $2,500 in gold coins in a blanket under a creosote. The money was just another rock, too heavy to carry. They were becoming like Manly or the Shoshones, abandoning money and things in order to survive. Several of them even tossed aside their guns. They had seen nothing to shoot for weeks. A few days later in the Panamint Valley, an Illinoisan who had exhausted his spoonfuls of flour offered a group of Mississippians a $5 coin—more than $100 today—for a single biscuit. Finding no takers, he wept into the sand over his money and his Knox County hog and corn farm and the last strings of rancid jerky he had left to eat.

Not all of them were so far gone. One man who kept his gun was Jim Martin of the Bugsmashers. He apparently had deep reserves and a case of Western fever so virulent that he would literally take a piece of the desert with him. On the far side of Tucki, he noticed chunks of silver float—surface ore—and put one in his pocket. When he made it through to Mariposa (or Los Angeles, depending on which story you read), he took his rifle and the piece of float to a gunsmith and asked him to replace the front sight of the gun, which had come off on the crossing, with the bit of souvenir ore. It was thereupon discovered that the rock was so heavy with silver that it might as well have been fresh out of a smelting furnace.

Whether this actually happened, and whether the nugget in question was pure silver or mostly lead or just a greasy stone, doesn't matter. Because people *believed* the story. And the story spread, until prospectors and speculators all over California and Nevada were talking about the Bugsmasher and his gun. That pebble of ore sprouted and grew until it was the top point of a whole mountain of pure silver way out in the desert just waiting for the right set of eyes. It became known as the Gunsight Lode, and when people went looking for the silver mountain and couldn't find it, it became the Lost Gunsight.

Another tale: Two Germans traveling with the Jayhawkers, John Goller and a companion, found nuggets of gold. The men were starving, thirsting, shuffling through a ravine somewhere beyond the Panamints. Goller showed up in Los Angeles with three bits of red-orange gold and a story that told like a hallucination. Or maybe he didn't even have the nuggets, just the story. One way or another, Goller could never quite remember where he and his nameless friend (who died down in San Luis Rey or got rich and moved to Maine) found that gold. So people began to hunt for the Lost Goller, too.

The fairytale logic of these stories sounds absurdly thin now. But at the time, beginning in the late 1850s and continuing for the rest of the nineteenth century, people scoured the desert for metal with a certainty that passed mania and became doctrine. God had made the desert specifically to stuff it with mineral wealth. Otherwise, what was it good for? The certainty that men like Goller and Martin had already found and lost the treasure inflamed the searchers. Clues and maps and riddles cost men decades, all in the quest for that one stone they needed to kick over to find the top of the underground mountain of silver. Even Manly came back, in 1860, to look for Goller's gold. New stories got told. Lost mines multiplied.

The desert faith was practiced just as fervently in the cities. Hucksters dreamed up a dizzying parade of shell companies and stock scams. They made outlandish guarantees, describing miners at work in gold holes so rich the miners were walking on the stuff. "Investors" dutifully contributed their dollars because anyone who was anyone in America had to ascribe to one gold mine or another.

Early in the twentieth century, the frenzy began to unwind. Whites in the West have been living this same story of boom and bust since they first arrived. Derelict mills and half-started diggings scattered across the Death Valley backcountry look ridiculous now—just like the unfinished plywood and plastic sheeting of abandoned strip developments in 2009's suburbia. Building houses when there's no one to occupy them, digging mines where there is no ore—that's the tradition of the American West. World War I briefly spiked the price of antimony, causing one last scramble for war metals. By the end of the war, Death Valley had emptied out. A few isolated mines remained, along with the most hard-bitten prospectors and a couple of big borate operations along the Tonopah & Tidewater Railroad east of the Black Mountains.

Walking between the mountain and the sand, I could see Jim Martin and John Goller stumbling through on their way to spark the human wildfire of mining in Death Valley. The men who followed them swarmed the mountains and valleys, chewing through the ground like the caterpillars I'd watched munch the springtime bloom.

No matter where else I steered them, my thoughts all seemed to loop back around to eating. Manly, pass the hawk! No, there were pancakes in one of the boxes ahead. But those boxes stayed stubbornly bee-sized. That's the trouble with the desert when you have a destination. You'll see where you're headed for a good long while before you get there. I tried to imagine what I'd look like walking out of the creosotes. Dark. Thick of beard, tan, and dust. Photographs of the early desert miners show men and women burnt brown to the bone, even those who started out as lily Yankees or fair Southerners. It's hard to see how they could have thought of themselves as white-skinned.

After I ate, maybe I'd take a couple of my bottles out into the sand and have a shower. Then again, why fight the dust? One of my desert heroes is the kangaroo rat, a nocturnal ball of fur with huge eyes and hind legs, which lives in the sand and hops just like its namesake. It doesn't fight the desert. A kangaroo rat may live five years and go its entire life without drinking a sip of water. It takes in all the moisture it needs from eating seeds, and it bathes in the dust. I kept walking, willing breakfast closer.

Another portentous visitor passed through here, on the edge of the sand, just as the mining culture went into full decline. She was Edna Brush Perkins, a six-foot-tall suffrage agitator from Cleveland with a lean face and a fine, big nose that looked purposeful, like a railroad spike. She was a mother of four, a member of the extreme upper crust of wealth and class, and an occasional adventurer. She and Charlotte Hannahs Jordan came to Death Valley in 1920. The two friends took a train to Beatty, hired a mule-cart for their food and a local to guide them, walked down through Daylight Pass, crossed Salt Creek and the sand, curved around Tucki Mountain, and climbed high up into the Panamints. They were among the first trickle of tourists to Death Valley, arriving after seventy years of pioneers, prospectors, and miners had crisscrossed the desert and faded away. Their journey was brief, a few weeks, but the book Perkins wrote about it should have been mandatory reading for the flivver-driving dandies who followed her.

Perkins and Jordan first traveled to the Mojave in 1919, and they came by car. On that trip, they wanted to visit Ballarat, in the Panamint Valley, but didn't because it had been abandoned and there was nowhere to stay. They had the whole wide, clean desert to sleep in, yet would go nowhere that lacked a hotel. But on their 1920 trip, they renounced the car because the noise and speed drowned out the Mojave and their dependence on gasoline had made them feel tethered. They wanted the desert underfoot and in their faces. No machine would come between them and the land, an impressive turn of thought for Eastern socialites at the dawn of the Roaring Twenties. Back home, they practiced by sleeping nights on Lake Erie beaches. Halfway through their Death Valley expedition, they discovered that they wouldn't sleep inside even if given the choice. They couldn't be shut away from the stars and the sand. One night near the end of the trip, they opted to sleep outside under ponchos and snow flurries instead of in a miner's hut.

The desert got inside Perkins's head. The barriers, physical and psychological, came down. "We had never seen the outdoors, never really seen it," she wrote. "We had thought we saw it . . . a place for pleasant dalliance when work inside the walls was done, or a sort of glorified gymnasium." I think wilderness is still generally viewed this way—as a place for recreation, vigorous or otherwise. Death Valley opened Perkins's eyes in a way she hadn't expected. "The outdoors," she continued, "is the awe-full, magnificent universe moving along, inexpressibly fearful and beautiful."

Perkins had reached a new understanding of land. The desert is more than a scenic drive-through. A mountain should be more than a pull-up bar. These are places for coming to terms with physics and time, the rhyme and meter of the universe. Places that offer a window into the art of the planet. Alone in a canyon, hands pressed to a yard-thick layer of cool blue stone representing ten thousand years, I can imagine the atom-by-atom accretion that makes dolomite and stars. It is impossible to look at the artifacts of humankind in the same way afterward—or to take them very seriously.

I hit pavement. A two-lane asphalt string draped itself over the desert. One end trailed off into the sand, the other ran up between Tucki and the Cottonwoods. I felt vaguely bovine, stopped at a line in the ground like a cow stalled out in front of a painted cattle guard. Back on pavement, it seemed like I had just stepped off a boat, with brain sway from walking on nothing but rolling rocks.

Ranger station, gas station, motel (with bar, restaurant, and pool), RV park—that's Stovepipe Wells. There's a halfhearted attempt at Old West kitsch, wagons and skulls and POIZIN WATER signs. But for the most part, the place is a straightforward economic transaction between Xanterra—the park service's concessionaire—and a captive audience of vacationers. The first person I saw was a pink, sweating Santa Claus of a man coming out of the gas station store wearing a Death Valley National Park baseball hat with the price tag fluttering off the back. He shuttled six steps to the parking lot, donned his carapace, and zoomed away. Few visitors, then or now, have followed Edna Perkins's lead and traveled the desert afoot.

I slipped my petrified second pair of boots into a garbage can, along with some handfuls of trash I'd picked out of the creosotes on the outskirts of Stovepipe Wells. Then I went by the ranger station and retrieved the food box I'd mailed there. One of the rangers had kept it for me in a closet. I thanked him twice with a sputtery tongue—I was out of practice talking to anyone but myself. The square little room with the man behind the counter seemed fake, like a stage set. I was having trouble readjusting to my role, so I paused to give him a chance to rescue me and ask where I was headed. He said nothing, and the pause stretched, so I took my box and knotted tongue back to the gas station and occupied a picnic table in the shade of the building.

My timing was bad. Pancakes like rafts in syrup had floated through my head all morning, but the motel restaurant had just closed for breakfast. My box held the same durable calories I'd been eating for the past five days, which were not what I had in mind. I stepped into the gas station store. Plastic-wrapped sandwiches. SpaghettiOs cans. Madame Tussaud's apples. My fantasies crumbled. I settled on a strip of Kozy Shack pudding cups, a banana, and an ice cream bar.

Back at my table, eating tinny pudding and ice cream, I watched Tucki. The mountain stared back, hugely, impassively, a red and brown eruption of cliffs stacked so high I lost all track of scale. And I couldn't even see the whole mountain. Tucki held back its upper curves. You'd never know of the green rollers just over the rim.

I try to sit at these benches whenever I pass through Stovepipe Wells. They're generic, industrial park service boards, but they've acquired enough personal history that they feel contoured to me. The first time I sat here was the first time I came to Death Valley. Ashley and I had been together only a few months. We pushed into the far backcountry of the Grapevines: tunneling through canyons, scrambling behind twisted, purple mountains, finishing with an open crossing in noon sun, during which we both about lost our minds. Flushed with the desert and each other, we sat here and watched the heat rise around us while eating through a sack of oranges that had miraculously stayed cool in her Honda.

It's a good spot to find out whether the desert will call you, invite you deeper. Stovepipe Wells is perfectly situated to be negligible. A few rocks to the mountain, a few grains to the sand. The basin curves around it as if the world were a fish-eye lens and the village just a speck on the glass. The desert butts right up against the bee-box motel buildings. The RV park and campground, on the other side of the road, are simply gravel rectangles where the creosotes have been evicted.

People milled around, most of them penned in by the asphalt and pointing cameras out into the desert. Safari vests and shorts were in fashion, which made for a lot of wrinkled white elephant knees on display. A school-bus-yellow Toyota SUV bedecked with off-road lights pulled up by my table. A family of four jumped out, ran inside the store, and a few minutes later were back in the car with baseball caps all around. The gas station must go through hundreds of those things. German, French, and Japanese voices mixed outside the store. On the other side of the building a man with a sharp goatee and barely blue sky-eyes held a cardboard sign that read: 3 DAYS STRANDED. PLEASE HELP.

The placement of Stovepipe Wells is ideal as far as I'm concerned. It's right that people should feel like the desert is pushing in on them, watching them. Bob Eichbaum, who put Stovepipe Wells here, originally had a much grander vision of a resort perched up on the eastern rise of Death Valley. The hotel would look out across the mountains and down into the sand, where a damp spot had turned into a hand-dug water hole visited by Indians crossing the valley and miners traveling between Rhyolite and Skidoo. The winds liked to bury the well, and the miners, lacking the water sense of the Indians, marked the spot with a length of abandoned stovepipe. It would have been an impressive site, but one of Eichbaum's trucks loaded with building materials mired in the first stretch of dunes on the opposite side of the valley. The other drivers stopped on solid ground at the edge of the dunes, waiting for Eichbaum to come and tell them what to do. He took a look at the stuck truck and the five-mile expanse of sand they'd need to cross, and being a practical Californian, he told the drivers to drop the lumber right where they were. The spot suddenly looked as good as any other.

The year was 1926, the mining boom was dead, and tourists were the new ore. The processing techniques were novel, but the goal was the same, to separate gold from the ore-body. The Furnace Creek Inn, a creation of the borax and railroad companies, opened the very next year. Airplanes, Studebaker triple phaetons, and private cars brought in visitors to see the hellish, mysterious, menacing valley that had killed forty-niners, bewildered miners, dazzled poets, and cured the sick of tuberculosis, psoriasis, and ennui. Promoters had once screamed headlines about miners wallowing in gold holes. Now they invented lost civilizations and mysterious lights in the sky—and city folk continued to buy their fantasies.

New roads began to unspool across the desert. Prior to 1926, a tangle of miners' tracks—mostly wandering ruts with a habit of disappearing—had been the only routes for mechanized travel in Death Valley. But tourists now came in Model Ts, and it was preferable for them to arrive, alive, sooner rather than later. Eichbaum, who busted flat as a gold miner in 1907 and reinvented himself in tourism with a goat cart on Venice Beach and later a sightseeing operation on Catalina Island, spent the end of 1925 and the beginning of 1926 building a road from Darwin to the sand dunes. His technique was simple. He hired half a dozen men with shovels and drove a caterpillar tractor with a grader directly over the desert. Road complete, he charged a toll of $2 per car and $0.50 per person, and Stovepipe Wells was the end of the road.

Once Eichbaum had added people to his village of canvas bungalows, he devised entertainments for them. A broken-down borax wagon became a "lost wagon" of 1849. He played a "lost" whisky ruse while touring guests through the sand: An employee would pretend to stumble upon a buried cask, and Eichbaum would tell the story of a teamster who had disappeared in a sandstorm with a shipment of booze. The tale would cause much excitement among his prohibition-era guests until the keg was raised from the sand by the employee and found empty. Eichbaum even invented a lost continent called Mu and spoke of a canyon in which he'd found an ancient tablet covered in hieroglyphics that described Mu's disappearance.

At my picnic table, I drank water by the liter, trying to plump my cells back up. I planned to give myself the rest of the day off, and my back and legs thanked me, but I felt antsy. Plus, I was making my kidneys cranky. A couple fit-looking, gray-haired guys sat down at my table, and one of them told a story from when he was young and had hitchhiked from Panama to Chicago. I asked if he would do the trip again. He shook his head. Not a chance. He figured anyone who would stop for a hitchhiker these days was probably worse news than the hitcher. The Chicagoans moved on and were replaced by a group of college kids doing a week-long geology field study. One told me that the caterpillars with the tail thorns turn into sphinx moths, which come out big as hummingbirds. A young woman offered me a bag of snap peas from a cooler. She seemed alarmed, though not unhappy, when I ate the whole pound.

I read for a while from *The Grapes of Wrath*, my other paperback, which I had picked as an antidote to Zane Grey. In Steinbeck's epic, the Joads crossed the Mojave in the nighttime in their sagging Hudson Super Six, going twenty-five miles per hour, fearing the dawn and the heat and their boiling engine. I put down the book and looked at the cars all around me, the way they slid through the desert without noticing it. Then I talked to the man with the cardboard sign and got a convoluted road story of another kind. His ponytail and goatee were pure gray, but he didn't look older than forty. He'd hitched south out of Vegas, only to discover (too late) that he had left town going north instead. He spoke with a rueful sense of irony, as if, of course, you couldn't expect to leave Las Vegas going one way and *not* discover yourself going the other. A second ride took him over mountains and dropped him off here in the middle of the night. He was trying to get to his girlfriend's place in Burbank. Did she know he was here? Yes, he thought so. But she didn't have the means to retrieve him. He wore yellow and green Bermuda shorts and leaned in when he spoke. A Malibu beach or cut-rate Vegas hotel would have suited him—the desert dust hadn't stuck to him at all. His irises were so clear they looked like panes of ice.

I sat on a bench outside the store with a trio of middle-aged Louisianans. One, a red-faced man in a T-shirt and jeans, asked if I was German, a conclusion he'd formed because my English was too clear and all Americans had read *The Grapes of Wrath* in high school. It turned out that he hadn't read it, either, only seen the movie. But he was enthusiastic about my trek, and even more so when he found out I had a philosophy degree because he had studied philosophy in college, too. He wanted to know what I had been thinking about while crossing the desert, whether I had answered any of Bachelard's questions about history and psychology, whether I understood the universe any better. Of all the people I had talked to, he was the first to ask me where my mind went when I walked. What could I say? How could I explain about the sheep, the salt, the dolomite? I didn't understand them myself. And I'd never read Bachelard. I think I disappointed him. He perked back up when he found out about the cards I was mailing Ashley. He insisted on sending one for me. He had a high, smooth, honey drawl, and while I wrote he said, "Ah, now he's writing sweet things," and this seemed to be immensely satisfying to him, like he'd run into some kind of wandering troubadour. "You know I'll read this," he said, holding up the card. I was glad to be able to give him something.

One of the other Louisianans, a woman with an appealing tone of no-nonsense sympathy, said she was worried about the man wanting to get to Burbank. She asked him to change his sign so that it would at least say what he needed—a ride, money, a sandwich. He thought this a good idea. They had a long debate over whether he should write LOS ANGELES or BURBANK on the cardboard.

"None of us'll know where Burbank *is*," she insisted.

"But I don't want to go to Los *Angeles*," he said. "Anyway, looks like I got a job. Man says he needs a cook at the restaurant. I used to cook all the time. Big fryers." He grinned, elusively. Later, I overheard him talking to a guy in a green Xanterra shirt about the dishes he knew. And it made me wonder how many workers in modern Death Valley just happened to drift in and stick. That's certainly how it used to work. The man in Xanterra green disappeared into one of the boxes across the road. By late afternoon, he hadn't returned.

The sun sank and turned the air fire-orange. The color drowned us. We breathed it in and out. Creosotes, sand, people, buildings— all submerged in the same light. The man with the sky-eyes trekked away from the gas station, toward the sun, carting all of his things in an old woman's wheeled shopping basket. He was headed up the Mosaic Canyon road, where he had slept the past two nights. He winked at me as he passed by. "Home's where I roam," he said. I guess he listens to Metallica, too.

I filled my bottles and repacked the goblin with the contents of my food box: tortillas, figs, nuts, peanut butter, honey, chocolate, granola, powdered milk. I'd start in the morning with ten liters of water and food for nine days—I hoped. I'd given up on the restaurant for myself, regardless of who was in there doing the cooking. The pudding cups had killed my appetite.

The sun fell below the Cottonwoods, and night rushed back into Death Valley, as if the desert had drawn a breath and sucked it in from over the Grapevine Mountains. I gave Ashley a call from the gas station pay phone and found out that the cards I'd sent, including the one I had put on the Subaru's windshield, had already started to arrive. I was tired, she was tired—we made quite a conversational pair, like two affectionate pieces of plywood leaning against each other. I told her about the top of Tucki, the green waves and phantom sheep. She told me stories from her day in the emergency room. She had seen the usual, which meant gunshots and stab wounds and homeless addicts with maggoty feet and crushed limbs from freeway accidents—the damages of collective living, of too many primates packed into the same cage. After I hung up, the desert felt a little emptier than it had before.

I walked over to the campground to find a place to sleep. Darkness pooled at ground level, but the sky glowed with stars. Somewhere among the mostly empty sites, a woman began to talk to me. Her name was Edie. She worked in Yosemite in housekeeping and had driven down to Death Valley for a few days to take photographs. I sat at her picnic table, and she smoked cigarettes and spoke in bright, angular syllables, describing what she'd shot: cactus flowers, sunflowers, the mountains, and the sky. She pulled out her laptop—and I groaned inwardly, imagining three hundred snapshots on parade—but her work impressed me. She'd found colors and shapes I didn't expect. A symmetry of cloud and hill. Streaks of chocolate brown so rich they seemed to crumble off a cliff. Blue flowers like flashbulbs.

Her friend, also a photographer, returned from a star walk, and they made dinner. He had climbed some in the Sierra, and we talked mountains and Yosemite. If I went silent, their dialogue found its way back to light and color. They tossed locations and times of day back and forth, almost as if they were discussing the habits of different bird species. One of them asked me where I was headed, and I told them about my walk, and Edie said "God bless you, dude!" about a half a dozen times.

They turned in early, planning a predawn start to beat the sunrise to Twenty Mule Team Canyon, where certain colors would appear, they thought, for a few minutes at first light. I wanted an early start myself to beat the heat across the sand. I laid myself down in the campground dirt and watched the stars until I faded out.

▲

Good as their word, the photographers were up and gone in the dark. I realized I hadn't ever seen their faces. We'd sat together for over an hour, and I wouldn't recognize either of them in daylight. I drank an extra half-liter of water to top myself off and sloshed out into the sand. The goblin was heavy and the sand loose, but my legs felt good.

The air moved so lightly past me, it barely seemed to exist at all. The Cottonwood Mountains shuttered the west, their highest peaks just catching the first heat off the top of the sun. From up on Tucki, the Cottonwoods had looked like a pile of bunched burlap. Now they looked steep, high, densely convoluted—a barrier reef of limestone and dolomite. Miles of unseen canyons and deep passages wound through the range, showing from the outside only as hidden spaces between peaks and ridgelines. It looked like the kind of maze where you could hide out for years.

One obvious gap cracked the mountain front: the gate of Cottonwood Canyon. Five miles of sand and three miles of alluvial fan separated me from the canyon mouth, which opened cavernously despite the distance. I had no trouble imagining the canyon digesting mountains and spitting them out. The fan spilling past the canyon's chin spanned so far I had to readjust my sense of scale just to recognize it. I looked miles to the right to find one edge, and miles to the left to find the other. Then its shape clicked in my mind and it rose, gently, up out of the desert, a slice cut from the side of an immense and strikingly geometric cone. Its lines were perfect, almost soothing, and hard to reconcile with its maker, the canyon spigot puking out millions of yards of crushed-up mountain.

The sand rippled ahead of me, herded by the wind into long ridges like ocean breakers. The liquid shapes of the dune bodies made it clear the sand was on the move, even if its motion happened on a timeline too long for me to track. Baked-hard mud, cracked into tiles, surfaced in troughs the wind had brushed bare.

Sunrise shadow on the sand.

Large, dense creosote tangles pushed out of the sand every forty feet. The creosotes created their own dunes around their roots and stems, piling the sand as much as ten feet deep. At the bottoms of the dunes, animals had dug holes of all sizes to nest in the creosote roots. Tracks walked up out of the holes and zigzagged across the sand.

Stovepipe Wells dropped away behind me, diminishing once again to a pile of boxes placed by chance where the sand met Tucki. I could see four mountain ranges and about 250 square miles of flat creosote desert and sand, and the only interruption was the one small clump of walls and roofs. From where I stood, they looked ready to wink back out of existence and let the desert have its way.

Brown-eyed evening primrose congregated in the sand, looking a little creepy in their uniformly starched white petals, like fundamentalist door-knockers too cheerful for their own good. One or two out of a hundred had rusted bright pink or crimson. Darkling beetles did headstands as I passed by. A pair of smaller black and white beetles looked dressed up as Halloween skeletons. They mated slowly end-to-end on a leaf. Sleeping green stink bugs clung to flower stems. Mounds of black ants began to stir. As far as I could tell, they had dropped with the night—winding up scattered around their holes wherever they happened to be when the temperature dipped below their threshold—and were just now starting to pick themselves up.

The Cottonwoods hardened to their daytime orange and brown. The morning light spilled onto the desert floor, washing across the sand like an incoming tide. The tops of the creosotes around me went pink, then the color tipped down and caught me, too. The sand seemed to glow. It could have been flesh with a pulse. The tracks multiplied. I saw snake lines and swishing lizard

Tracks in the sand.

tails, rabbit-foot dots and kangaroo rat claws. Dune burrows let loose highways of inbound and outbound traffic. Pitchforked bird feet of all sizes landed, spiraled, flew off again. There were collisions, standoffs, circlings. A hole and a spray of sand showed where a ground dweller had been taken from above.

I saw no animals except for the bugs and a mummified chuckwalla. Zero. The sand was alive with them, but I drifted through outside and apart, a ghost again. It was maddening. I wanted to stake out a hole under a creosote and just sit and wait until something came out. But the sun was headed in the wrong direction for that project. The soft morning light had vanished. All the creatures with any sense would be spending the day below ground.

Here is what Zane Grey missed when he came to Death Valley. He came looking for a symbol of death, claimed the salt as a sepulchre, and called the place ghastly. But the Shoshones did fine here. The kangaroo rats are quite comfortable. It's only whites who are unwelcome—or better put, irrelevant. The desert wasn't trying to kill Zane Grey. It didn't even notice him. And whites tend to take offense when a landscape has no place for them. We fill it with poison and murderous intent, our own worst qualities. Grey had plenty of company. To writers of his era, the desert seemed almost to be a personal insult.

Edna Perkins is a partial antidote to the men and their macabre fixations. Her desert lives—and lives in full color. She found every shade of blue in Death Valley, from the big, black indigo of twilight to the pale blue shadow pools on the sand. The colors in her writing are large and dazzling, just like the land. Lamps come down out of the sky at night. White heat sizzles at noon. The colors confounded Perkins. Part of her wanted to sing and clash cymbals at sunrise. Part of her was wounded by a show of light that left her feeling boxed and claustrophobic behind her own walls of brain and skin. The desert was too big for her to grasp, too foreign to make familiar, too beautiful to turn away from. She spent a lot of time "tongue-tied . . . mute and bewildered." And these are the right things to feel in Death Valley. She forced nothing onto the desert and put the burden of awe on herself.

Herbert Hoover created Death Valley National Monument in 1933, and that seems to have dried up the pens of the writers who followed. The most interesting work since has been done by historians and photographers. Storytellers like Zane Grey and Dane Coolidge had the benefit of premixed drama—stick a man with

Sphinx moth caterpillar.

a gun and a pickax down in the desert, and a tale can't help but follow. Take away the weapons, make people do something other than fight the land and each other, and those easy storylines fade. I'm still looking for the novelist whose characters walk the salt to look below the coverlet of the world.

The earth turned to give the sun a cleaner shot at me. The color line left me behind, the sand turned flat, yellow, and hot. The air felt combustible. Insects buzzed up around the yellow creosote blooms, and I tracked the sand under their hum. I left the sand behind and trudged up stones on the gradual rise of the fan. The caterpillars reappeared. And I felt instantly bad for accusing the primrose of being too perky. Because I remembered something else the students had told me about the caterpillars—that their favorite food was evening primrose. Sure enough, not a single brave little starched-white flower remained, only bare skeletons with grossly obese caterpillars napping through food stupors on the stripped branches. Caterpillar feces piled high on the ground, and more caterpillars swarmed through the black shits looking for any shred of leaf the ones above had missed.

The mouth of Cottonwood Canyon unhinged itself. It would swallow me like a whale gulping a single plankton. Dark and cool, the shadows invited me inside. The sun was starting to pierce my hat and get into my head, and it was barely midmorning. A dirt road swung in from the south and threaded itself through the canyon mouth, and I saw a Jeep ahead, bumping slowly down the wash. I walked over to the road, flagged it down, asked the driver if he would put a card in the mail for me. Then I stepped through the gate into the mountains.

Chapter 5

COTTONWOOD MOUNTAINS

"When I go out, every time my foot touches the ground, I think 'before the sun goes down I'll be worth $10,000,000.'"

"But you don't get it," I reminded him.

He stared at me with a sort of "you're-too-dumb" look. "Who in the hell wants $10,000,000? It's the game, man—the game."

—Shorty Harris,
in William Caruthers, *Loafing Along Death
Valley Trails*, 1951

Crossing into the shadows felt like diving down to the bottom of a lake on a hot day, only here, I could breathe and stay. I took the goblin off on a wide bench of gravel by the jeep track and flopped myself beside it. I pulled out some tortillas as an excuse to stall awhile.

I heard a two-part *crunch crunch* from up-canyon and looked up to see a man and a woman with fanny packs trekking down the road. I'd noticed a van parked at a wide spot in the creosotes outside the canyon mouth. Maybe it was theirs. I waved at the hikers and said hello. I got no response, which I thought was odd. So I waited for them to come closer. Then I waited a little longer. They walked right up next to me without a hint of recognition on their faces, and I realized that they did not see me. I was twenty feet off the road, sprawled out by the goblin in the gravel with a peanut butter and honey burrito in my lap, and they walked right past me.

Spooky. I was beginning to blend with the desert. If I were a sociable person, I guess I would have announced my presence and had a good laugh with the hikers. But I couldn't help myself—I wanted to test the boundaries of my invisibility. So I whistled one loud, low note. The man perked up and looked around. I whistled again. He turned all the way around and looked everywhere, including right through me. Then he shrugged to his companion and they kept walking.

I ate and leaned back on my elbows in the gravel. The gray and orange walls of the canyon shot up straight and high above me. Whenever I looked up, I felt like Alice drinking shrinking potion— the stone jumped and I dwindled. The water ghost (present everywhere and nowhere) had cut the canyon wide, too, and the entire bottom was filled with flood-tumbled rock. I put away my food sack and heaved the goblin back up on my back. Feeling pretty anal about my no-trails mandate, I crossed to the other side of the canyon from the jeep ruts and walked the unaltered river bottom.

Limestone walls are made of shells—in this case, trillions upon trillions of little Paleozoic sea creatures from three, four, and five hundred million years ago, when the coast of North America ran through Nevada. Brachiopods, ostracods, clams, corals, algal mats. They lived, they died, they settled on the bottom and became a few grains of bedrock. Some left impressions in the stone—the Cottonwoods are filled with fossils—but most simply disappeared into the structure of the land. I'm not sure which end of the time telescope is more mind-bending. Looking through the small end, at full magnification, I watch the earth build a mountain range a single ostracod at a time. Looking through the big end, I see a hundred million generations of creatures—whole evolutionary branches—compressed to a few thousand feet of stone in a single mountain range left high and dry in the desert. I wonder if all the *Homo sapiens* who ever lived would add up to even one rib of the Cottonwoods.

Tectonic plates jostling against each other in the late Paleozoic, a few hundred million years ago, ended the tropical calm and the local production of limestone. Volcanoes erupted and pushed back the ocean, an early salvo on the modern Ring of Fire. Down in the volcanic subbasement, gigantic chambers of magma cooled, crystallized, and became granite. The volcanoes weathered away, the granite surfaced, the Sierra Nevada was born. The old limestone ranges look to the west at the new granite, which blocks them from water in more ways than one.

I passed through the neck of Cottonwood Canyon and the land opened up. The jeep track followed the Cottonwood Wash to the left; I detoured through low hills and ravines to the right. Several big canyons gather here at a miles-broad valley, a kind of stomach of the Cottonwoods, where juices and gizzard stones from all directions merge and roll around before funneling out the canyon mouth.

The heat began to wear me down. The sun seemed to be dissecting me. I'd find myself standing motionless, staring at throbbingly green desert trumpet branching and rebranching out of the gravel. The plants looked like dinosaur ganglia lit with pinprick yellow flowers. And I'd have to force myself to get my feet moving again, having no idea how long I'd stood there. The goblin slurred through off-key songs and labor slogans about mules on strike and the revenge of the jackass.

Washes, gulches, and side canyons poured into the valley from all directions, each offering another doorway into the maze. In their day, prospectors prodded the nooks and crannies, searching and dreaming. How many years could you spend convincing yourself that Goller lost his gold just around the next twist? And—more importantly—if you ever did find a joint in the rock toothed with reddish gold, would you be happy? When you traded the quest for a reality of rocks salable for some particular number of thousands of dollars, would you be satisfied with the deal? Or would you keep looking?

John LeMoigne, the man who died north of Badwater in the sand under the mesquite with his burros—the one I think about when I'm trying to hide out from the sun under branches designed to be solar sieves—passed the latter half of his life out here in the Cottonwoods. He was a Frenchman with an education, born Jean LeMoignon, and he turned up in Death Valley in the late 1870s or early 1880s. Pictures show a dignified, long-boned man with a full white beard and cheekbones browned almost black. Frayed cuffs don't detract from his gravity, though by all accounts, he could be warm in the right company—particularly if the right company came along only infrequently. One story has it that he'd come to work borax and arrived to discover that his partner and sole connection had committed suicide during his transit. Lacking the means for a ticket back to France, LeMoigne began prospecting the Death Valley country and never found a good enough reason to leave.

Though he had claims scattered across the desert, his best was a lead-silver mine in a canyon that now bears his name a few miles south of Cottonwood Canyon. The cabin he built there still stands—I once spent a long day walking up to it and found a tiny structure, half dug from a hillside. The back wall was naked rock.

Raw juniper posts supported the wallboards and corrugated tin roofing. There was enough room to walk in, turn around, and lie down. Baling wire did more work than nails.

The isolation I experienced in LeMoigne Canyon the time I visited Old John's cabin felt fully geologic—like the same pressure that turns shells into mountains pushed back against the outside world. Gray-banded limestone crags clawed out of the hills. Nothing moved—the only inhabitants seemed to be the Joshua trees and wind. Out of the V of the canyon a wedge of sand was visible five thousand feet below and fifteen miles away. LeMoigne lived there before Eichbaum ever conceived of Stovepipe Wells. For LeMoigne, to go to "town"—the Furnace Creek Ranch, or later, Skidoo—meant a two- or three-day burro trip. He may have been mining lead and silver, but he must have truly prized being alone.

LeMoigne became a local folk hero. The younger men looked up to him, a desert rat version of the wise old hermit cloaked in mystery up in the mountains. Since he wrote nothing about himself, others' stories of him are what remain, and the contradictions are endless, down to his age and the ratio of lead to silver in his mine. There was one man in particular who wrote the story of Old John. Frank Crampton, the black lamb of a wealthy New York family, ran away from home at age sixteen and hoboed west to begin a successful life of mining and prospecting. He played Plato to LeMoigne's Socrates, doling out wisdom received from observing Old John at work. Crampton was also one of the men who found LeMoigne's body and buried it in the sand.

Crampton credits LeMoigne with a kind of mental diviner's rod when it came to finding ore. LeMoigne searched obscure strata no one else had bothered with, and he usually turned up dirt that would pay. He'd leave a location notice in a can, but rarely bothered with monuments or boundaries or documenting his claims at the recorder's office—though somehow his name *did* show up all over the county mining records. According to Crampton, people just didn't jump Old John's claims, and Crampton wasn't even sure LeMoigne would have cared if anyone had. The searching and the finding made him happier than the business of filing and selling. Besides, whenever he needed money, he just went back to sack some more ore from his lead-silver prospect, which Crampton called LeMoigne's "bank."

Crampton claimed to have seen a fat vein of pure silver down in LeMoigne's diggings. Some true believers thought it might be the Lost Gunsight itself. Others saw only a low-grade lead pit. Reportedly, LeMoigne wanted a quarter of a million for the mine, though that number sounds more like a used-car salesman's opening than a serious price. In the end, LeMoigne just didn't seem to have much interest in selling out. The mine gave him a fixed place in the desert with work to do and a trickle of income. He had no hurry in him. Rather than bother with a windlass or contaminate his solitude with an employee, LeMoigne built a series of steps inside his excavation and shoveled his ore step-by-step up to the surface. That was hard, slow labor for a man who kept his shovel moving into his seventies.

In his shack, LeMoigne was supposed to have had a shelf of French, German, and English classic literature. Given the dimensions I saw, there couldn't have been many titles. I wish I knew which books he kept. I've yet to find anyone who named them specifically. *Gulliver's Travels* would suit him, a stranger marooned in far-alien antipodes. Fossil mountains by day and *The Origin of Species* at night? *Faust*? Rousseau's *Reveries of a Solitary Walker*?

I shuffled on through the gizzard gravel in the open valley, feeling like a barge floundering upriver. Colonies of beavertail cacti unfurled outrageous pink flowers. I imagined LeMoigne rattling through here, reading the rocks, finding strands of metal in the seams between the stones. He hated money, a trait told through an array of stories, each more fanciful than the last: He wouldn't recognize checks or paper currency. He ran a store in which people paid whatever price they thought right. He had a mansion built from mining royalties and blew it up in a fit of antimaterialist disgust. What sense did it make for a man with no taste for money to spend his life digging for gold and silver? How could his name be attached to so many prospects scattered across the country while the man remained so poor?

Crampton said LeMoigne simply didn't care. He turned LeMoigne into a philosopher, a Death Valley ascetic who needed only empty space and the quest. But Crampton sidestepped into fantasy often enough in his storytelling that the legend of John LeMoigne can be hard to reconcile with the hermit in his cabin. Maybe LeMoigne was just poor and stubborn, not monkish. Maybe there's no difference between those qualities—two sides of the one coin of which LeMoigne had a pocketful.

Death Valley turns out to be remarkably fertile ground for lies. Dig a little, and half-truths wiggle up out of the gravel and sand. Pinning down simple historical facts can be as difficult as parsing meaning from an old Shoshone legend. Among other things, it seems that too many men found and interred LeMoigne's body, unless they all converged there at once, like buzzards appearing magically in the sky above a carcass. Harry Gower, a longtime borax man, also claimed to have buried LeMoigne, in exchange for $40 from the county coroner. Of Crampton, he wrote, "The guy who is going to have a tough time getting squared with me is the alleged author who claims to have been associated with LeMoigne, and buried him on the desert. If he gains a bit of notoriety by his statement I have no objection as I got paid for my work. I'm sore because I doubt if he ever had the guts to dig a hole two feet deep in Death Valley in August."

Striped cliffs gathered on the eastern edge of the valley. Another canyon mouth opened to greet and swallow me. I dived back into the shadows like a happy amphibian. Alternating layers of light and dark limestone stacked the years above me. Over the narrows, immense gray crags built into mountains which I saw only in snatches out the top of the canyon. The gravel felt deep below me. I had the impression you could dig far before hitting anything solid. Explosions of apricot mallow came up out of the canyon corners, stiff green leaves and salmon-colored cups on long stems. Galaxies of crinoid fossils swirled through the walls: bits and pieces of flower-shaped seafloor animals polished to glass.

The walls closed in. Strange chert nodules, like socketed eyeballs, stared back at me from the stone. They were made of recrystallized silica—amalgamations of the skeletons and spicules of ancient radiolarians and sponges turned to flinty bulges.

A huge noise ripped through the canyon, a tearing sound, part wings, part rockfall. I looked all around. Nothing. The canyon stood perfectly still. No dropping stones or diving talons. I began to feel a little paranoid. There were things happening around me I couldn't account for. Even the *walls* were watching me. The desert felt alive and observant. I wondered how many unseen eyes had tracked me today.

I turned a curve in the canyon and saw a huge granite boulder wedged across the narrows at the end of a long straightaway. The rock was smooth as a river cobble, a twelve-foot quartz monzonite egg. Trapped against the limestone walls, it looked out of place, as if it had taken a wrong turn back in the Paleocene. The closest possible source was the Hunter Mountain pluton, a lonely batholith of Sierra-era granite shoved up through the Cottonwoods. But Hunter Mountain was still far away, and this gigantic boulder had not only found its way down into the canyon, but then been carried miles downstream. I tried to imagine the pressure necessary to move it, let alone send it traveling. Galloping water ten feet deep? Twenty? It would have been titanic weather.

I dropped the goblin and walked up the long corridor to the stone. Evening had leaked into the canyon. The boulder was cool and sleek against my hands. It felt solid, fixed. How long since the last storm big enough to send it wandering?

On my way back to my pack, a raven landed in front of me. It stared at me with one black eye-bead, then waddled down-canyon and stopped and cocked its head back at me again. I wasn't trying to follow it, but where else could I go? I walked behind the raven. Every few steps, it would stop and look back and wait, as though it had somewhere to take me. When I returned to the goblin, I stopped and the raven stared at me for a long moment with a distinct look of disappointment. Then it lifted off and dissolved into the half-light.

I sat in the gravel with my back against a curve of stone. Squabbling emerald-green cliff swallows poured out of the rock. They collided and wrestled in midair, dropping straight to the ground, wings whirling, chirped curses flying; a few feet off the gravel, they released and zoomed apart. For half an hour they dashed back and forth through the canyon, and just as the gray hardened to black, they disappeared back into the stone. I stretched out in my sleeping bag and watched the thick stripe of stars visible out the top of the canyon. Gusts of wind tumbled between the walls, bringing sounds like breaking branches. This was only strange when I began to wonder how close the nearest branches were, but by then, I was half asleep.

▲

I woke early to a cool, muted morning. The sun was a rumor, the air the same steel blue as the rock. The light made everything look submerged. Above the boulder, the canyon tightened down. The stone crested over my head in two opposing waves, one on either side of me, as if the water ghost had clapped its hands and parted bedrock. Which it had, a miracle that left me more than a little overawed. I trailed my fingers along the glossy stone, feeling the minor curves, the waves within waves. The narrows twisted through tight, deep S turns. Orange and tan streaks poured down the rock. Demented nonpatterns of white lines and warped rectangles looked like Escher and Dali arguing over tiles.

The corridor ended, and I walked out into bright sunshine. It was early still, but the light felt less jagged—I had gained enough elevation to take the edge off the sun. Wind gusts surged back and forth through the canyon. The gravel underfoot turned to sand, which set about a systematic bludgeoning of my legs. Parasitic dodder strangled clumps of sweetbush in the middle of the wash. It looked like piles of neon-orange spaghetti dumped on top of its host.

The canyon wash swung back and forth through wide arcs. Cliffs buttressed the outside of each arc; on the inside, steep, rocky scrub rolled up into the mountains. Clouds flew fast across the sun, so that the morning felt stroboscopic. A few raindrops fell and evaporated the moment they touched down.

Petroglyphs appeared on the cliffs hemming in the wash. Bighorn sheep walked next to me, masterful abstractions carved into the stone. A few lines suggested horns, limbs, motion. They reminded me of why Picasso studied Spanish cave paintings.

Bighorn petroglyph.

Rattlesnakes shimmied up the walls. Figures with human heads and torsos and enigmatic lower extremities held each other arm in arm.

A substantial body of research shows that the Shoshones had a complex system of metaphors and vision quests. Bighorns, for example, were the spirit helpers of rain shamans. Killing a bighorn lubricated the sky. But that didn't mean organizing a hunting party. The rain shaman *became* a bighorn and died in his trance, passing from human to bighorn and back again. Native tobacco or jimson weed helped him to transform his body. The drugs loosened the grip of surficial reality, made his skin tingle with crawling insects or growing fur, stretched his head, drew horns from his skull. The shaman passed to the world beyond the world through a natural doorway—a spring or a crack in stone that opened to him as he peeled off his own worldly husk. The tunnel between the realms might be guarded, often by supernatural rattlesnakes. When the shaman returned to his physical body, he cut glyphs of what he had seen, using a stone knife or chisel.

All the elements surrounded me: the snakes and sheep and human figures slipping into or out of other bodies. Old stories, half-heard, echoed around the canyon. I could imagine a wide-eyed man coming back from the dead, back from the world of power, and pecking into the canyon walls the images of what he had seen and who he had been. Just like us—shuffling symbols around and trying to make sense of the universe. Walking the desert, away from the rigid logic of machines, feeling just outside a whole secret world of happenings, had brought my latent genetic paganism bubbling right back up to the surface. A single raven landing in front of me and staring me down at the end of a long, strange day had been enough to make me wonder.

I passed the petroglyphs and trudged through the sand. Cloud fragments continued to fly by overhead. I found out later it was storming on the Sierra; the clouds were the shrapnel tossed out over the desert.

The land began to curve again. Jagged peaks and outcrops retreated behind me, replaced by sky-high bulges. Arms of the canyon multiplied and reached back between the hills. More granite flotsam rode the sand. At the junction of a big side branch and the main canyon, on a triangular boulder planted in the wash, I found a petroglyph of another kind: big, faded block letters reading GOLDBELT, with a leftward arrow below. A mini-rush happened here from December 1904 to January 1905. Prospectors hurried through the Cottonwood gate and up this canyon to the newly christened Gold Belt District. This empty wash was a thoroughfare—road signs, traffic, braying and cursing, scruffy miners and their mules funneling through, racing each other to the new digging just in case it turned out to be the next bonanza.

The first claims were located on December 15, 1904. "Lousy with free gold" read the report in the December 30 *Inyo Independent*. A "crowd" of gold chasers had already massed in the area. The article speculated that it wouldn't be long before the whole district was parceled out. A January 12 *Inyo Register* spot added that the ore was stained with iron and copper. Another *Inyo Independent* piece, on January 20, confirmed a reddish color for the ore, which must have caused an uproar among the followers of Goller. The article concluded with a last bit of hype: "The promoters of Gold Belt are already making plans for a townsite, and they predict that the new camp will soon rival the mushroom towns of Nevada."

A final *Independent* article came out on February 3. It called the Gold Belt one of the most promising new finds of an auspicious spring in mining country. "Every report that comes from the new district is favorable," the paper said. Immediately following was this curious sentence, apparently offered without a bit of irony: "Nothing has yet been done beyond surface work." And that was it. There *was* no appreciable gold below the surface. The Gold Belt disappeared out of the papers and became one more obscure name on the Death Valley map.

It took me a while to understand the mechanics of a rush. If you uncovered a quartz ledge spitting out chunks of gold, wouldn't you keep it a secret? So how does gold get found on December 15, and talk of a townsite show up in the newspapers by the end of January? News traveled in the desert, sure—the empty air seemed to work better than fiber-optic cable for announcing a gold strike. But what if there were no message to begin with? At some point,

I realized that a *miner* might want to hush a mine, but a *prospector* thrived on an inflating bubble. Excavating, drilling, sorting and sacking ore, financing a mill, establishing supply routes—none of that held any interest for a prospector. How could he move around if he were tied to a hole in the ground? His million-dollar find was waiting for him in the next canyon over. He didn't want to stay put, digging up metal like John LeMoigne. He wanted a buyer. And for that he needed excitement, hype, newspaper articles: enough fever in the air that some investor from Los Angeles or New York would hand him $1,000 or $10,000 or $40,000 just on the off chance that he truly had kicked the top rock off the underground mountain.

Frank Harris made the strike that began the Gold Belt excitement. Born Scotch-Irish in Rhode Island in 1857 and orphaned into poverty as a boy, Harris went west, alone, at the age of nineteen. He drifted through Leadville, Coeur d'Alene, Montana, Frisco, Tombstone, always looking for a fortune, before falling into a permanent orbit around Death Valley. He was a desert leprechaun: somewhat south of five feet two, with big ears, blue eyes, and gold-plated front teeth. He liked to speak about himself in the third person as The Short Man. Everyone else just called him Shorty.

Harris was a prospector—in the 1930s, at the end of his life, he called himself the last of the single-blanket jackass prospectors, a phrase written on his grave marker at the edge of Badwater. He hurried everywhere, driving his burros furiously around the desert, searching and searching, though his critics might add that he was so busy going places and chasing rumors that he seldom bothered stopping long enough to actually look for ore. Nevertheless, his name is associated with some of the biggest discoveries in Death Valley country: Harrisburg, Bullfrog, Greenwater. But little of the money sloshing around those camps ever wet Harris, unless it came out of a bottle of O Be Joyful. His destiny was to make other men rich and stay closer to the dirt himself.

The story of the Bullfrog, on the east side of the Grapevine Mountains, is typical of Harris's business strategy. Harris and his partner Ed Cross discovered handsome turquoise ore chunked with gold. They knew right away the ground was rich and so were they. Straight off, they beat it to the county seat to register their claims, then ended up in the town of Goldfield, sixty miles away. Harris flashed an ore sample at anyone with a dollar to buy him a drink. In a matter of hours, he had a rush under way like nothing anyone had seen. Company miners, clerks, and waiters dropped their tools or trays and raced each other in buckboards and wagons to the new ground. The whole town seemed to be on the move, like an ant colony relocating. Harris recalled seeing one man on the verge of tears because he couldn't find a jackass to buy despite offering $500. Others simply loaded their gear into wheelbarrows and set out on foot.

Shorty Harris was not in the stampede. He was in a hotel room in Goldfield in the middle of a titanic bender. A saloon man kept Shorty in liquor for six days, and when he dried out enough to care, he discovered that he had sold his interest in the Bullfrog to the barkeep for $1,000. Harris's signature was on the paper next to the names of six witnesses. Ed Cross made enough from his share to buy 120 acres of prime orange and walnut land near Escondido, where he settled with his wife. Harris took his $1,000 and bought champagne and beans for anyone who would join him until the money was all but gone.

I found this story painful when I first came across it. After so many years of poverty and search, why shouldn't Shorty Harris be set for life on a spread of walnut and orange? But then I read more stories of the same pattern, with only slightly lower stakes. In each,

Shorty found interesting ground and sold out fast or foolishly and poured away any money he'd made in the deal so quickly you'd think it poison. His habit went far beyond a little problem with gambling or profligacy. I realized that maybe Shorty didn't want to own a walnut farm. When he had money, he wanted a crowd of friends and a band and a bath in about a hogshead of whisky. And then he wanted to go back to being a single-blanket jackass prospector. Can you be a prospector with $10 million or even $10,000? Maybe not. What reason would you have for driving your burros across a place built like a blast furnace if you already had the gold in your boot?

Shorty stayed in Death Valley right up to the end. He lived in an abandoned adobe schoolhouse in Ballarat, the ghost town

Frank "Shorty" Harris stands in the salt.

at the western base of the Panamints. Edna Perkins had wanted to visit Ballarat on her first desert trip, but hadn't because she'd been told it was uninhabited. A box nailed to one wall was Shorty Harris's cupboard. He'd chinked the broken window panes with old underwear; he had a hole in the roof and a rocking chair held together with baling wire, that ubiquitous desert glue. The year before he died, he accidentally pulled a wall of his shack down on himself and was nearly crushed to death. He recuperated at a friend's house near Pasadena. When he returned to Ballarat, he greeted his broken-down schoolhouse and said, with complete satisfaction, "Well, haven't I got a dam' fine home?" A comfortable life in Escondido was not on The Short Man's agenda.

Shorty Harris and John LeMoigne differed in nearly every respect—personality, education, height. But they shared the same dysfunction when it came to money. Old John wouldn't touch the stuff, and Shorty burned through his cash as if it were a sickness that had to be purged. They were the men in the ground, two of Death Valley's most entrenched seekers, but it seems they wanted the seeking much more than the gold. Once the government stamp got put on the raw coinage they dug, the quest became a materiality of bank accounts, interest rates, diamond pinkie rings. Money was the one thing that could take them from the desert and put them behind a stack of papers and a desk in a ranch-house office.

I detoured into a side canyon to get water from a spring. Five minutes up, I found the end of the flow, sinking straight down into the sand. A few minutes higher, and the water made a clear, fast creek lined with willows, cat's claw, and cattails. I filled seven bottles—fourteen liters—enough for two and a half days of clear pee or four days of dry mouth and headaches, all depending on how fast I reached the next source. I thudded back to the fork, having gained thirty pounds in ten minutes. My legs and back told me to plan on being thirsty. The main canyon teased me. A temporary string of water burbled right through the sand in a trench of its own making. I stopped and dumped some water from my bottles to ease my back, then drank and dumped more because it felt so good. Tiny orange butterflies filled the air and brushed past my face. Then the stream parted ways from me and disappeared up another branch, and I had to collect water all over again and regorge the goblin.

The sand got deeper and looser as I walked higher up the canyon. Joshua trees appeared in ones and twos, first on the north facing canyon rise, then on both sides. The green bayonets quilling their limbs made hands and crowns—court jesters bent into outlandish, exaggerated pantomime.

The brush in the sand thickened, coming up waist-high. I followed narrow leads between the sage. Small tracks—mice, rabbits—dashed crossways through the open space. Hoofprints—deer, bighorns, wild burros—followed the leads with me. I looked up for a moment to pick out the path of least resistance; when I looked back down, I'd been joined by lion tracks. They were fresh. *Really* fresh—the prints seemed barely settled. I put my hand in one, and my palm didn't cover it.

I looked up and all around and realized that I would never see the cat unless it wanted me to. The sage was so thick a two-hundred-pound mountain lion could have been five feet to my left or right and invisible. I walked on, feeling like the desert itself stalked the canyon ahead of me.

I am not ideal cat food: too big, too strange, and when the tracks were before me, I felt fairly secure of my inedible-ness. But when the tracks disappeared into the sage on either side, I had to work harder to ignore the reality that although I wasn't a deer, I was still juicy, slow-moving meat. After a few minutes, the tracks would reenter my lead and slink along through the sand, and I'd breathe a little easier despite myself. Mountain lion tracks usually run shallow, befitting a perfectly balanced animal built like an antigravity spring. But these prints pressed deep, and I struggled to fill them with a cat of the right size.

I meet black bears all the time in the mountains, and I'm easy with them. They're like big, hyperintelligent dogs, with expressive faces and postures, who'll let you know exactly what they're thinking. Mountain lions offer nothing. There's no interspecies communication, no mutual recognition. Their eyes are withering, like something out of the night sky. Deep off, old, paralyzing. I don't see them often, but when one looks my way, I'm not sure whether it sees man, food, or nothing at all. Just like the desert.

I followed the intermittent cat tracks for nearly an hour. I stopped worrying about when the cat had eaten last. I only hoped for a glimpse, a moment of tawny reality to fill those prints. Too many secrets, too many signs—the feeling of constant nearness was getting to me. The sage hills, repetitive, endless, crested up toward the sky, and the sun dropped behind them. A tall, upright figure backlit by the sun stood on the profile of one hill. Somebody out here? No— the silhouette didn't move. Its shoulders and head convinced me I was seeing some kind of carved idol, stuck there in the ground for cultish reasons that I could only imagine. I came closer and found a lanky, anthropomorphic Joshua tree grinning at me.

The canyon corkscrewed through steep, scrappy cliffs, then pushed straight through a bottleneck between two hills into high, open ground beyond. The sun had gone over the horizon for good by the time I made the Gold Belt District. Evening gathered in the sage. Cold air pooled in the ground hollows and in my lungs. I was back up to five thousand feet and glad I'd thrown a warm hat in my food box before I sent it to Stovepipe Wells.

Four collapsed cabins clustered on a short hillside. A flipped car, sporting tail fins and a chrome bumper, disintegrated into the sand next to a rotting mound of empty tin cans. A small cargo truck rusted picturesquely on a rise—a 1940s-era K-series International, bug-eyed, about the size of a modern F250, only with a cab that would barely seat two, one of whom would be straddling the yard-long stick shift. Behind the truck, a dense colony of wild rose showed the location of a spring, though a machete and a Kevlar bodysuit looked to be the minimum requirements for reaching water.

The story of the Gold Belt could be told, with different details, about most Death Valley mining districts. Surface gold and a heedless rush. Boosters bragging of a townsite one week, the district emptying the next. Ten years later, in 1916, with World War I

Cargo truck in the Gold Belt District.

in full swing, Shorty Harris came back through and found some tungsten, an element suddenly demanded by weapons makers who needed its high melting point to harden the steel of large guns. He managed to stay in one place long enough to sack and ship a few hundred pounds of ore—worth $1,500—but that was about all the ground had to give. Another thirty years passed. Talc miners opened several diggings in the area. The wreckage I saw was theirs. The talc men had more staying power, but by the 1960s, their last productivity petered out. A couple wollastonite mines may have stayed active into the 1970s. A very few Death Valley mining camps, like the Bullfrog, made millionaires. Most, like the Gold Belt, produced some piles of rusting junk and a few hundred tons of talc.

I poked around the cabins in the last of the light. They had been well made. Red tar shingles on the roofs, double-layered wooden floors that would have kept out winter cold and summer snakes. A Royal Rose propane range stood upright among shattered boards. A broken door retained a knob and keyhole. Each of the cabins, in the end, simply leaned over, the roof outliving the corner beams and joints. Two had gone uphill, propping their intact roofs against the hillside. Two went downhill in explosions of snapped lumber. They all showed the same insane optimism, that this place could be made to produce money.

The history of men trying to make money in Death Valley is far richer in irony. The forty-niners came to California looking for gold and nearly died trying to escape an area that would become famous for gold rushes. The rushes? They were pipe dreams and promotion scams, fueled by urban money pouring into the desert instead of the other way around. In the end, the reliable mines mostly produced decidedly unsexy clays and salts and other blue-collar minerals.

I was shivering, and twilight made it too dark to see, so I settled into a gravel patch uphill from the overturned car, feeling unusually fastidious about my spot. It's a funny thing—I could live, sleep, and eat off the desert for months without feeling the slightest bit dirty. But put me in an old mining camp, and I start thinking of lice, cobwebs, rats' nests, asbestos, tetanus shots.

I cocooned myself in my sleeping bag and rubbed away the chill. Then I stretched out and stared up at the sky through the cinched collar of the bag. The stars were thick, like a drift of snow burying me.

▲

The newspaper articles about the district all bragged of the geologic boundary between Hunter Mountain and the Cottonwoods, the central avenue of the mineralized zone (such as it was). Here the twenty-mile bubble of Sierra rock that had wandered off course miles below and millions of years back bobbed up to the surface in the Cottonwood Range. Where the new granite squeezed and heated the old limestone, it metamorphosed. Pressure and temperature turn pure limestone into marble. But sandy, dolomitic limestone— the rock in the Cottonwoods—becomes more interesting mineral species, like steatite talc and wollastonite. More importantly, at least to Shorty Harris, the boundary area during the time of metamorphism would have been shot through with fissures leaking superheated water vapor from deep below—vapor that transported particles of metal, including gold and tungsten.

The geochemistry of contact metamorphism would have been hazy at best to the boys of 1904. What mattered to Shorty and the rest was that quartz reefs bearing gold tended to be found along these joints in the earth's surface. What mattered to the newspapers was getting people's attention, and for that, all the papers had to do was gloat over the fifteen-mile contact zone in the Gold Belt and the ledges of quartz being unearthed there.

Every up-and-coming boomtown had a rag or three: the *Rhyolite Herald*, *Tonopah Bonanza*, *Skidoo News*, *Coso Mining News*, *Beatty Bullfrog Miner*, *Goldfield Gossip*. Along with a scattershot of national headlines, the paper told you who was in town, who was getting married or recovering from the measles, what the railroad bosses were up to, how best to bend brass pipe without kinks, and where to buy land, beef, or overalls. Editorial styles ranged from stuffy to snarky, though each paper took itself and its own indispensability quite seriously. Some were even real journalistic enterprises, with standards and history—Western history, anyway, maybe as many as three or four years of continuous copy. The residents might all still be living in canvas tents, but you knew the town was going right if it had a bank, a cathouse, and a couple of printing presses banging away somewhere. Writers were basic infrastructure on the desert, right alongside prostitutes and bartenders.

One of the most entertaining of the desert papers was the *Death Valley Chuck-Walla*, a brash twice-monthly printed on brown butcher paper. "A magazine for men," the front cover proclaimed, under the title. "Published on the desert at the brink of Death Valley. Mixing the dope, cool from the mountains and hot from the desert, and withal putting out a concoction with which you can do as you damn well please as soon as you have paid for it. PRICE TEN CENTS." A mix of desert lore, sulfurous opinion, macho Western materialism, sarcasm, copper-boosterism, and occasionally even a news piece, the *Chuck-Walla* boasted twenty subscribers on Wall Street and distribution to each of the forty-five states by the end of its ten-month run in 1907. Eastern urbanites were sinking money into "prospects" three thousand miles away—prospects about which they knew nothing. Everyone with money in a mine—which, according to Edna Perkins, meant anyone with money and some without—wanted the facts, and the *Chuck-Walla* promised to "call a liar a liar, a thief a thief, or an ass an ass."

The papers all had the same dilemma. Everyone knew that many desert claims would amount to nothing and that some were out-and-out scams. But each town depended on one or two principal mining prospects for its existence, and the newspaper in turn depended on the liveliness of the town. So each newspaper felt a natural survival pressure to be liberal about roasting wildcat claims, particularly in other districts, while cheerleading the mines and miners of its own.

The *Chuck-Walla* perfected this double standard. Though it generally affirmed the Death Valley area as God's own treasure horde, it would merrily scorch a hustler or sham prospect. But never Greenwater, high up in the waterless Black Mountains, where the *Chuck-Walla* made its home. There were only two questions about Greenwater: How soon would it exceed the production of the copper king, Butte, Montana? And would Greenwater become a town of ten thousand or a city ten times as large? Three railroads were on their way, each racing to be the first. Millions were already being made—on paper, in stock certificates. For miles, the ground was practically pure copper. Capitalists were gathering like pigeons. In defense of the two men behind the copy, Carl Glasscock and Curt Kunze, they walked out broke just like all the others who rode the Greenwater bubble till it popped. No appreciable shipments of ore ever left the mines. Years later, Glasscock wrote that he felt "a little ashamed" of what he had written in the *Chuck-Walla*, though at the time, he believed in Greenwater with absolute faith.

I walked west along the contact line in the Gold Belt. The land opened up. Cresting hills and peaks encircled wide, flat valleys. My eyes told me I could reach out and touch horizons miles away. Which made for slow walking at a human stride. I'd passed through the Cottonwoods, gotten myself one range closer to the Sierra. More had changed than just the extra water I'd seen in the canyon. The whole color scheme shifted. No more reds and purples and corkscrew mountains. Gray, brown, silver, and sage draped pleated hills. The feeling of being at the bottom, underwater, was replaced by an expansiveness that went to my head. I felt pressed up into the sky.

The sage and shad brush covered the ground like short, stiff fur, shin-high. I could never really see where my feet fell between the plants. I obsessed about rattlesnakes even though it was much too cold for them to be aboveground. I probably could have stepped on a snake without its having enough blood heat to react. But it would have been a truly bad place to get bit. I wasn't even sure which direction I'd go to find the nearest person.

A few coils of dirt road connected the former Gold Belt diggings. I crossed these tracks, following the larger pattern of the contact line, then walked up a slow rise to the rim between two valleys. The sun got bright without delivering any heat. Hidden birds filled the sage with music. The air stayed dry and fine—massless, as far as I could tell, as if it were made of nothing but light. I still wore all my layers but couldn't get warm. Small Joshua trees, not much taller than me, gathered in clonic groups connected by networks of underground rhizomes. A family of leaning, reaching, bowed Joshuas looked so alive and alert I wouldn't have been shocked to hear one ask for the news.

Joshua trees provoke strong feelings in people. They're a kind of test for desert lovers. William Manly enjoyed their company. He

Joshua trees beyond the Cottonwood Mountains.

called them "brave little trees." Other forty-niners torched Joshua trees for sport, pausing in the middle of wandering through the desert just to watch them burn, as if they could revenge themselves on the Mojave through its avatar. Edna Perkins surprised me. Joshua trees repulsed her. She called them "monsters masquerading as trees."

Joshua trees mean as much to the desert as sequoias to the Sierra or redwoods to the coast range. Seeing their spiked heads outlined against a pink-hued, Armageddon sunset, listening to the whispers that seem to leak from their hairy trunks, makes me proud of the earth for engineering such wonders. Joshua trees grow on the Mojave, in a zone between two and six thousand feet, and nowhere else in the world. Like all yuccas, they descended from the lily. So they're proper Westerners; they've wandered far from their origins.

They are "trees" only for lack of a better word—their trunks don't have growth rings, just thousands of interlocking fibers. Their springtime blossoms, which require a particular pattern of rain and freeze, pile up on the ends of their branches in wild profusion, with all the ornament, color, and sexual overtones of wedding white. The bloom is a buffet for desert dwellers. The Shoshones collected the dense, nutritious buds. The larvae of the tiny white yucca moth, the Joshua tree's pollinator, live on its seeds.

Down the other side of the pass, I walked through the middle of the Ulida Flat. Even shadscale had trouble growing here. A few clumps struggled up through loose, grainy soil streaked white with alkali. The brush shriveled back the closer I came to the center. On all sides, the basin curved up to the sky, enclosing a huge space ringed by steep waves of brown hill and mountain. The sun finally reversed the night's inertia and the morning quickly turned hot. I shrank under the eye of the sun at the bottom of that enormous lens of earth, an atom of blood and muscle anchored between a planet and a star.

Across the flat and back on the contact line, I walked beside a spur of darkly varnished granite. A gap in the hills led me west, and the land dove down toward the Saline Valley, four thousand feet below. On the other side of the valley, still twenty miles away, the massive black wall of the Inyo Mountains tore up the sky and shut away the distance. No point staring and wondering at them now—I guessed I had two more days before I'd be pressed up against those dark peaks looking for safe passage to the other side. I'd come to the middle of my crossing, and the desert felt deep on all sides. I could see for miles and days, and the journey still stretched out of sight. I floated past silvery, skeletal outbursts of shadscale. Lonelier than the salt or the sand, this high domain of Joshua trees and distant mountains cut the anchors off my bones.

I gave up the horizons and looked back at my feet. Stones twisted up out of the ground. A red-tailed hawk spiraled above me. I walked down a shallow ravine full of weathered granite boulders and hoodoos. Close by, guarding the true edge of the Saline Valley, the head and body of Ubehebe Peak climbed up into view. At its base, like an artifact of alien visitation, the three-mile-long, perfectly flat Racetrack Playa slid slowly into place.

Chapter 6

SALINE VALLEY

Coyote . . . came to some red berries. As he sat eating them, a
rattlesnake bit him. He wanted to tell somebody that he had
been bitten. He found a man, and told him to tell the people.
The man went a short distance and came back. Next time
he went farther and came back. He kept doing this until he
finally got tired. Coyote died while the man was going back
and forth.

—Patsy Wilson,
of the Saline Valley, as told to Julian Steward, 1935

The Racetrack Playa is one of the weirdest things I've ever seen.
I walked out to the rim of the granite ravine I'd been descending
and had a seat. Broken cliffs dropped straight down below me a
thousand feet to the edge of the playa. I had a perfect view of the
entire oval length of dry lake bed, but I still struggled to get my
mind around it.

The Racetrack is exquisitely, dizzyingly flat. Scientists with surveying gear, I found out later, have measured elevations and found
one inch of decline from the north to the south end. That's one
inch out of three miles. The flatness disoriented me—I might as

The author at the Racetrack.

well have been staring at television static. My eyes knew something was wrong with the signal and kept searching and waiting
for a picture to emerge.

Ubehebe Peak, a steep, black-varnished pile of granite, heaved up
on the other side of the playa, directly across from me. As the Cottonwood Mountains step down into the Saline Valley, the Racetrack
occupies one long bench interrupting the decline. Cottonwoods,
Racetrack, and Ubehebe make a deep, boxy opening in the earth.
Imagine a gods-sized horse trough perched on a mountainside,
bone dry, with the leftover silt at the bottom flattened to a geometric
ideal. I picked myself up and reentered the ravine, working down
between coarse granite boulders turning to sand in the bottom of
the V. The ravine swung around the far side of the cliffs I'd sat
above, and brought me down to the level of the Racetrack shore.

I about fell over when I first stepped onto the playa. The ground
wanted to skate out from under me. The footing was perfectly

firm, but perceptually slippery. The playa surface cracked itself into knobby, palm-sized polygonal tiles—billions of them according to a pen-and-paper guess I made. They *looked* close enough to infinite to set my head spinning. I'd never felt vertigo in vertical places, so it seemed kind of ironic that something horizontal would get me. I walked out onto the playa, and the shore where I had started receded without anything else coming closer. I was swimming through an overly symbolic dream: a landscape reduced to abstract shapes, tiles multiplying to blurry endlessness, forward motion with no discernible change. If I had any facility with graphic comics, I'd put Freud, Jung, and some dueling pistols right here.

The playa was interrupted by one outcrop, a miniature Ubehebe made of the same black granite and named the Grandstand. I could see the Grandstand, even individual boulders, but it was impossible to gauge how far away it was. What could I use to judge distance? I started walking toward it and figured I'd get there sooner or later.

I began to see people. A long, bad, washboard road connects the northern end of Death Valley to the Racetrack (and, I discovered, it was Saturday). The sweet loneliness I'd felt up above faded. Cars trundled along the road below Ubehebe, throwing off rooster tails of dust. A few people wandered around the Grandstand and scrambled over its boulders.

I walked past the Grandstand and fell in step with a man who carried a tripod over one shoulder like a lumberjack with a spruce log. We talked photography, while the Racetrack slid below us and Ubehebe clawed up into the sky, until we reached the edge of the playa and the road. He asked what kind of GPS receiver I used to track my route. I was curious, so I asked him why he assumed I'd carry one. "Might save your life," he said, skittishly, as if I'd just sprouted horns. I tried to suggest that it would be pretty hard to miss my bearing, whether or not I had help from satellites. The sun sets in the west, the mountains were that way—plus, we were in the desert, where you can always see where you're going, often more of it than you'd like. He tossed me a hasty good-bye, jumped in his pickup as if I were a train wreck he wanted no part of, and drove away. I might be physically incapable of getting from one corner of the desert to another; it might be too far, or a mountain or the heat might stop me. But to get lost, I'd have to forget which way the earth turns.

It was late afternoon, and the light began to mellow. I had time to explore, but a rough-hewn park service bench had been front-rowed, all on its own, on the edge of the playa. It looked totally out of place. And so inviting. I sat on the bench with my book open facedown on one knee, watching the ripening light animate the billion tiles.

A man and a woman walked by. They had a kind of lean, upright scruffiness I recognized, so I struck up a conversation and we talked while the light moved through all the colors of a salmon's underbelly. They both worked at REI headquarters in Washington State and were in the middle of a Death Valley sampler: hiking, canyoneering, sightseeing. They asked if I had enough water to make it to my next source. Had I realized I'd show up at the Racetrack on a Saturday, I might have hauled less water out of the Cottonwoods, but as it was, I still had close to ten liters. My food sack, however, had deflated like a leaky bal-loon. A moment later, the man returned with a couple of gra-nola bars, a slab of chocolate the size of a hardback book, and a cold beer from a cooler in their car. Comrades! They drove away waving, and I settled back into my seat. I thought of all the times Shorty Harris had told a story for a sandwich and a drink, and felt I was in good company.

An hour later, the shadows had crawled down off Ubehebe to the edge of the playa. A final trio walked back from the Grandstand to the last car parked at the roadside. I got two questions, rapid fire: Where'd I come from? Where'd I get the beer? One man asked me, mock sternly, whether I was going to carry out the empty bottle. Actually, I'd hoped he would take it. Outmaneuvered, he accepted the empty good-humoredly.

The Racetrack turned pink, and I had it to myself. I walked back out to the Grandstand and climbed up to the highest point of rock, a standing pinnacle maybe eighty feet above the playa. My shadow stretched out across the sea of pink tiles. I waved my arms and jumped up and down to watch my long double boogie across the flatness.

▲

I woke early when an owl mistook itself for a rooster. It was barely light and bitingly cold, but the insistent hooting pulled the crank on my brain, and once I was conscious, I couldn't lie still. I left my gear and descended to the edge of the playa. I found a full plastic water bottle set upright on the roadside, and it was frozen almost solid. The water had probably been left on my account; I think I made folks uneasy.

I stepped out on the Racetrack and headed south to visit the wandering rocks. Fresh legs, no pack, and a perfectly flat, even surface meant walking felt like flying. Before I knew it, the three miles had slipped out from under me. Down at the southern end of the oval, a few shivering photographers in down parkas and hats had tripods set up to catch the sunrise light on the playa.

As if the Racetrack weren't strange enough on its own, there is this additional bit of witchery: stones travel on its surface. It's no trick, and the motions aren't subtle. The rocks plow long tracks that end up baked into the dry mud for a few years before dissolving away. Remember that the playa is perfectly flat, unless you count the inch of decline from north to south, in which case, the rocks are actually moving *uphill*. The stones come mostly from a crumbling buttress of dark dolomite standing right above the south end of the playa, which is why the tracks congregate here. Individual rocks range from softballs to suitcases. Many look to weigh eighty or a hundred pounds, some even more.

The stones have been sailing around the Racetrack for at least as long as whites have come here to gawk at them. They look organized. I caught enough of a pattern to be teased by hints of choreography. An American majority of the rocks (say, 40 percent of them) headed north thirty or forty feet, then made a sharp westward turn and walked a similar distance toward Ubehebe. But others turned east, or doubled back on their own tracks, or zigzagged through indecisive swerves. Where the rocks were dense, the tracks crisscrossed and showed collisions, rocks striking other rocks and tumbling like snowballs bouncing downhill.

Geologists interrogate the travelers regularly, but the rocks, being shy or puckish or simply toeing the Death Valley code, move only when they're not watched. Some winters, no rocks move at all. Other times, they move en masse, and some individuals slide a few feet while others go on drunken wanderings, leaving tracks hundreds of feet long. Often, one rock will light off on a journey while its near neighbors remain stationary.

A lot of ink has been spilled on the riddle of the rocks. Some pretty outlandish ideas got floated in the 1950s: magnetic anomalies, vibrations, gravity tides (not to mention aliens and airplanes). Ninety-mile-per-hour winds and cloudbursts turning the playa surface to super slick mud are now the generally accepted causes. Ice also plays a role, either by attaching itself to individual stones to give the wind more grip—literal ice-sails—or by moving rocks together in floes. The prevailing winds and the likelihood of ice sheets moving groups of rocks together explain the parallel tracks and unsettling sense of organization on the playa. But researchers haven't had any luck predicting when exactly the wheels under the rocks will turn. What precise combination of mud, ice, and wind shear brings the stones to life is still a mystery. I walked among the tracks, moving rocks around in my mind, thinking of the mountain lion and the bighorn sheep, of bone-dry canyons made by sudden rivers, of the shaman tapping visions into the walls. The desert would be such an easy place to believe in a parallel world of power, where *things* happen and the earth shakes and bighorns are go-betweens and stones get up to stroll around. What's even better, that world of power is *our* world. Getting there isn't a question of leaving the here and now so much as opening our eyes.

I walked back north up the playa with the same feeling of the earth turning fast below me. The sun topped the Cottonwoods, and the temperature immediately jumped with it. I stripped down to my T-shirt and shortly began sweating through it. The whole Racetrack Valley seemed built like an old-fashioned sweat lodge: feverish days and icy nights instead of hot rocks and a cold river.

The rocks had put me in a good mood. It's a cheerful scene, dolomite bricks scooting around their ancient lake bed, playing an elaborate game of red-light, green-light with geologists. It made me happy to think that no one had yet caught the stones in action. It's a losing bet for anything on earth to evade our scrutiny, but still, it's good to think that these rocks, hidden behind gales, ice, and bad roads, have a chance to preserve their mystery. Here's an instance of a secret whose solution will mean nothing but another dead secret. So I'm rooting for the rocks.

I collected the goblin and continued north under the declining wall of Ubehebe. Up ahead, the granite ended and blue limestone began, with a stark vertical line dividing the two. My map, scaled at three miles per inch, wasn't good for much more than general suggestions, but it hinted at a pass at the contact line, and I liked the idea of descending into the Saline Valley between the rock species, along the edge of the batholith.

I walked through a large, flat, sandy area dotted with round, butter-gold flowers angled up like satellite dishes. In the middle of the flowers, I came across an old camp: a holey ammo can, some wire and rust and broken glass, a metal box I couldn't open. The long-dead camp, out in the sand and flowers and already far removed from the Racetrack road, made me think of the people I'd encountered so far. In nine days, I'd seen people in four places: Badwater, Stovepipe Wells, the mouth of Cottonwood Canyon, and the Racetrack. None of them, except the couple with the fanny packs leaving Cottonwood on the road, had been out of sight of their cars. So where were the desert rats? Where were the bearded vagabonds and harmonica-toting drifters? I like being alone, and I don't need any more rusty camps, but the Shoshone-Manly-Harris line of desert foot-wanderers seems to be dwindling toward extinction. The desert might not miss them, but I do.

I walked up a tilted field of stones that led to the pass, a blue-sky portal in the Ubehebe ridgeline. When I stepped through to the other side, I found a plunging limestone canyon with deep walls that blocked out all but a thin slice of the Saline Valley. I had forgotten how far I had yet to descend to the Saline's floor, another three thousand feet. Seemed like the canyon was in a hurry to get there.

I couldn't see more than a few hundred feet ahead. The entrance chute twisted once, twice, then dropped out of view. The canyon gave me a powerful feeling of gathering momentum, of angle dropping away from horizontal as the canyon fell down into the Saline. Still, nothing in sight would stop me. So I tipped into the decline and kicked down curving slides of blue limestone on the canyon's floor. The rock seemed dense and massive. It gripped my boots as though they'd been magnetized. I felt like a spy walking down the side of a building.

The canyon cut deeper into bedrock. High cliffs, towers, and buttresses leaned out above me. Wild blue and white layers warped my perception of the architecture. I've read that zebra stripes cause the animals to blend into one big beast with many heads and hooves in the eyes of a lion, and when I tried to dissect the limestone mob squeezing in on the canyon, I believed it. Only I was more of a beetle down around the ankles of the herd. The canyon floor spilled out from under me. I walked through empty molds carved by a coursing, foaming rush. Vacant hydraulics and plunge pools scooped tornado shapes out of the rock. I could sense the whole canyon tilting toward gravity. So it wasn't much of a surprise when the stone ended and a deep column of air opened below me. The top of the fall was undercut—looking over its lip meant looking straight down 150 feet into hammered white stone at the bottom.

I left the goblin and scrambled up on top of a single fang of rock jutting out from the northern canyon wall. The height of the pinnacle gave me a wider view of the Saline Valley, of sand and creosotes and salt, all coming closer, rising up to meet me. From a notch behind the pinnacle, a high ledge edged around a buttress and brought me to a narrow gash dropping down through empty space into the amphitheater below the fall. Sheer walls enclosed me. I leaned out and considered the chute. I was going to have to get down somewhere. I'd be dead if I fell, but what else was new?

Mentally, I played forward some climbing moves to test the line: A little stemming (exposed but okay). Some rails for hands and feet (good holds, happiness). Vanishing holds with cracks in the chute's corners (hand- and finger-cracks, possibly doable). A steep bottleneck and flaring, heel-toe chimney in shiny, water-polished rock (gulp).

I backtracked along my ledge and studied the opposite wall of the canyon. A wandering bypass shaped up piece by piece (by piece). It would be ten times longer than going straight down. By the direct way, I guessed I'd be at the bottom of the chute eating a Snickers bar in seven minutes. I killed off the temptation. The canyon could hurry along without me. I climbed back to the top of the fall, collected the goblin, and booked passage for the long way round.

Ledges and broken rock. A dirty gulley. An unnerving traverse through crumbling limestone shelves. Steep ground, loose gray plaques of rock in my face, tipping me over backward. I'd left the good rock down below. A concave ridgeline turned slender, then knife-edged. A rusty, scrappy knife, a ladder of stacked blocks. They vibrated when I moved. They were attached to . . . what? No, they were just balanced there. I could see air space behind them. I thought featherweight thoughts, tried to turn my bones hollow. I didn't catch a normal, heavy breath until I teetered off the last loose rung and reached a broad shoulder of wretched, but level, rock. This was my reward for being wise?

I'd gained five hundred feet over the top of the fall. I skirted the edge of a drop to a ramp that led down to talus. The rock seemed afflicted by mood swings, a personality disorder. Down below, it had been so solid, so smooth and massive. And it was the same striped limestone up here, but cracked, shattered, splintered into cubes like outsized crushed glass. Thin bands of surgically sharp

striations lined the blocks, so that handling the rock felt like grab-
bing the edge of a broken window. I surfed down the talus, trying
not to put too much rock into motion, trying to keep my ankles
clear of the stones that did roll. At the bottom, I crossed back over
the personality threshold and the rock settled into its enormous,
smooth curves. *Hostile?* it asked. *Jagged? Who, me?* I followed gra-
cious blue slides and baby-fat curves to the canyon's mouth.

The canyon deposited me at the head of a giant wash. Hundred-
ton boulders rubbed shoulders with rock fists and sand grains and
every size between. The piles of crushed mountain, grooved with
dry river cuts, wound down for two miles and lost another thousand feet on the way. Beyond the wash, the Saline Valley spread
itself like a massive delusion, looking too big and bare to be real:
an inland sea of sand, salt, and rock. On the other side, the Inyo
Mountains—a black wall 11,000 feet high, the last range I'd cross
before the Sierra—blockaded the west. The mountains were fifteen
miles away but already looked impossible, monsterish. Nothing
interrupted the 10,000-foot rise between the bottom of the Saline
and the freshly whitened summits on the crest.

Smaller mountains—with a visible rise of only a vertical mile
or so—encircled the Saline to the north and south. The land felt
deep. Dark summits flew above me like wings. The horizon, those
summits, looked impossible to reach. Too high, too aloof. All the
same, I could see every mile of sand between me and the mountains' feet, and every cliff and canyon stacked up to where rock
and snow met sky. The mountains made me puny, a brother to
the sand grains, but the desert opened my eyes so painfully wide it
seemed I could see everything all at once.

It had been eight years since I'd last been in the Saline Valley.
That time, I had driven the long jeep road from the south with a
friend, and we'd spent a few memorable days exploring canyons in

the Inyos and having near misses with rattlesnakes. The canyons were deep, wild, filled with wet and dry falls, and we'd brought ropes and climbing hardware. Now I'd be on my own with nothing hard but my head. Apprehensions muttering in my ears foretold dire outcomes.

Pygmy cedars scratched up from between the stones on the wash below Ubehebe. Out in the open, without canyon walls to anchor them, they looked contorted, their branches flung into the afternoon sun. I staggered down the wash, riding gravity and suddenly apathetic legs. The rocks underfoot turned to sand, and the implacable creosotes reclaimed the field. North and south, the Saline tilted up toward the mountains, which reached down into the basin with gravel fingers. Straight ahead, the Inyos ratcheted higher and higher into the sky as I trudged toward them.

The Saline Valley probably doesn't deserve to be called eerie, but the reputation sticks, anyway. It looks like an open bear trap with black mountains instead of teeth. And it doesn't help that Charles Manson and the Family prowled around here, first in 1968 and again in 1969, when Manson began scheming a bloody end to the Summer of Love.

Death Valley was the one place in California wild enough for Manson and his followers to operate without interference. At their dusty squatters' camps, they mixed sex and drugs, Satan and Jesus, love and death. Manson called his followers children (and many were in fact teenaged girls), and he armed them with knives and guns. In turn, the "children" spoke openly of him as Christ descended and attributed him with miracles.

The stark struggle of the desert—the hyperawareness of a coyote, the blades of a yucca, the rattle of a snake, the very name of the place—turned Manson on and made his followers cling to him. He told the children beautiful, violent fables about the land and the future. Among the hot springs bubbling out of the northern end of the Saline, he expected to find a hidden passage to a subterranean land of milk and gold, where they would weather the approaching apocalypse and emerge to repopulate the earth. He conducted nighttime war games in dune buggies, supposedly in imitation of Rommel's desert tank corps, the Nazi division that tore through North Africa. Manson had cross-referenced lyrics from the Beatles' *White Album* with verses from Revelations and come up with a kind of spiritual instruction manual. It directed him (among other items) to incite a black-white race war, which, he hoped and expected, whites would lose while he was underground out in the desert.

Manson roved back and forth between Death Valley and the outskirts of Los Angeles, 250 miles away, where he had another camp on a dilapidated movie ranch, used once upon a time for Westerns. Manson used it to launch his revolution. After members of the Family killed Sharon Tate and her friends in the Hollywood Hills and wrote messages on the walls with their blood, the Family disappeared back into the desert. They might never have been found, but one night, Manson and a few others torched a heavy earthmover sitting idle on the Racetrack road, and a small group of park rangers and local police tracked them down. Manson and twenty members of the Family were arrested for arson and credit card fraud in Death Valley before being charged with mass murder in Los Angeles.

Reading about Manson is enough to make you want to take a shower and go to sleep with the lights on. The brainwashing, the knives, the nighttime "creepy-crawling" raids on random houses. He is the nasty underbelly of 1969; long hair and free love transformed into a seriously bad trip. Seeing newspaper photos of him forty years later, in prison, decrepit and gray-haired, a limp swastika carved in his forehead, you are hard put to see something dangerous. Trouble is, the thirty-year-old Manson still walks the roads of our collective imagination, especially in the desert. The looks I've gotten out the windshield glass tell the story: behind every beard and thumb stands the killer. Each scruffy hitcher waits on the roadside in Manson's shadow. Until Manson's face hit the newspapers, hitchhiking was easy, a way of life. Then, by all reports, the rides dried up practically overnight. Manson didn't spawn a revolution and he wasn't the second coming—his legacy is two generations of frustrated hitchhikers.

Again I found myself hunting for shade under bony creosotes. I'd returned to the heat. It wasn't as strangling as at the beginning, on the salt, but it still stunned me, made me feel like a dumb animal, a cow looking for help from a wire fence. I kept moving. The snow capping the Inyos looked like a fever trick, a heat shimmer. I tried to tell my eyes that it was fifty degrees colder up there, but they persisted in tagging the white frosting as a hoax.

The creosotes enveloped me. There weren't even creature tracks in the sand between them. A half mile ahead, to my left and right, tight dust tornadoes kicked up out of the sand, random eruptions spiraling up two hundred feet and churning along for five, ten minutes before fading away.

I lost track of time and distance. I couldn't see any change in the middle ground. Ten miles of sand and creosote looked identical to eight or twelve. The only changes were to the mountains, the Inyos, which kept unfolding and rising—and to the sun, which slid down into the west, so that it looked as though the mountains were actually leaping up to impale it.

I stopped just before the Saline bear trap caught the sun. I didn't have any particular reason to stop where I did, but then, I had no particular reason to keep walking, either, and once I started thinking that way, I found I wasn't moving anymore. I dropped the goblin in the sand and stretched out next to it, waiting for the mountain shadow to take my patch of ground. When the shadow came at last, it felt like cold water spilling over me.

I watched the light play out over Ubehebe's western front. Orange diagonals zoomed by overhead. I absolutely believed I could see them shooting over the Inyos. For a few minutes on Ubehebe, every burnt water track, cliff, and rock stood out from all the others, the visual relief sharpened to a cutting edge, as if I'd just remembered to put on my 3-D glasses and the whole mountainside jumped out at me. And the colors! Pastels I wanted to eat. Tan, blue, white, orange, chocolate. A sharp, vertical line slicing down through the mountain divided the blue-white sherbet of limestone from the dark varnished granite. I picked out the notch through which I had descended. The canyon below looked wild. From down in the Saline, I never would have believed a person could sneak through there.

The sun left Ubehebe, and I thought about the rusty camp I'd seen past the Racetrack. For all I knew, it could have been the leavings of Manson and his Buck-knife-wielding zombies. But I'd prefer to imagine a few unhurried individuals stretched out in the sand and flowers, watching the light, thinking about scale and the heft of a lifetime, maybe playing some music.

An air force jet came howling by, shaking the air until the noise felt more like rockfall. The plane hugged the desert. It flew so low I could see stains on the fuselage and the pilot and his oxygen mask through the cockpit glass. Manson isn't the only one to have used the Saline Valley for war games. The Edwards Air Force Base sends its planes on almost daily runs into the Saline. Manson may be a psychopath, but he only caused the deaths of a handful, which is more than can be said for the sane faction of America. I felt worn out and surly, and went to sleep before the stars had finished taking their seats.

▲

I woke up sweating. It was becoming harder to get up each morning. The sun had caught me in bed. I fed myself and did some halfhearted knee bends to try to work the lead out of my legs. Then I levered the goblin up on my back, and straightaway, something connective gave out inside my shoulder. I imagined old fabric tearing at a seam.

Lurching forward through the sand, I watched the Inyos, hoping that they would come closer without getting any bigger. No luck. They kept rising and revealing more of themselves. Canyons fell down between the peaks in steep, parallel lines. Keynot Canyon, Craig Canyon, Hunter Canyon—each offered its own gate into the mountains. Rusty, dusty giants' gates, clearly not made for monkey man, which made them all the more appealing to me. Away in their darkest places, I knew those canyons to be three thousand feet deep and so tilted that flat ground becomes a noble concept, a half memory of someplace else entirely.

I'd been up Craig and Hunter before. Craig was stoppered with cathedral rooms of curving, overhanging walls. Hunter had vertical falls, wet narrows, and sections of outrageously loose and dangerous rock. I was scared of them both. But more than that, I wanted new ground. Not just new, but completely unknown to me. Every elbow bend should make me think. I wanted the canyon to pry open my eyes and awareness as wide as possible. So I'd looked at the map and chosen Beveridge Canyon, the next opening north of Hunter, as my route over the Inyos. The only things I knew about it came from the two inches it occupied on my map. One dot showed an old mining camp high up above the tree line. Another marked a talc mine perched on a ridge overlooking the canyon. That was all I had to go on. I'd been careful to preserve my personal sequestration. Not a hard task, as it turned out. Top to bottom, these canyons are big bites to chew—thick, raw cuts of mountain with a flavor acquired by only a few.

I began to see animal tracks in the sand. Like Badwater, the Saline is wetter on the west side. The Inyos, next in line to the Sierra, pour water down through the canyons, and it spills out at the edge of the Saline. In the central salt flat, a shallow lake of brine turned green, blue, orange, and brown, depending on my angle. The plants swelled in size. The creosotes lost their grip on one-party rule. Desert holly and pickleweed met on the margins of the alkali. Cottonwoods took hold and became real trees.

I passed by a thirty-foot wooden tower built with four timbered feet gripping the ground, relic from another desert lunacy. The Saline Valley runs true to its name; it offers good, clean, white halite. Table salt. And salt wasn't always dirt cheap at the grocery store. Old salt roads crisscross Europe and North Africa. Wars were fought, and transcontinental trading routes created, over the stuff. So when White Smith came to the Saline in the early 1880s and realized he was looking at an unlimited supply of salt, he had visions of empire.

Smith was a Tennessean who moved with his parents and brothers and sisters to the Owens Valley, where he settled, married, and had a daughter. He found work, initially, as a teamster for a modest borax interest in the Saline Valley. There he became acquainted with the dazzling white lake of salt that Owens Valley residents had long been carrying out in buckboard-loads for their own use. Locals called it the best in the world. Smith began filing mining claims and spent the next forty years, until his death in

1927, trying to turn a profit out of the halite floor of the Saline Valley.

The mountains were against him. The Saline was (and still is) about the most inaccessible spot in California. A railway ran through the Owens Valley, not more than ten air-miles away, but the 11,000-foot crest of the Inyos literally walled off the outside world. White Smith's salt might have been pure as snow and plentiful as sand, but he still had to move it to the tracks before anyone would give him a nickel for it.

By the time Smith was ready to tackle the logistics of putting the salt in motion, years had passed and much had changed. Smith worked in Bishop as a lawyer and land broker instead of as a teamster. In 1903, he created the Saline Valley Salt Company. The arrival of the twentieth century meant new thinking. There was a machine for every problem, the bigger the better. A precipitous wall of jagged mountains was not an obstacle; it was more like the necessary backdrop for a truly grand gesture. The company decided to run a tramway right over the top of the Inyos, connecting the Saline and Owens Valleys with a 13½-mile line of towers and cable—all for the sake of hauling 800-pound bucket-loads of salt over the crest and down to the narrow-gauge railhead at Swansea, near the edge of Owens Lake.

The usual sale of stock and hype hit newspapers in 1910, and construction of the tram began in 1911. Materials included 650 tons of nuts and bolts and fasteners, over one million board feet of Douglas fir, and roughly fifty miles of steel rope and cable. Mules and donkeys hauled the material up into the mountains. The animals even had to haul water to mix concrete for the footings of the towers, not to mention food and water for the men who built each tower (162 in all) by hand. They ran the line right along and over Daisy Canyon, one thousand feet deep and so steep that building supplies had to be let down to certain stations with ropes from above. The tram topped out at an 8,700-foot pass where the Inyos began their decline toward Cerro Gordo.

The vast machine strung across the mountains could not fix the deeper problem for White Smith and the Saline Valley Salt Company. In fact, the machine itself signaled the inevitable outcome of the venture. It was not the Middle Ages anymore. Salt roads and empires were relics in the cellars of modern nations. In 1913, when the tram delivered its first 800-pound bucket of salt to the railhead in the Owens Valley, the price of salt was $2.31 per metric ton. The tramway itself had cost in the neighborhood of $500,000. Its operation required electric power from a new dam in the Owens Valley and the diligent care of engineers to keep the wheels turning and the buckets from falling off the cables, which happened a little too often for anyone's liking. Down in the Saline, a small army of men with shovels dug salt all day long to keep the buckets full, and they had to be fed and paid. The economics proved less surmountable than the Inyos. For two decades, salt companies went into and out of bankruptcy, and the tramway changed hands like a fancy car no one could really afford to drive. None of the companies made a profit. Now the tramline is returning to the earth—the towers have fallen or been burned or blown away.

Jets flew back to bludgeon the sky. Two of them chased each other through multi-g rolls and dives. I reached the edge of the Hunter Canyon fan and turned uphill. I'd experimented and found that my shoulder wouldn't jab me so long as I didn't move it or make it bear weight. That wasn't much help, so I followed my remaining course of treatment, which was to ignore it. I walked up the Hunter fan until I found the outflow creek from Hunter Spring. The water ran so clear it seemed to barely touch the ground. It was only three inches deep, but I wanted to lie down in it full length and see where it would take me. Willows and cresses bowed down at its edges.

I sat on a rock by the spring, feeling used up. The sun drummed down. Biting flies buzzed and bit. I kicked the goblin. It barely budged. It took me a long moment to find this strange. It should have been empty. I looked inside and found big, sweating bottles full of water. I tried to remember when I'd last had a big drink, but all I remembered were headaches, heat, and creaking joints. I tried to pee, and a mustard-colored trickle came out. I sat down again and started drinking. One liter went down, and it felt like a spoonful. The second liter made me feel a little damp. By the time I killed a third liter, I'd slowed down enough that it took me four or five minutes to finish the bottle. I saw Shorty Harris shaking his head and telling yet another story of a greenhorn dying on the desert with a full canteen.

I left the goblin and headed downhill to look at the Hunter Spring arrastra. An arrastra is about as far from a salt tram as can be imagined. It is stone-age gold-mining technology, the hardest, crudest way to separate gold dust from rock. For a one-man operation, the miner lays out a circle of flat stones, say, three to eight feet wide, and lines the rim of the circle with raised curbstones. He puts a post in the middle, which only needs to be a thick branch. Lashed crosswise to the top of the center post go more branches with rocks hung from their ends. He puts ore and water on the arrastra surface, harnesses his mule to the crosstree on the post, and drives the animal in an endless circle so that the suspended stones grind over the ore—the world's most primitive, one-man rock crusher. Once the ore is "refined," the miner adds mercury to amalgamate with the gold, or simply pans out gold dust in the creek.

The Hunter Spring arrastra is six feet wide—just big enough to lie down in. The stones were polished to marble from their endless grind, and they still felt glassy. With the whole Saline Valley sweeping around and the Inyos piled ten thousand feet above, the one circle of flat stones looked superbly lonely. Imagine the Saline Valley before Smith's salt tram, without the jeep road or the jets. Just six feet of stones drowning in the desert, and a hairy fellow in greasy clothes turning circle after circle under the sun.

Possibly W.L. Hunter, for whom Hunter Canyon is named, built the arrastra originally. He filed some of the first claims in the Inyo canyons. It could have been used by different men in different years. In any case, anonymity seems appropriate, a monument to all the dirt-poor miners who came this way. Above ground, their histories are interchangeable: watch the man pull rock brick by brick out of the mountains, walk it down to the spring, grind it, pan it, and repeat the process until time or frustration catches him, and cheap metal and machines pass him by. What inner demon drove him to that kind of labor in this kind of place? That's what I'd like to know. Glory and fortune? That might bring you to the desert, but I don't think it would make you stay.

I walked back up to the goblin. Three ravens imitated the jets, playing tag in the wind. I could see the air pluck their feathers, but they made no sound.

The ribbon of water floated past me. The arrastra is here because of the creek—you need running water to pull gold from ore. So it's no coincidence that upstream lies a parallel artifact from another way of life. On top of a huge rectangle of dolomite—one of those mountain boulders that must have needed something like a biblical flood to roll it down into the Hunter Wash—are mortar holes made by Shoshones pounding mesquite beans with pestles. Women handpicked the bean pods in late spring. Young, tender pods could be eaten fresh. Mature pods were stored or taken to the grinding stone. They separated the seeds from the pods and pounded both into meal for cakes, which they carried up into the mountains for the summer. Each spring, the women returned to sit on top of the grinding rock and talk and work at the mesquite beans to create bread for the next season. Some of the mortar holes go a foot deep into solid stone.

So here are three desert-borne psychologies in a mile of the Saline Valley. There's over-the-top-lunacy: riding White Smith's salt tram, literally trying to bend space, time, and the cost curve with one grand machine. There's longshot lunacy: in the arrastra, one man against the desert, trying to crush rock with rock. And in the background, on the grinding stone, there's the slow, cyclical persistence of California's elder civilization, where the will to live became an elemental force that weathered rock over centuries. I'm not sure which sounds tougher, grinding desert beans for flour or rock for gold. At least you can eat the flour.

Petroglyphs and pictographs cover the sides of the boulder. Most have faded to spots and shades. Soon they'll be completely gone. If I squinted, I could see two upright figures leaning their heads together.

Back in the 1860s, when whites began appearing regularly in the Saline Valley, about thirty Shoshones lived by Hunter Spring during the cool half of the year. They went up into the Inyos for pine nuts and deer, they gathered seeds from sand grass on the basin floor, and the spring watered the all-important mesquites. They called their location *Ko'o*, which means simply "deep place." They long predated White Smith's claim to the salt, which they exported on foot to Paiutes in the Owens Valley (the Paiutes in turn traded it over the Sierra with tribes farther west). In autumn, neighboring Shoshones gathered at *Ko'o* for a rabbit drive and fall festival.

But then the gold hunters and borax teams and salt enthusiasts arrived. Whites burned mesquites for fuel, grazed their animals on the seed grasses, used the water to wash their salt and gold. The Shoshones drifted away. Many ended up in the Owens Valley, working on road crews or ranches or as laundresses—selling work for money to take to a store to buy food trucked in from elsewhere.

In 1935, Julian Steward caught up with a few of the survivors of the displacement and listened to their stories. Steward would go on to chair Columbia University's Department of Anthropology and become one of the preeminent names in his field. But in 1935, he was thirty-three, recently married, and between teaching jobs. The Great Depression had a stranglehold on America, so when Steward won a $500 research grant, with matching funds from his connections at UC–Berkeley, he and his wife Jane packed their Chevrolet and drove out into the desert.

They hoped to make their thousand dollars last for months, maybe a year. Steward had ambitious plans for an ethnographic history of the Shoshones. He and Jane drove dusty, rutted roads between ranches and camps, looking for old Indians who would agree to be interviewed. In the first month, they drove from Berkeley around the Sierra to Owens Valley, then out into Death Valley, Panamint Valley (where Julian talked with George Hansen), and then back to the Owens. Steward knew the desert and had come prepared with tanks of drinking water and evaporative cooling bags for their pre-air-conditioning car. For high, cold nights, he wrapped a bedroll made of ten pounds of wool batting in a tarp and tied it to the front bumper of their car. Jane, despite being city-born and city-bred, called that time of wide-open days and starry nights *Eden*.

George Hansen.

If it was Eden for Julian and Jane, it was the hard end of the fall for the Shoshones. In a single generation, their way of life had disintegrated and their homeland would no longer even feed them. The interviews were bizarre intersections: a young, upwardly ambitious white man, working in a young field, questioning ruined Shoshones twice his age who had childhood memories of whites appearing like aliens out of the sky. When vague or contradictory answers to Steward's abstract questions about kinship relations filtered back to him through his translator, he became frustrated. He fretted over the days slipping by and the cost of gas and his other expenses. The Shoshone past was about to fade entirely into the desert, and if Steward wanted to prove his theories about primitive societies, he needed mountains of data. Meanwhile, some of the men and women sitting across from him found themselves closer to starvation than their parents ever had been on the desert. The Great Depression, the gut punch at the end of the white invasion, hit the Shoshones particularly hard. After insisting that Indians give up the land and work for money like civilized people, the whites then told them there was no money to be had. In the new economy, selling their pasts to Julian Steward for $2.50 a day was the best deal going.

Back in the Owens Valley, after a month on the road, Steward met a Shoshone woman named Patsy Wilson. Members of her generation often took the name of an employer, and Jane Steward remembered the Shoshones being noticeably reticent about giving their trueborn names. Patsy Wilson, born in the Saline Valley, was sixty-six and told Steward myths from *Ko'o*, wild stories of Coyote, the trickster-hero of the arid lands who took on different roles and powers for different desert peoples. In the Saline Valley, Coyote shape-shifted with clay, populated the land out of a water basket, and acted as a local Prometheus, handing out fire. Coyote also flew, threw the sun in a campfire, and ate his own brains. The stories were violent, full of casual death and dismemberment and rebirth. Jane called them "really amusing" though she felt she missed some of the fine points. Julian didn't know quite what to do with the stories—he wasn't much interested in myths, and the ones Wilson told didn't fit into the sociopolitical thrust of his research—but he wrote them all down as best he could.

Alone by the grinding stone, I listened carefully to Patsy Wilson. *Amusing* was not the word I'd have used for her stories. Gripping or grim seemed more apt: a slapstick combination of Genesis, Greek tragedy, and a Warner Brothers cartoon. From where I sat on the rock, I thought I could understand just enough to glimpse meaning, like a kid with a keyhole view. Strange history ghosted past me, a deep human current running through the harshest of places, the muddy days of origin told through sun-blackened humor. There is something exactly right about Coyote dying from a rattlesnake bite while the man he tells walks uselessly back and forth, even if I'm not sure where exactly the rightness lies.

I collected ten liters of water from the spring. I suspected I was wasting my time and needlessly burdening my back. From the outside, Beveridge Canyon looked like a promising home for living water. All that snow I'd seen up in the Inyos had to go somewhere, and Beveridge looked deep and dark. I imagined springs and creeks bubbling out from cracks in the canyon walls. Still, if the canyon proved dry, I didn't want to lose hours walking back through the rubble fields. So I watered my load and saddled myself, an exercise in backwardness that I'd become resigned to but which might have killed Shorty Harris from laughter at my expense.

I rolled along the curving fans spilling out of the mountains, headed north, parallel to the crest, for a few miles to the mouth of Beveridge. The debris flushed from the canyons had buried the joint between the basin floor and the Inyos. The surges of stone rubble wrestled with and overlapped each other. I turned west up the Beveridge fan, headed for the gate, a narrow crack in the diorite front of the mountainside. I passed one of the several parcels of private property in the Saline, where someone has amassed a collection of huge, old earthmovers, including a crashed and gutted dump truck that looked embarrassed to be a flyspeck on the edge of the biggest earthmover of all. And then I stepped up to the canyon mouth, where I found not a spring or a seep, but a full-throated waterfall shooting out between Beveridge's lips.

Chapter 7

INYO MOUNTAINS

No part of the district is penetrated by wagon roads. Rocky trails alone, climbing in places to the face of tremendous cliffs, and overhanging giddy depths barely wide enough to receive the feet of the patient mule and burro, lead into this mountain fastness.

—"Work in Beveridge,"
Inyo Independent, December 30, 1882

Across the whole desert, I'd been haunted by the water ghost, and now the Inyos were after me with a fire hose. Water exploded off the top of the fall. It poured down the back of a shallow amphitheater, throwing mist and echoes into the desert. For eight thousand feet, this water had fallen down from the snowline through the canyon, and here it moved as if under pressure. I drank a liter, and dumped six. Thirteen pounds lighter, I scrambled up crumbling ledges of black rock around the right side of the fall.

Above, I entered another world. The Saline Valley disappeared behind the first twist in the canyon. The rock enfolded me. The current of water tripped and splashed below my feet.

The plants—willows, ferns, cat's claws—turned lush. Imagine the luck of being dropped here as a seed. Chirping birds hung out in the greenery. I watched a swallow try to snag a gigantic moth in midair, but the moth, being about the same size as the bird, shrugged it off and the two of them duked it out around a bend in the canyon and out of sight. People had been here before me. There was something that was not quite a trail but not quite my imagination either. I slipped through the growth at the water's edge, finding openings just when I expected to begin fighting the brush.

I turned a corner and hit another fall, a two-story face of moss and dashing water. An easy ramp in dry rock led up to its top and a dense thicket of black-banded horsetail, a hundred-million-year-old dinosaur of a plant that looked right at home here. Rich, warm, chlorophyllous smells filled my nose. Another step in the canyon made another waterfall, this time more of a water *glide*, past maidenhair ferns and over smooth slides of polished stone.

The canyon tightened down. Sheer white walls of marble, seventy feet high and ten feet apart, squeezed in on me and the water. Above the marble, the canyon walls continued up gargoyle cliffs and cresting waves of shattered rock—for two thousand feet, according to my map, though I couldn't see the rim so the number hardly mattered. Down in the bottom of the narrows, I'd run out of elbow room. I slipped into the current, which came up to my knees. Then, feeling ridiculous, I took off the goblin and dumped all the rest of my water except for one liter. If I got thirsty I'd just bend over.

Muck slid up my ankles and my boots filled with silt. Water plants I didn't recognize bobbed around me. I felt as if I should be carrying a machete or at least a snorkel. At the end of a corridor, another cascade filled a plunge pool. I waded into water up to my crotch and climbed directly out of the pool up slick stone next to the waterfall.

A big *uh-oh* thought-balloon hovered over my head and tugged along after me as I plowed through mud and water above the fall. I could practically feel the ground tilting under my feet. The walls climbed higher overhead. I was dwarfed and soaked and completely overmatched. The canyon was so much bigger than me, and it would take so little for it to turn me back. Twenty feet of blank stone would do, a forgotten pebble in the canyon's pocket. And I didn't care. To be in the presence of something this massive and wild—to be carried for a time in the crease of the palm of its hand—put me in the company of something much larger than my brief journey. My gate had pulled me through into ancient architecture, an elemental place: stone, water, sky. I couldn't have been happier. The canyon could do with me what it wanted.

And it did. After a few hundred yards, another waterfall blocked me, a fifteen-foot-high curtain of liquid white noise. The walls were so close that water poured over the whole width of the drop. It crashed and foamed over funky, blobby stone. I stepped up to the spray, bracing for immersion.

Two ancient ladder legs leaned against the back of the fall. The rungs were long gone and the wood felt slimed and rotten. In places it looked as though the stone had actually grown around the wood. I reached through the curtain of waterfall and the rock felt curvy and fungal in the way of stalactites and other living stones.

I climbed the rock next to the old wood. The waterfall came right down on top of me, pushing me down, making it hard to breathe. I could feel the stone better than I could see it. Water sluiced down my shirt sleeves and past my armpits, searching my nooks and crannies. When my hands froze, I groped around feeling doubly blind, hunting for in-cuts I could trust with slithery fingers.

I burst up through the top of the fall, shaking off water, imagining, for a moment, what a spawning salmon feels to clear another hurdle. The white walls of the canyon rippled past me and curved overhead. Huge hands seemed to be cupping me. Here the water has *loved* the stone. That's the best way I can describe the smooth rounds it has made of the canyon walls. The stone glowed pale like the moon. The sky became a crack above. Muddy and disheveled, feeling like a hobo in a cathedral, I sloshed forward through the mountains' vein.

The hint of trail, a few cut branches, the ladder legs—all of those signs might have given me hope that the canyon was passable. Actually, they suggested the opposite to me. I couldn't believe people would consider this a thoroughfare—so if people did come up this far, it was to see something special. And in a stone box inhabited by a small river, something special was bound to be a big, bodacious waterfall.

Two more turns in the canyon proved my hunch right. I heard it before I saw it, a sound that echoed and redoubled. Around a final bend, I found the engine of the rumble and the end of the line. A free-dropping spout of water poured down a complex of sheer, square walls seventy feet high. If I'd been dry and warm I might have stayed there a long time, watching the water come apart in the air. But I was wet, cold, submerged, and wondering what to do with the seventy feet of waterfall and eight thousand feet of mountain stuck between me and the Owens Valley.

Up above the polished marble, on the south wall of the canyon eighty feet over my head, I saw a hanging ledge walking along the rim of the narrows. It floated above the lip of the fall and disappeared from view. It looked elegant, perfect, a catwalk bypass made for me. The ledge continued downstream, suspended at the same height over the canyon floor, until I lost it in the bends of the canyon.

The stone between the ledge and me was overhung and glassy. I'd need suction cups or a team of giant geckos to climb it. I put my back to the waterfall and waded back down the narrows, looking for a weakness that would take me to the ledge. The walls ran smooth and steep and offered nothing so much as a finger-hold. I returned to the brink of the previous fall. A narrow apron of stone dropped from the ledge to the water. It was steep but not completely blank. I could see edges the water hadn't worn away. If the canyon saw fit to open the door just wide enough for me to squeeze through, it seemed ungrateful not to accept the invitation. I balanced the goblin on a step in the rock above water level, took out my coil of cord, and tied one end to the goblin's grab loop and the other to my ankle.

I pulled myself out of the water, pawing up the clean, white marble, not sure I could trust my mud-logged boots. I seemed to be carrying about a pound of river bottom in each shoe. One stone edge put me just in reach of another and another. The rock felt smooth and solid in my hands. I screwed my feet into the holds, trying to press the water out from between boot rubber and rock.

Forty feet up, a little porch stuck out of the canyon-side. I pulled the goblin up and sat it there, where it wouldn't roll. I restacked the rope, watching for tangles, hyperaware of the shape of the coils, the grain of the rock, doing all the small things with attention. The canyon had put my eyelids on the rack and stretched them wide. The details mattered. I feared the rope hooking a rock on the ledge or snagging and toppling the goblin because I feared getting jerked off the canyon wall like a toy on a string.

The apron of climbable rock bent to the right and narrowed. I left the goblin on its porch and cast off toward the rim of the narrows, angling across on more foot and finger edges. The marble wall curved away below my feet, so that when I looked down, I looked straight down sixty feet to the canyon bottom. I wondered how much padding I could get from knee-deep water. I thought I could maybe ride out a fall if I got my legs under me; the goblin figured I'd find just enough cushion to live long enough to drown. A gap opened up between toeholds. I dug my fingertips into the marble and brought my foot to my waist, knowing I'd whittled my margin of error skinnier than I should. But I was close. Some balance, a few more holds, and I was up on the ledge system I'd eyed from below.

Reality did not live up to expectations. I'd pictured a marble sidewalk with nice sharp corners and maybe a handrail. Instead I found a leaning skid row of shattered rock. The ledge angled out toward gravity—in places it was more slide than ledge. At first I couldn't even find a stance solid enough to free my hands to haul the goblin. I moved some loose rock, put my back to the canyon wall, dug in my heels. Then I undid my ankle leash, leaned as far back as I could, and pulled. The goblin swung out into space, a giant nylon pendulum bob. I hadn't realized how far to the right I'd traversed. I could feel the cord scraping across the stone and the goblin swinging freely out of sight below.

I hauled in the goblin, dragged it over the rim into the scrappy rock, worked the cord back and forth to thread a path through all the little stone hands reaching out to grab it. I cleared a few more loose stones and wedged the goblin behind a solitary cactus sprouting from the rock and shaking its finger at me like a Dr. Seuss character. *Run along, you don't belong*, it told me.

I tiptoed out along the drunken lines of the rock, lacking handholds but keeping my feet on the ledge and my body pressed close to the stone above, happy to have a trial run first without the goblin pulling me over backward. The climbing wasn't difficult, just unnerving, with crumbling bricks underfoot and the drop into the narrows right below that. Broken rock welded into cliffs piled up above me, until I lost the individual features in the immense walls of the upper canyon. The ledge swung up and down, but mostly it stayed close to the marble rim of the narrows, eighty feet above the canyon floor, and it ran true to the step in the canyon where the waterfall went airborne. A final ramp climbed above the level of the fall. An updraft of noise blew past me. I scrambled to the top of the ramp, relieved to have made it there, eager to see where the canyon would take me next. I stuck my head through a notch in the rock. And looked straight down a blank cliff. My stomach dropped. The ramp ended. No more ledge. No stairway back into the narrows. Nothing but sheer white walls below my perch and the water corkscrewing up into the mountain.

I had been a true believer in the sidewalk I'd invented from below. I would follow my wide eyes along a gleaming white passageway to the other side. The canyon had wanted me to go this way; it had told me so.

I shuffled back along the crumbling ledge to the goblin and the cactus and looked down the apron of rock I'd climbed from out of the water. It looked bad. And if I survived the downclimb, where would I be? Right back in the water with no progress made. Going forward required wings; climbing back down the blank step with the marble curving out from under me had me calculating odds. That left up. The rock above looked to be a nudge away from collapse, scary bulges with dark teeth leaned out overhead, and the cactus perched on its ledge sniggered at me. Still, I could see weaknesses, climbing lines, and I wanted to cross these mountains, not retreat back toward sea level. High above me ran ridgelines I'd studied from the Saline Valley. If I made it onto one of those mountain spines, it might carry me where I wanted to go.

About that time, I began to appreciate the full ridiculousness of my situation. Eighty feet below, a late-spring flood of mountain water tumbled by. In my pack, I had the one liter I hadn't bothered to throw away. It didn't matter—I was going up, anyway. The canyon wall pulled me along like a hooked fish.

I eased the goblin onto my back and scrambled up into the broken rock. A chute splitting a headwall had looked benign from below. When I arrived at its downspout, I found it steep and rotten. I wedged the goblin behind a block and tied the haul-line around my ankle again. The rock above felt leprous, sloughing its skin wherever I touched. I pressed and palmed and babied the stone while the cord connecting me to the goblin dangled below. I popped up through the headwall at the end of the chute, hoping for a ledge, but finding instead narrow ribs of brown stone slanting down toward me. I wrapped my legs around one rib, riding it horseback, in order to hold myself while I pulled in the goblin.

I climbed higher. Even when I didn't look, I could feel the vacuum of that gigantic empty space at my back where the earth was cracked open. Below me the canyon tapered to a dark shadow. I'd gained a few hundred feet, and already it looked bottomless. The cliffs and passageways of the canyon wall began to blur together. Absurd, vertical rubble fields, stuck together by nothing but habit. Buttresses bowing at strange angles. Tributary ridgelines that would have been whole mountains on their own if they hadn't been minor structural flourishes of the canyon. I straddled a blade of chalky white rock with big air on both sides. It was so fragile that chunks broke off each time I moved. I looked over my shoulder and saw that I'd come level with the Snowflake Talc Mine, cut into the crest of the opposite canyon-side. *Great*, I thought. *I'm climbing talc.* Higher, the rock became granite, but it was ugly, scrappy granite that gave no relief from the feeling I had of climbing on eggshells. I changed my wet, muddy socks on a ledge—a bad idea. The cargo of river muck in my boots overwhelmed my only spares, and they too became filthy squeegees before I thought to save them.

The sun sank behind the Inyos. I began to wonder if I'd make it off the canyon wall by nightfall or end up curled behind a block with my feet dangling off an edge somewhere. I started looking for a place to sleep, just in case, even though I didn't want to stop. The single bottle of water in my pack spurred me along, pushing me to arrive somewhere definite before taking a drink. I felt wrung out, like I had sweated a gallon since leaving the narrows. The idea of sucking on my socks didn't seem nearly as bad as it should have. The question of stopping turned out to be moot anyway. I barely saw places to sit, let alone lie. The canyonside was relentless, never pausing in one place long enough to make a ledge.

Just before dusk, I crawled over the rim of the canyon. The ridgeline I found wasn't much less steep than the canyon wall had been. Loose gravel shot through with weathered spires and broken horns, all made of granite, marched relentlessly upward to the distant snowline. Sage and shadscale made patchy cover, though their hard, knotted branches seemed more mineral than vegetable. I was about four thousand feet above the floor of the Saline Valley, and five thousand above sea level. I'd gained much of that elevation—more than two thousand vertical feet—climbing from the narrows to here. The Inyo summits sailed into the west, in plain sight, right on top of me, but six thousand feet over my head. I found one narrow, flat space on a little promontory and declared it home. I upended the goblin and poured out my gear. The moment I sat down, a plague of black gnats rained down out of the empty air. *No way*, I thought as I stirred through my things, hunting for my head net. *Nothing else is up here! What do they live on when they're not served human?* They multiplied enthusiastically, until I couldn't tell which was darker, the bugs or the twilight.

Directly below my little gnat-infested aerie, the canyon yawned open. It was so big and steep I began to fall just sitting there looking down into it. The wind whistled in my ears. The earth tilted. I couldn't get enough of the sensation of the canyon sucking me down. Proud ridgelines dived with me through the vertical half mile. The canyon floor was an angry snake, twisting and thrashing against the marble. I've never seen a more fractal place—unnamed canyons cut through the walls of Beveridge, and each side canyon had its own canyons, and the grandchild canyons branched into gorges made by cliffs split by widening erosion cracks. A maze without end.

I peeled off my boots and socks. My feet looked deceased— white, wrinkled, drowned. I took some small satisfaction from wiggling my toes and noting that the gnats wouldn't touch them.

I hefted my water bottle. Maybe a little more than a liter in there. I tilted it up, cautiously, pretty sure I could empty it with a swallow if I weren't careful. One, two, three unsatisfying sips. I put it away.

Between my water predicament and the risky climbing, I felt a little foolish. I'd made some damned interesting mistakes. None of it would have happened if I'd pried into the secrets of the canyon while sitting at home. But that wasn't what I had wanted. If I had dug up the guidebook snippets in Hart or Diggonet beforehand, I'd have seen what they saw, and crossed Beveridge off the list altogether. And then I wouldn't have arrived here, at an outpost floating in space, with the wind whistling in my ears, the canyon grooving my brain, and my eyes stretched wide open. I slid under cover in a steady rain of gnats, too worn out to look anymore.

▲

I turned myself out of my sleeping bag in the predawn murk after dozing through a night of red, dry, tonsil-busting dreams, hoping for progress toward water before the sun began cooking off my juices again. I made some repairs to my feet with cloth tape, then stuffed them into tar-paper socks and stuccoed boots. The explorers of old usually wound up filthy and exhausted, with pieces of their feet falling off. At least I was in good company.

The sun touched the mountaintops and brought them to life. The crest looked close. If I were a bird, I'd have been there in twenty minutes. But straight lines don't exist for us ground creatures in the Inyos. Like Sisyphus, the Greek who irritated his gods one too many times and wound up spending eternity pushing a stone up a hill only to watch it roll back down, I expected to have to roll myself right back down the side of Beveridge. I began to think I should adopt Sisyphus as a patron saint, given my preoccupation with climbing one side of a mountain range in order to go down the other.

I worked a sip of water around and around my mouth, trying to wet down all my salivary plumbing. Then I buried the bottle with my last half-liter in the goblin. Being so dry meant I had no appetite, which was just as well because the food bag looked suspiciously flat.

I had a plan, more or less. Up on the ridge, high over my head, I could see snow sparkling in the descending curtain of sunshine. Water source number one. Down in the bottom of Beveridge ran water source number two. Neither choice made me want to lose a drop of spit. I had no stove, so my only means of turning snow to water would be to fill my bottles and stick them in my armpits. Plus then I'd be up in the snow, with a lot of steep, white mountainside between me and the crest. But I wasn't too eager to charge back into the canyon either. If I chose my line wisely, I'd walk straight down and keep on till I was chin-deep in the creek. If I chose poorly, I'd end up cliffed-out above the narrows again, and then my personal drought would begin to look pretty desperate.

Either way, whether I decided to go all the way to the snow-line or return to the canyon somewhere above the narrows, I had to start uphill. The broad, round sage and granite ridgeline pushed on toward the summits, and I aspired along with it. The angle never let up. I walked where I could, and climbed through notches between outcrops of stone horns. The ridge gathered and narrowed. Beveridge carved out its immense depths to my right. Hunter Canyon did the same to my left. Just one canyon like Beveridge would be enough. Eight of them, lined up in parallel, each one falling from near ten thousand feet down to one thousand, made me feel a little dazed—maybe like Sisyphus, when Zeus finally cornered him and gave him the hill and the stone. At my back sprawled the length and breadth of the Saline Valley. Dunes. Salt. Rock.

The sun wheeled up over the Grapevine Mountains on the far side of Death Valley. The morning slipped by. I topped a rise and walked a few hundred feet of level ground on the ridge crest, while the two canyons tumbled away below my feet.

One narrow arm of Beveridge reached up the canyon wall. While I walked I looked down into it, trying to gauge its character. Ahead of me, the ridgeline steepened into cliffs peopled with daredevil pines. It could have been the subject of a Chinese scroll painting—it looked that fantastical. Did I believe the canyon could stop me a second time? I guess I didn't. I dropped off the ridge, headed back down into the depths.

I scrambled down a gigantic bowl of sage and rock funneling into a broad, V-shaped trough. Bare talus filled the bottom of the ravine. I kept my feet, barely. The floor tilted so much I couldn't understand how all the loose rock stayed put. It felt like a gravity well. The canyon pulled me down, reeling me in.

The walls climbed higher and higher above me. I could sense the approach of the main canyon, but couldn't see it. Horizontal bands of bedrock sliced through the talus. Ragged sage plants made a mean living probing the rock for water. I wondered if at some dim, biochemical level, they sensed the water running freely below and yearned for it as I did. One enormous old pine had apparently found somewhere good to stick its roots because it grew up out of the stone floor, shaggy and fifty feet tall, the only one of its kind, the largest living thing I'd seen in days.

My side canyon cut down through cliffs and layers of rock, all the way through to the canyon floor. I emerged by the creek, in the sun, under a waterfall, with willows all around. I stuck my face in the current and heaved in water—and microbes or macrobes, for all I cared—until I ran out of breath and surfaced, snorting and shaking off drops. Once I'd drowned my thirst, I could consider the insanity of what I'd done, circumventing one eighty-foot fall by climbing two thousand vertical feet up the canyon-side, and fifteen hundred feet up the ridgeline, then giving back a couple thousand and change to return to the canyon bottom. The waterfall that had blocked me couldn't have been more than a half mile downstream.

I found a long chimney system above the pool where I'd made a siphon of myself. A hundred and fifty feet of clean, brown-varnished granite bypassed the golden hose falling through the sun. I practiced it once without the goblin, then came back down, riding a solid rehydration buzz. I tossed the goblin on my back and scooched back up the chimney, left hand and foot pressed against one side, right hand and foot pressed to the other.

Now that I no longer felt like a salted snail, I was all enthusiasm, almost jittery. The canyon would open up for me now; I was sure of it. I couldn't wait to see what would happen next. Somewhere ahead lay the Beveridge mining camp, built by gold miners who came clear over from the opposite side of the Inyos and as far down the canyon as they could reach. I tried to imagine what I'd find there. Without really looking, I stuck my right foot higher against the chimney wall. My foot shot out from under me, along with a dinner plate of loose granite that popped off and clattered away. I fell for a microsecond. Then my arms locked across the two planes of rock. All my frisky thoughts rushed back into the barn. My worldview clenched. When I continued, I existed in six feet of spotlighted rock, and I saw every bit of it. Looking too far ahead, I decided, was a good way to see your own end.

The stone got even better once I started paying attention. It wasn't shattered limestone, not blank marble, not even the egg-shell granite from the ridgeline. This was clean, white, Yosemite-style granite, and it felt like the ribs of the mountain to my fingers. Above the first waterfall, I turned a corner and found another. I climbed a slab at its side, up good, square edges and a splitter crack, with the water cartwheeling past me. I curved around another turn, and the canyon straightened into a long, gradual ascent under tall granite walls.

The rock on either side stayed sheer and close, pressing in on a fifty-foot-wide stripe of living green below. In a willow thicket I found an enormous iron cook pot that looked to have tumbled down the canyon in a flood. The canyon floor turned lush. And vicious. I'd never seen such a tangle of electric greenery and spines and thorns. Never mind concrete and razor wire—you could fence prisons and demilitarized zones with the Beveridge brush. It didn't look like such a good idea to water desert plants like this.

The native claws drove me up onto the walls of the canyon. It was easier to climb across the granite than fight the jungle. I traversed on cracks and edges, ten feet above a crash pad of thorns. I stemmed across corners, changed levels between shelves, dinked my feet along little nicks in the stone. An overhanging buttress ended my fun. I could see friendly ground on the opposite canyon-side, so I lowered myself into the weaponized shrubbery.

The twenty-minute bird flight I'd imagined to the crest? It took me longer than that to cross fifty feet from one canyon wall to the other, and I was no closer to the crest than I had been in the morning. Wild rose—living whipcords bearded over with half-inch needles—knit together willows to make a solid bunker fifteen feet tall. I tunneled through, lurching and wrestling, branches snagging my pits and crotch, leaves in my mouth, thorns everywhere. I received the full sumo-acupuncture treatment. Somewhere near the water, I left the ground completely, suspended by bouncing softwood and the connective rose vines. Tall, ripe cattails found room to thread their stalks up through the green chain-link. Each one I brushed sent an explosion of seed fluff showering over me.

I emerged on the other side too spent to be enraged. I pushed on because if I stopped I'd want to eat, and I didn't have enough food for that. Wind gusts poured through the canyon bottom, ruffling the jungle and sucking the air out of my mouth. I followed crumbling shelves through cliff bands pleated into accordion folds on the northern canyon wall. The sky slipped from blue to gray. Clouds thickened and blocked out the declining sun.

On a ledge a hundred feet above the canyon floor, I turned a corner and saw my first Beveridge machine. Maybe I felt something like the Shoshones when the whites first arrived with their carts and cattle. I sat on a rock and dug out the last of my tortilla and honey, which disappeared before I remembered to conserve. I had imagined that a mining camp up here would mean a couple shacks and some tunnel entrances. But I was looking at a double-decker aerial tram terminus, with an ore chute and a grinder, built against the bare rock of the canyon-side. Other chutes dropped through terraces and granite retaining walls to the canyon floor, where two fifteen-foot-wide cyanide catchment tanks, built of redwood planks hooped together, collected flood debris.

I descended talus and recrossed the creek at a prominent bare spot just below the two cyanide tanks. The tram cable crossed the canyon high over my head. It was a jig-back tram: a single bucket lowered to the terminus by gravity and a braking mechanism, then winched back up to the mine by hand. One worker stood on top of the wood-frame structure of the terminus and dumped each bucket of ore into a jaw crusher, which fed the two massive drums of the Huntington mills bolted to the terminus footings. A plate on one of the Huntingtons bore giant lettering: THE F.M. DAVIS IRONWORKS CO. DENVER COLO. A geared pillar inside the drums turned iron bars to pulverize the ore. Added water created a slurry that passed through metal screens when the particulate became fine enough. Just looking at them, I could feel the bone-shaking noise those crushers must have made. Mercury added to the drums amalgamated to the gold, separating it from the rock. Three or four ounces of gold per ton of ore would have been a fair return. The remainder, the tailings, were dumped down the chutes into the cyanide tanks to leech out every last particle of metal.

The tram terminus, spliced together from timbers of all sizes and looking like a bundle of sticks but still very much upright, stood close to twenty feet high. The Huntington mills were iron beasts. Metal pieces were scattered around the mill terrace. Some of the bits and pieces, I could only budge. A square iron block I didn't recognize had to have weighed over two hundred pounds. A section of wheel weighed as much as the fully loaded goblin. And all I could think was, *How did they get all of this in here?*

I wandered up the canyon in disbelief, trying to visualize mule strings, engineering specs, labor forces. It turns out that Mexican prospectors found the first gold in the Inyos. They arrived in the big canyons on the eastern slope of the mountains by the late 1860s, possibly earlier. After all, California *was* Mexico until 1846, and Mexican miners knew their trade better than most of the gringo greenhorns bumbling in from the East. The newspaper editors were all white, so Mexicans in Beveridge received little attention in print, even though they lived and worked there for the better part of five decades. The social section of the *Inyo Independent* might report that Pat Keyes or Charles McEvoy had come to town with bullion or to buy supplies, but the Mexicans were almost always just "the Mexicans." The names they did leave behind are the names of their mines—like the Trinidad, Santiago, Junietta, Barranca, and La Cueva. Over a quarter of the 111 mines and prospects of the Beveridge district had Spanish names.

While Mexicans were making the first strikes in the high Inyos, William Hunter, Hunter Canyon's namesake, and John Beveridge were running a mule packing outfit supplying the booming Cerro Gordo mines a few mile south. Oftentimes, the provisioners—grocers, packers, bartenders—were the people who made the most reliable money from mining because the one guarantee in the desert was that men would want beans and whisky. Hunter and Beveridge did well in their line; at one time Hunter drove two hundred mules to and from the camps. The two men were close right up until Beveridge's death in 1874. Hunter fixed his partner's name to the canyon as well as to his own son, Beveridge Hunter.

William Hunter officially organized the Beveridge Mining District in 1877. He hosted the meeting at his Big Horn Spring mine in Hunter Canyon. I've been there. It's as remote as any canyon bottom in the Inyos, but all the miners in the area came to take part nevertheless. The canyon walls and Inyo summits towered above, and down among lush cottonwoods and shade, the men crafted articles and bylaws governing their claims and the use of wood and water. Hunter led the proceedings. In a picture of him taken later in life, he has a thin face and big ears and a huge, flowing white beard that forks below his collarbone. In his place, at his mine, he must have looked like some kind of gnomish canyon creature. I like to picture him up on a stump with the wind in his beard.

The mining district they created covered a huge quadrangle of the Inyo Mountains: fifteen miles north to south, and from the Saline Valley floor to the Inyo Crest. Between $1 million and $2 million in gold left the canyons for the cities, at a time when gold was congressionally fixed at $20.67 per ounce. But Beveridge never had a speculation boom. Capitalists became something of a joke in the district—rare, awkward birds feathered with more rumor than substance. The Owens Valley papers, which had rooting interests in the Inyo mines because their produce fed the miners and the bullion flowed out into their banks, roundly damned the investing class as a gaggle of fainthearts who were afraid to take a little walk in the mountains. The goading made no difference. The district became one of the few made by labor instead of speculation.

The first mine I came to, with the jig-back tram and the Huntington mills, produced a small part of the district's total figure, somewhere in the neighborhood of three hundred ounces of gold and a further thousand ounces of silver, dating back to 1885. The numbers are fuzzy. Different miners worked and reworked claims over the years. The two cyanide tanks may well have been later additions to the original mill site, built to reprocess the accumulated tailings. A trickle of work here continued all the way through to the 1980s. An incongruously modern shovel and wheelbarrow left on one terrace showed the accumulation of artifacts to be ongoing.

I continued up the canyon, past a sheet-metal cabin filled with a century's span of miners' trash: bits of old glass and newspapers, magazines and technical manuals, broken lamps, batteries. The clouds sagged down and began to spit rain, making a god-awful racket against the corrugated roof.

The rain slacked, and I entered a narrow part of the canyon that was filled with machines. Wild rose braided the willows. Cottonwoods hung screens of green and brown off their branches. I'd part the curtains, step through to another canyon hollow under the rock and dripping branches, and find new artifacts, each more improbable than the last. Heavy, three-inch-diameter pipes connected broken-down vats to a set of three rectangular zinc boxes made of milled wood and propped on stones and pinyon logs. The miners mixed ore crushed to a fine sand with cyanide in the tanks, then piped the mixture into the zinc boxes to precipitate the gold out of the cyanide solution. A four-cylinder car engine propped on timbers and slowly sinking into a bog powered pumps to refill the vats. Willows and ragged belts on wheels draped a higher set of tanks. Thick toothed gears drove shafts and rollers.

I slid through skinny leads between the granite walls and wild rose thickets. The brambles weren't as thick as they had been lower, but I still felt like an escapee crawling past barbed wire. In places a few feet of old miners' path remained between walls of growth. Everywhere, I saw the earliest signs of the processes undoing the miners' work. Willows bursting vats, tunnel mouths

Aerial tram in Beveridge Canyon.

collapsing, rust sinking into iron. It will take a long, long time for the canyon to reclaim itself.

At the junction of a rocky side canyon, I reached a second aerial tram, this one much longer than the first and made to run as a continuous loop. Built about 1880, it stretched for three-quarters of a mile up the canyon-side. The intermediate towers along the line were built of bare, native pinyon logs left rough and round. Essentially, they were sticks lashed together, making me think of the house of the second little pig. But these towers had stayed upright for 130 years and still held their cables. An ore bucket dangled from the return track at the lower terminus, like a single chair at the bottom of a ski lift. To support the terminus against the strain it had to bear, the miners tensioned it to gigantic granite stones in the side canyon, making their anchors by girth-hitching one-inch cable around the boulders.

How did the Beveridge miners get their iron, timbers, tools, food, and cyanide into the canyon? The way miners did everything: labor, months, mules. Their trails came from the south, on the axis of the range. A wagon road connected Cerro Gordo with the Burgess Mine at nine thousand feet, at the far southern edge of the district. From there, the mountains became hopeless for roads, so miners created their own footpaths and hoof-paths along the crest and down into the canyons. Where the canyon walls ran sheer, the men built and blasted trails into the stone. Stories of epic individual constructions trickled out into the newspapers. One man invested $1,800 in the last quarter-mile of trail to his mine, building stone support walls twenty feet tall. Sections of similar masonry exist through the cliffs above Beveridge, between slides and washouts and places where the stones have simply fallen away. Over and above the money, the miners spent more in sweat and craft than they could reasonably have hoped to be repaid by their ore. In their own way they must have loved these projects and the wildness of a canyon that compelled such outsized creations.

Even with the trails, material traveled into and out of the Inyos at a crawl. A mule could carry 300 pounds all day, or 450 pounds for shorter stretches, and every beam, plank, and pound of nails had to arrive on an animal's back. Timbers in the tram terminals had to be spliced together because mules couldn't carry long lengths of lumber around the hairpin turns of the canyon trails. I saw pieces of wheel marked with roman numerals showing which ends fit together—a DIY mill kit, assembly required. The Beveridge miners mastered recycling and improvisation. Fuel cans became ore chute patches. Packing crates became shelves. A broken drill steel could still be a crowbar. The cables for the aerial trams were a special problem because they came in continuous lengths. One description of mules transporting metal cable in another district was so reverent in tone, it could be a Bible verse:

> Transport of this rope . . . was accomplished by dividing the rope into ten lengths, each length made up into seven coils, with an intermediate length of ten feet, and each of the coils in each length was loaded upon the back of a mule, the entire train being composed of seventy mules, and three men being provided to each seven mules.

I passed a short fall by scrambling up past the tram terminus on big blocks of granite. Then I returned to the canyon floor and walked into the center of the district. Bed frames rusted on flattened terraces. A table and chairs waited for its people to return. Branch-roofed stone huts mushroomed up from bedrock. A chemical shed stood mid-collapse in a jungle of willows. The walls of a one-room wood-frame house had peeled away, leaving nothing but the skeleton. An outhouse squatted over the empty air of a crack in the canyon-side. Miners literally walked a plank to this closet of sheet metal and had a seat on a board with a hole cut from it, while the canyon wind whistled up from below.

Rising out of the willows on one side of the canyon floor and looking down on the other structures stood a wood and iron beast, a five-stamp mill, in a gigantic timbered frame. All of its cranks, shafts, and pistons were there, intact. It looked ready for a mouthful of ore if you'd only give it a wash in a lake of WD-40.

A man named Lasky, a grocer from the Owens Valley town of Lone Pine, built this mill. It took him months and mules uncounted to drag the pieces over the mountains and into the

Lasky's mill, Beveridge Canyon.

canyon. Just the individual stamps—the metal shoes that actually crush the rock—reportedly weighed 750 pounds each. To carry one any distance, a mule would have needed repeated rests while a portable support structure took the weight off its back. When the mill was finished, miners brought Lasky ore, paid him a fee or a percentage, and he crushed and processed their rock and handed them back their ounces of bullion. Just like arrastras, stamp mills needed water, and most of the mines in the district either couldn't afford to build a mill or didn't have the water to run one. So the men came to see Lasky, and his mill became the rumbling, shuddering heart of Beveridge.

Even with a hungry iron dinosaur, crushing rock into sand takes time. An ore run often took days. Usually the miners simply waited nearby with others who had congregated there, talking, laughing, probably gambling, while the mill throbbed away, twelve hours a day. The ore could never have been far from their minds. Had they struck it rich? Had they found $100 per ton rock? $200? Or had they wasted months sacking and hauling $9 junk? I imagine a holiday atmosphere, empty time between labor and payday. A store and saloon opened by the mill—though this could mean that someone simply laid some cans of food or glasses on a plank and declared himself open for business. The store doubled as a polling place for the 1884 election.

Like other Western mining towns, like America itself, Beveridge was an international catchall of immigrants and wanderers. The miners brought their names from Mexico, Ireland, Canada, Dalmatia, Scotland, Switzerland, Germany, France, and England. A few tantalizing artifacts of families have turned up—some shredded wallpaper, a child's shoe, a doll. Three leather-bound Shakespeares were found in the rafters of one cabin, inscribed in 1896 with the name Virginia Twigg. But most of the residents were men, many working alongside their brothers or sons. A sense of neighborliness connected the individual mines despite the distance and terrain between them. News and stories traveled freely. The miners knew the workings and happenings of each other's mines. They often traveled down to Independence or Lone Pine for one holiday or another. Sometimes they celebrated together up in the mountains. One *Inyo Independent* article mentions a man headed back up to Beveridge for Christmas with a turkey and gallons of flavor extract for mincemeat.

By the 1890s, Beveridge had already slumped into its long decline, though the district, compared with most of California's desert prospects, was a success. One mine in particular, the Keynot, became a local legend, producing $500,000 of gold and keeping Lasky's and another mill in the next canyon north occupied for long stretches of the year.

I left Lasky's and headed higher. The canyon opened up, pushing me closer to the leaded sky. The plants changed. Pines, juniper, and sage came down to the canyon floor, though willows still held the water borders. Sections of wooden water pipe, made from boards wrapped in wire, began to turn up under the sage, and on terraces, and half-buried in the coarse granite topsoil. To stay in production year-round, Lasky brought water a mile and a half down the canyon to his mill through these pipes.

I saw an arrastra and the remnants of many more stone cabins. Most of the cabins were built against bedrock, so the miners got one wall each for free. From there they laid raw country rocks, stone upon stone. Granite isn't light. The rocks they handled were mostly head-sized, mixed with a few hulking, hernia-worthy pieces placed at the ends and corners of their walls. Some walls were mortared, some simply stacked. A few remains stood over my head. Most had survived to my knee. With long, flat stones that

Remains of stone cabins, Beveridge Canyon.

looked as though they could have been pulled from an arrastra, the men created windows and mantles. I saw one ingeniously designed chimney stacked against a natural lean in the bedrock. After all the rusting metal and machines, this area of sage and stones felt quieter, and older, though that was an illusion. I liked thinking of men handling these rocks, methodically putting them one at time into a wall, finding the interlocking edges that fit just so.

Of the 111 mines in Beveridge, there was only one Keynot. Other diggings brought in a few thousand dollars here or there. Most did nothing but give a few men some big ideas. The miners living in these stone cabins and grinding ore in arrastras maybe made wages, maybe not. And when they did have a strike and a pocketful of bullion from Lasky's mill, they followed the desert pattern and headed down into the Owens Valley to tour the bars until the gold trickled out of their pockets and into the currents of a world economy on the gold standard. When their pockets ran dry, they returned to the mountains.

I just don't believe they were here for the gold, at least not in the worshipful way the outside world hoarded and banked it. There must be a hundred easier ways to make money than to dig it out of the ground. And if they weren't here for the gold, the only thing left is the canyon and the mountains. Which means they were here for the same reason that I was, to wrestle with the brambles and water and rock.

Early twilight poured down the canyon. The clouds hardened into shelves of black and gray. I found a ledge of dry needles under a pine and set up camp. My body cooled off fast when I stopped, and I ended up in my sleeping bag on my back, staring up into a low sky full of leaks. Rain whistled down and changed to snow, then back to rain. I pulled my bivy sack out of the goblin and slithered inside. The wind ran laps up and down the canyon, blowing the rain and snow in all directions and snapping the fabric of my nylon sleeve.

One of my favorite Mary Austin yarns features her recurring character, a miner called the Pocket Hunter, traveling from the west arm of Death Valley to the White Mountains, the northern half of the Inyos. In Death Valley, he wades through sand and heat on a short water ration. A few days later, up in the Whites, he is hit by a late autumn storm. The snow blinds him and piles around him, and he trudges through the dark, seeking shelter. He stumbles upon a hollow below a few bent cedars and hears the sighing of a flock of sheep. Thanking luck that some hapless shepherd has also been overtaken by the storm, the Pocket Hunter wiggles in among the warm bodies and sleepwalks from cedar to cedar through the night with the flock.

In the morning, he awakes on his feet to bright sunshine and a white world. And he finds he has no shepherd to thank: "Then the very soul of him shook to see the wild sheep of God stand around him, nodding their great horns beneath the cedar roof, looking out on the wonder of the snow . . . The leader stamped lightly on the litter to put the flock in motion, suddenly they took the drifts in those long light leaps that are nearest to flight."

I had no such luck. One huge-eyed pack rat kept me company in the storm, running under the hood of my bivy sack every hour or so through the night to see if anything was worth stealing out of my beard.

▲

The morning dawned clear and calm, but at ground level, everything was still wet. Drops splashed from my pine. A few pads of snow slushed into the ground. I felt muddy.

I passed the top of the water, where a narrow creek bubbled up out of the sandy floor of the canyon. Plants crowded in on all sides to greet the flow. Miners built a house of stone and wood here—it survives intact—and they planted walnut trees and mint by the spring.

Above the water, I walked granite sand through sage and Mormon tea. The sun brightened the morning without doing much to warm it. The main arm of the canyon curved in toward north-facing slopes and deep snow on the side of New York Butte, a broad pyramid near eleven thousand feet dusted in a billion new twinkling snow diamonds. The granite gave way to a parade of metamorphosed layers, limestones and schists twisted and tortured then heaved to the surface. I took a steep side branch due west, making for a pair of curves on my map that showed a pass through the Inyo Crest.

Talus. Pines. A few cacti shivering in pockets of new snow. The ground pressed up relentlessly. I willfully ignored faint loops of old path drifting through the scree and trees. Instead I crawled straight up bare stones at the bottom of the ravine, an exercise in stubbornness that turned my legs into pudding. The Cottonwood Mountains stretched out behind and below me. The Saline Valley showed a white triangle of salt through the cut of the canyon. Ahead, the Inyos tilted up and up, rising to meet the sun.

I pulled over the pass with the sun straight above and plopped down to rest. Mesozoic slates clanked under my butt. I picked up a few, broke one in half, then another. Each flat, palm-sized stone had an individual weathering rind painstakingly applied by grandmaster time. Black slate and tiny scintillations made the inside layer; the outer skin was brown and gray and exactly the same thickness on each piece—they looked like candy bars, a million of them, chocolate dipped in caramel. Apparently my stomach had hold of my eyes.

I'd been waiting for the view west from this spot for days. From my 9,600-foot pass, I'd stare across at an orchestra of 14,000-foot mountains. Granite would fill the air. The gray-blue isosceles of Mount Whitney would preside. I'd sensed Whitney in the west, felt its rain shadow, chased it blindly long enough, and now I wanted to see it staring right back at me.

I was going to have to wait. Black clouds cut the Sierra from the scene. Something massive lurked in there, that was plain. But the clouds allowed no hints to escape. No elbows or crowns of granite showed through the curtain drawn across the other side of the Owens Valley.

West to east, my view at the moment was an illustrated primer of the desert I had walked. The Sierra pulled the storm to itself as if it had the clouds magnetized. A few dry shells, high and white, drifted over the Owens toward me. I sat in the bright sun beside pockets of snow slumping and trickling into thirsty ground. To the east, brown and purple mountains baked in the noon heat. I knew which trench Death Valley inhabited, and I could practically see the thermal glow coming off the ground there. Dry, drier, and driest, all visible from my seat on the Inyo Crest. I saw the work happening, each mountain range sucking the last moist breaths from the sky.

I dropped down off the crest with gravity finally on my side. The only limit to my speed was how much pounding my joints would take. I tumbled down the first thousand feet in a matter of minutes, plenty pleased to let gravity do the work, then took the second thousand slower when my knees began to squeal.

A new canyon shaped up into a broad box between cliffs. A deep water track cut through the floor. One prominent trail climbed out of the canyon at a spot where the northern wall broke down. I ignored it, too. I had used the canyons as my highways all along. I figured I would stick with them to the end.

The western slope of the Inyo Range tilts less than the precipitous east. And the Owens Valley is higher than the Saline, so the mountains on this side have 3,000 fewer feet to shed (though for those keeping score, including my knees, that still amounted to a 6,000-foot drop). Given the gentler angle and vertical decline, the western canyons of the Inyos should be shallower and better behaved than their big sisters on the other side. That's what I was telling myself about the time I hit the top of the first fall—a slabby, holdless ramp that stumped me on the down-climb until I put together some wedging jujitsu in a flaring corner on one side.

The canyon narrowed, and opened, and narrowed again into a slot. The floor dropped away over chimneys and falls, and I thought I'd be turned back many times because the walls rose sheer on both sides. But then I'd look over the edge and find a thirty-foot ladder of holds or a set of scoops like a waterslide. So I kept tunneling deeper into bedrock with the canyon. The holds egged me on until the very last fall, where they quit altogether. I could see the canyon mouth below me, and the upper edge of the Owens rising to meet it, but sixty sheer feet of polished pink marble cut me off where I stood.

Maybe I have some skeletons in my karmic closet, some penance to work off, because here is the one type of climbing I seem to be made for. I call it The Bullshit: fifth-class climbing with no climbing shoes, a heavy pack, weird route-finding through miles of bad rock, the consequences of a fall unthinkable—and I gravitate to it like a dung beetle to a road apple. There seemed to be a lot of road apples between Death Valley and Mount Whitney. I ferreted out a meandering, hairy, utterly unlikely bypass to the sixty feet in question. I crossed a mountain of pink rubble and catwalked into a whole separate drainage. By the time I was done, it seemed like traveling from A to B by way of Timbuktu.

When I arrived back in the canyon, the creosote shadows stretched east and my legs had had enough. I walked out to the canyon mouth, where the outer rim of the Owens Valley curved up to the base of the Inyos. The clouds had lifted off the tops of the Sierra. The highest peaks all sported half-mile-long plumes of silvery snow blowing from their summits. Snow banners!

John Muir loved snow banners. He wrote about a winter day in the Yosemite Valley in 1873, when a wild "norther" shook his cabin and brewed up the perfect conditions for banners. Muir dropped everything and charged up to the rim of the valley— a four-hour, 4,000-foot climb through deep snow in Indian Canyon. From a ridgetop, he set himself against the hurricane and watched the highest mountains of the Yosemite backcountry flying perfect white silks off their tops.

To watch my banners, all I had to do was sit down and stay down. Langley, LeConte, Whitney, Russell, Tyndall, and Williamson—peaks I knew well—all threw their plumes into the sudden blue ten thousand feet over my head. Each banner began white and dense and finished diaphanous, unraveling across the sky. I felt ambushed by the mountains. They'd hypnotized me again with their latest magic, the equivalent of doves flying out of their hats.

For Muir, who is best understood as a poet-scientist—one of those brilliant mutts who transcends both his parental schools of thought—snow banners were the kind of multilayered phenomenon he could sink his teeth into. Good banners needed an alignment of wind, earth, and snow, and Muir, the ultimate observer, cataloged the details with care. The snow had to be dry and fresh, and the individual crystals had to be pulverized, their six sides crushed and sheered until nothing but a fine dust remained. The wind had to howl—and, most importantly to him, it had to howl with one steady voice from the north. The northern sides of the peaks had been scooped most deeply by their glaciers. Huge bowls and amphitheaters funneled the north wind toward the summits, concentrating its power until geysers of snow dust erupted off the very tops of the mountains.

Muir transmuted those facts into an insight about the rhyme scheme of the world. The glaciers bit deeper into the north faces of the mountains because the shadows of the northern hemisphere protected them. Therefore, the patterns of snow banners depended directly on the patterns of shadows—a phenomenon of light governing a phenomenon of wind, using glaciers and mountains as its intermediary tools.

My wind came from the south, and Muir scoffed at banners

made by a south wind, but they looked pretty good to me. The sun dropped behind the mountains, turning the banners yellow, then orange, then pink. To the north, the Sierra stayed wrapped in gray. To the south, Olancha Peak stuck its head into a thousand-foot-high triangular cloud, a towering war bonnet that made the mountain look like a god in a headdress. But all through sunset, the blue window remained open on Mount Whitney, and its neighbors, and their snow banners.

I rolled out my sleeping bag and ate the crumbs out of every corner of the goblin, except for a granola bar I squirreled away for breakfast. As twilight became night, the snow banners shriveled back and disappeared, except for one huge white jet blowing off the top of Mount Williamson, which stayed strong until the mountain turned shapeless below the stars.

Chapter 8

———

OWENS VALLEY

There it is. Take it.

> —William Mulholland,
> as water first flowed through the Los Angeles Aqueduct,
> November 5, 1913

The Sierra and Inyo lined up on opposite sides of the basin, as if the mountains were taking sides. The desert began. I could see it crawl out from under the Sierra rain shadow, pass under my feet, and harden into the bare, black triangles of the Inyo summits. The Owens Valley is an ecological crossroads, and also contested ground, a kind of Jerusalem of Eastern California. Races and creeds and massive presumptions of entitlement have crashed against each other here below the mountains and fought for control.

From the base of the Sierra to the base of the Inyo, the land unwinds a smooth, green curve. The sagebrush doesn't grow much above the waist, so no place in the Owens Valley is ever really out of sight. The mountains stand tall and the basin rolls up at the edges to meet them. Even on a day heaped up with clouds, the overwhelming attribute is *space*. The mountains gather the volume between them and make it tangible, breathable, like oxygen for the eyes. Creeks spill out of the Sierra through gates in the granite, and where the water runs, long lines of pine and willow follow. The water, having been pulled from the ocean, floated over the edge of the continent, scattered on the mountains, merges again at the bottom of the Owens. It is live, unghostly *water*, a genuine Styx on the edge of the desert.

Sudden blooms and hatchings splash across the land. Life cycles are close to the surface but ephemeral. An outpouring of flowers or flies will fizz up out of the ground and disappear in a week. For centuries, Paiutes lived under the mountains, following those patterns. They built semipermanent villages along the creeks and migrated to the outbreaks of fecundity. Grass seeds in the meadows. Pine nuts in the high groves. Fly larvae in the shallows of Mono and Owens Lakes. Bulbs and tubers in the floodplains of the creeks. Each harvest had its microseason.

When whites came along, they saw only a sea of empty and unused grassland. A perfect place for finishing cows. In 1860, just over the Nevada border, the town of Aurora roared to life as if spit full-blown from the head of a dragon. Miners flush with gold wanted beef, so ranchers in the southern San Joaquin Valley in California began driving herds over Tehachapi Pass and up through the Owens to the new boomtown. It was a 300-mile trip, and Aurora showed no sign of losing steam, so in 1861, a dozen cow men established ranches in the Owens Valley.

John Muir called domestic sheep "hoofed locusts," and I guess that makes cows roughly equivalent to hoofed tractors. Grasses that had sustained Paiutes as a primary food source for centuries disappeared. Springs watering bulb marshes turned into cow wallows. Seeing no declarations of ownership, no fences or walls, whites built their own, platting out cash crop farms on the most fertile ground and plowing under the native plants. The mountains and basin abide, but the cover has changed.

I ate my last granola bar in about two seconds and walked down the rim of the Owens into sand, sage, and dense runs of silvery green rabbitbrush, yard-high shrubs that exhaled bitter breaths as I brushed through them. Citizen rabbitbrush is one indication of change. It has always been a resident of the Owens, but it only began to dominate in the tracks of the cattle. It moves in where other plants have been weakened. In the fall, when the rabbitbrush blooms and turns square miles of the Owens Valley yellow, you could take yourself back a century and a half by erasing the bloom in your mind and filling it in with meadows.

In 1928, Julian Steward, then twenty-six years old and a graduate student in anthropology, interviewed a Paiute known as Sam Newland, born in the Owens in the early 1830s. Newland told Steward about the time before the cow men arrived. His stories hooked themselves to places. Instead of recounting his life story sequentially, moving forward year by year, he moved around the Owens in the telling, connecting his past to geography. When Newland was a boy, his father died in the pine nut groves near Glass Mountain, where the Paiutes also collected obsidian for arrow points. Newland remembered a fishing trip when the men dammed a creek and then used rocks to pulverize slim solomon, another distant lily relative, which they dumped in the water. The herb stupefied the fish and Newland scooped them up with baskets. He remembered bad winters when the snow buried the sagebrush and there were no pine nuts and they lived on the seeds they had stockpiled over the summer.

Steward called the Owens Valley Paiutes pre-agricultural, but for several years, Newland's brother-in-law worked as the annually elected irrigator. Each spring, he oversaw a work crew of twenty-five other men in the construction of a dam of boulders, brush, and mud across Bishop Creek. They jumped the flow into one of two broad ditches dug parallel to the natural channel. The irrigator visited the ditch periodically and redirected the water through small channels scratched out with a pole, wetting a large area of *tüpüs'i* and *náhavita*, important bulb and tuber plants. In the fall, the men broke apart the dam and harvested seeds and roots from the wet ditch. The following spring, they ran the creek through their second ditch in order to give the first a year to reseed and replenish. Each time they diverted water out of the creek or one of the ditches, they collected hundreds of fish left stranded on the suddenly bare creek bottom.

Newland's people hunted birds in the marshes around the Owens River, and deer higher up in the mountains. But Newland never caught on to the deftness of his friends, so animals tended to be safe around him. He had better luck pulling tule reeds and eating their roots with salt. Newland was also a lousy gambler, and gambling was the great love of his people. At their fandangos (as Steward called them), they'd play for days, in between dances, wagering extravagantly on the hand game, or dice made of colored sticks, or the hoop-and-pole game. Newland was unlucky and bad at hitting the rolling hoop with his arrows, so he watched, while the games often turned heated and occasionally bloody.

Newland lived a Huckleberry Finn life. At night he listened to bachelors and old men tell stories in the communal sweathouse. His nuclear family mattered less to him than his connection to The People. When Steward interviewed him, Newland couldn't remember the names of his mother or father or one of his sisters.

When he wanted to, he ran away with his friends up into the White Mountains, where they had adventures and were invited to Shoshone dances.

Clouds smothered the mountains again. I crossed several tiny playas of flat, dried mud. Springs used to surface all over the floor of the Owens, and large oxbows of the river attracted salt grasses and reeds. Now that the water table has dropped, bare, cracked mud prints are the only interruption to the brush.

The land, in Newland's stories, is like another one of The People, or maybe the sum of all The People. It has personality and moods. For Newland, that meant maddening deer and bitter winters along with high summer in the mountains and salty eats in the marshes. He was *of* this place, a part and product of its cycles, in the way an individual is made by a family. I'm a little jealous of that connection. I know this land pretty well, I feel intimate with it, but I couldn't depend on it for my life. Once the last granola bar is gone, I'm hungry. So I'll always be a visitor—along with most of us nowadays on whatever land we stake a claim to.

When the whites arrived and the seed plants disappeared, the Paiutes turned for food to the obvious replacement—the cows. Paiutes killed cows, whites killed Paiutes, and Paiutes killed whites. The army sent soldiers to this backwater edge of the desert in 1862. Indians were always worth fighting, and more pressingly, the cows fed the miners in Aurora, and the gold and silver reaped in the mines fed the Union war effort. The "warriors" the soldiers fought were men like Sam Newland, who remembered eating cows and horses and stopping a cavalry pursuit by killing its captain. Much of the killing was uglier than the skirmishes Newland described. Soldiers and militia wiped out entire camps of Paiutes, armed or not, while bands of Paiute men attacked individual ranchers and miners. No one in the valley remained a civilian.

The whites and Paiutes made pacts and broke them. Words never solved the fundamental equation of land use: Paiutes could die of starvation with the cows on their land, or die fighting the whites for the sides of beef. The two relationships with the Owens differed so radically that Paiutes and whites might as well have been looking at completely different valleys, even if they stood there side by side and shook hands. Occasionally, a soldier or government official would float the idea of a Paiute reservation, but in those years, whites didn't have much incentive for concessions. They had guns and Manifest Destiny on their side. Newspaper articles freely discussed the necessary and inevitable eviction of Paiutes from the Owens to make way for white settlement.

One day in late June 1863, Sam Newland returned home to Bishop Creek from an expedition to collect pine carpenter worms and heard that soldiers had summoned all Paiutes to Fort Independence with the promise of food, clothes, and peace. Newland joined the others at the stockade in the midst of a Fourth of July party, which was also the one-year anniversary of the erection of the fort. The symbolism of the occasion—whites shooting guns at the night to celebrate independence—should have seriously disconcerted Newland, but he remembered such a feeling of relief to be done with fighting that he simply enjoyed the show. The soldiers gave him and the others food, but no clothes, and then marched their captives en masse, nine hundred in all, south out of the Owens Valley. Newland assumed they would all be lined up and shot. Instead, the soldiers relocated them to an outdoor prison camp on foreign ground on the other side of Walker Pass. In groups of five or twenty, the Paiutes escaped—Newland broke free with four other men the following spring. The escapees returned to the Owens, and some continued to fight, but the serious Paiute resistance had broken.

The clouds thickened and clotted overhead. I walked down into the bowl of the Owens, imagining Sam Newland doing the same in the spring of 1864. He must have felt like he'd come back to a stranger. The land wasn't his to roam upright as he had. It wouldn't even feed him anymore. He sneaked through the quartz monzonite moonscape of the Alabama Hills, in the shadow of Mount Whitney, hiding from armed whites and trying to learn what he could of his displaced people and their new geography. Later, when the fighting stopped altogether and the land had turned thoroughly white, Newland began to work for the same men who had tried to kill and then exile him.

Likewise, the Owens Valley began its career as cultivated farmland. Whites grew wheat, barley, oats, corn, and grapes and kept orchards of apple, peach, and pear. The new breed of Sierra mountaineers looked down from the high summits through ten thousand feet of air and saw squares of green ripening through the summers. The produce fed miners in Aurora, Coso, and Beveridge, and some of it was shipped out to Los Angeles and San Francisco. Endless sunshine in the Sierra rain shadow, combined with easy water from the Sierra creeks, made for simple agriculture. In fact, the white farmers' irrigation techniques were about the same as the Paiutes'. They dug irrigation ditches and simply spilled the water out over the land and their plants.

Even with the farm runoff and the cows, the Owens River didn't much change. It swung through the bottom of the basin, wandering past oxbows, watering its marshes and tending its reeds. Drawn by the river, Frederick Coville came through here during his epic botanical expedition of 1891, a congressionally funded act of pure observational science. The botanists wandered through the Owens in just the right decade. Much earlier, and they would have been caught in the meat grinder of the war between farmers and Paiutes. Much later, and the river itself would have vanished off the map. At that settled time in between, it must have seemed like paradise.

Coville and the other members of the survey crisscrossed Death Valley and the Panamint, Argus, Slate, and Funeral Ranges, then visited Saline Valley and the Owens Valley before climbing up into the Sierra. Throughout the expedition, the scientists gave each other undiscovered flowers. When, for example, Coville found the white bear poppy in stony ground over the Funeral Mountains, he called it *Arctomecon merriamii*, dedicating it to C. Hart Merriam "as a token of his influence in the progress of geographic botany." These unself conscious acts of manly love—hairy, unwashed botanists away out in the middle of the desert finding outrageous new flowers and presenting them to each other—fit right in with the innocence of the time.

In the wet meadows around the Owens River, Coville made another discovery, a lavender star winking up at him from knee-high spikes of green. He must have had a soft spot for it because he kept this flower for himself, calling it *Sidalcea covillei*, the Coville mallow. The plant—like Sam Newland—was a child of the Owens, growing only under these mountains and by this river. There, at home, acres of Coville's sidalcea soaked their roots in the alkali bogs and purpled the river's floodplain with their blooms.

I walked through sage and sand. The river—a groove through the land, a fossilized snake track—wriggled away to the left and right and came close ahead. The Coville mallow is endangered now, along with all the other bog plants in the Owens. The basin has been wrung out and left dry.

The man who did the wringing, William Mulholland, first came to the Owens Valley in 1904. By then, Sam Newland was old and living with his daughter among the farms and white faces, and

Frederick Coville had returned to the East to help establish the Carnegie Institution's desert botanical laboratory. Mulholland was a tall, brusque man with a moustache, sharp-tongued and serious to his core about his work and his city. On that first trip to the Owens, he traveled by mule and buckboard with a former Los Angeles mayor and fellow engineer, Fred Eaton. Eaton had been waiting years to show off his solution to the expansion of Los Angeles, his plan to turn a dusty desert city of thousands into a metropolis for millions. Mulholland liked what he saw. Months later, as the grand plan unfolded, he told a friend: "Do not go to Inyo County. We are going to turn that country dry."

Mulholland had already watched Los Angeles grow from a village, essentially a Mexican pueblo, into a city of a hundred thousand, in a little over a decade. When Mulholland arrived among the angels in 1877, nine thousand people lived there and a smallpox epidemic had just burned through the Spanish quarter. Mulholland was then twenty-one years old and had attempted passage around Cape Horn as a stowaway. Along the way, he'd been discovered and jettisoned in Panama, which he walked across to save the $25 rail fare; from the other side of the isthmus, he sailed north aboard a Peruvian warship. As an older man, he said he'd still walk forty-seven miles to make $25. As one who would do it for free, I'm somewhat unimpressed by his parsimony. He seemed compelled in his adult life to fix everything with a definite cost, even memories from his youth.

At the time of his arrival, a private company delivered water to the streets and buildings of Los Angeles through the old Spanish system of canals, and Mulholland found work as a deputy *zanjero*, which translated, essentially, to ditch-minder. He cleared brush and dead animals out of the canals, dug new channels, kept the flow moving through the right capillaries of the network. All the desert communities of the era, white and brown, seemed to gravitate toward the same basic solution when it came to water: They spilled it through ditches. Mulholland's work differed little enough from that of the Paiute irrigator that he and Sam Newland's brother-in-law could probably have had a reasonable hydrographic conversation even if they couldn't speak about anything else.

Los Angeles fattened, along with the pride and wallets of the civic fathers. The Anglo transition meant more buildings, streets, machines, and people, and all of it, from the gardens to the skyscrapers, ran on water. Mulholland, meanwhile, studied geology and hydrography. He became a self-taught expert, the kind of man who could shovel mud with working stiffs or talk theory with engineers. He kept the plumbing for the entire city, down to individual pipes, in his prodigious memory. After ten years, the water company promoted him to superintendent.

Right from the start, Los Angeles treated its water like a kid with a hose on a hot day. The relentless multiplication of its spigots forced Mulholland to squeeze new tides out of the dry ground of the desert. By 1890, the city's population passed fifty thousand, then doubled again at the end of the century. In 1899, Mulholland figured the city used twenty million gallons of water per day. To catch every drop of the Los Angeles River, Mulholland installed vast underground filtration galleries and dams and huge iron pumps with dials, flywheels, and steam pipes—fantasy images of messy urban clockwork. But drought was the local average, and the Los Angeles River could only be counted on for so many gallons. Mulholland calculated serious water shortages beyond a population of 225,000, and no one in Los Angeles intended to stop the city there.

So Mulholland looked north, with Fred Eaton, all the way to the sparsely populated Owens Valley, where the farmers spilled the creeks over their orchards and the river strolled through the marshes. By then, the city had retaken control of its water from the private company, and Mulholland continued on as superintendent, though some went as far as to call him the "prime minister" of the water department. It was that time at the beginning of the twentieth century when good ideas were big ideas. But Mulholland's great insight was that in the desert, the most precious substance wasn't gold or salt or whisky—it was water. A thirteen-mile salt tram was a doomed operation, but a 240-mile aqueduct would succeed, spectacularly, because it carried the one thing no one could live without.

The idea of draining the Owens Valley to water Los Angeles caused an uproar both in and out of the city. One derisive member of the city council asked Mulholland whether he had ever personally been involved in anything like the construction of a 240-mile aqueduct across mountains, canyons, and desert. Mulholland replied that no such creature had ever been built. It would be one of the greatest engineering projects in human history. Of course, the people truly offended by the idea were the Owens Valley farmers, who howled bloody outrage and appealed to the state and federal governments to call off the urban bully trying to swipe the water out from under their feet. The land was theirs. After all, their parents had risked life and limb taking the valley from the Paiutes.

Unfortunately for the farmers, by the time they caught wind of the plan, most of them had already sold their deeds or water rights to Fred Eaton. Eaton used a variety of subterfuges to acquire all of the riparian land around the Owens River. Whether his tricks were strictly legal probably doesn't much matter. Greed ruled the ground, and the farmers sold out one by one.

One final question of right-of-way did have to be settled by Congress. The Owens Valley briefly became a presidential issue, a footnote in the old debate between Jefferson and Madison about the future of the country: Was America to be a dispersed nation of independent agriculturalists, or a nation of cities? Who had primary right to the land? Teddy Roosevelt, champion of national parks and egalitarian politics, sided with Madison. The interests of the Owens Valley farmers, he wrote, "must unfortunately be disregarded in view of the infinitely greater interest to be served by putting the water in Los Angeles." Congress followed Roosevelt's lead. Mulholland went to work. By then, he was being called the "biggest man" in Los Angeles. From 1908 to 1913, his crews built the aqueduct on a line barely deviating from the original route he traveled with Eaton in 1904. That buckboard trip had been a working holiday, and both Eaton and Mulholland had a taste for whisky with their water; the construction men joked that for survey markers, they only had to follow the empty bottles.

On a single day in the summer of 1913, Los Angeles's roughly four hundred thousand residents set a new record for themselves by consuming 69.4 million gallons of water in twenty-four hours. The following November, when the aqueduct taps opened and the water came pouring through the final spillway amid great pomp and celebration, Mulholland reckoned they'd have enough for a city of two million people. And Los Angeles obliged—just add water, and it grows and grows. Later, on its way to three and four million people, the city hooked its concrete arms into the Colorado and Sacramento Rivers, to boot.

I walked up to the vacant track of the Owens River, thinking of unctuous lawns and freshly hosed sidewalks and the thousand other ways I've seen the corpus of the Owens get frittered away. Imagine, for a moment, a Southern California in which Mulholland capitulated to his doubters or the farmers kicked Eaton out of town, and Los Angeles never grew beyond two hundred thousand. Mulholland himself said that if Los Angeles failed to take the water in the Owens Valley, then it would never grow big enough to need it.

What's left of the Owens River near Lone Pine today is a fecal ooze in a trench at the bottom of the old, sandy riverbed. The marshes are long gone. I saw no flowers of any kind, though I've heard that pockets of Coville mallow still come up for air in wet years. Compared with the original riverbed or with nineteenth-century photographs of a clear, stately flow or with John Muir's description of the water as unstimulating champagne, the remaining outflow is a brown thread that looks almost thick enough to shovel.

A thread, it turned out, that still ran twenty feet wide. I'd badly miscalculated when I imagined stepping over the last trickle of the Owens. Instead, I halted at a sullen, chest-deep trough of concentrated muck that looked like an open sewer. If I'd known the way to the nearest bridge, I'd have welcomed the concrete, my antiroad vows be damned. But my map ended at the Inyos and I hadn't bothered to bring one for the Owens Valley because I'd failed to imagine navigating anything more complex than a straight line.

Cattle trails and pies poked along through grass next to the sludgy moat. I chose south at random and followed along, hoping for the miracle of a fallen cottonwood while trying to psych myself up for a sticky wade. I reached an area of dense, dry reeds packed chockablock across a wide stagnation. The reeds had been standing seven feet high, but wind had bent them all over from one bank to the other. Not *exactly* a fallen log. I stepped out onto the reed mat. And the water gurgled up and swallowed my boot.

I scrounged three cottonwood branches from the grass and placed the first a few feet out on the reeds. I stepped on the branch, the sludge gurgled up—and stopped, just below my boot sole. All right. I put the second branch in front of the first and eased forward, then put the third in front of the second and retrieved the first to use again. I remembered playing this game as a kid in summer camp, though I think we just imagined a fire lake instead of the rotting corpse of an extinguished river. The reed mat bounced and creaked, and fat brown spiders swarmed up around my boots, chased from their homes by the rising sludge. We all were thankful when I reached the other side.

I continued west, toward the mountain in the clouds. The sand and sage became interrupted with trash and stretches of barbed-wire fence—sure signs of approaching civilization. Shotgun shells, plastic bags, rusting scrap. Every town has its particular corona of garbage. Not wanting to walk through anyone's backyard, I kept to the fence lines, which brought me around to the edge of the Mount Whitney Cemetery.

If you were inclined to be planted, this would be a good place for your relatives to visit you. Trees around the perimeter blocked out the pavement and litter. My eyes had nowhere to go but up into the Sierra and Inyos. Next to the mountains, the headstones were pebbles; life looked small and death ordinary. In the dark below my feet, men and women were returning to the earth, and from where I stood, the earth suddenly looked pretty good again.

Most of the graves had brass plaques or polished marble for markers. A few had uncut native headstones that looked like they had simply tumbled down and found a resting place. From Bellas to Levi to Patrick, the names told immigrant stories. Some old, flat, wooden headboards had burned and split in the sun. One gold-orange bundle of splinters that I particularly liked read:

Sam E. Ball

D: 5-29-1939

B: Abt 1862

a lifelong prospector

Spanish names lettered whitewashed wooden crosses. I caught this hint of a love story:

Arrona Martinez D: Feb. 1927. Buried by Pedro Martinez

Then, a few rows later:

Pedro Martinez D: 4-5-27

I passed through the main cemetery gate to the two-lane highway just north of Lone Pine. There was no avoiding asphalt now. I had a box waiting for me at the Lone Pine Post Office and a hollow belly. I walked the highway shoulder into town.

Clarence King, mountaineer and scientist—the man who gave Mount Whitney its name—came down the earliest iteration of this road in 1871. At the time, he was leading the 40th Parallel Survey through Wyoming, but he had unfinished business in the Owens Valley, so he caught a train to Carson, then made a 280-mile stagecoach run through Aurora (where the silver had just given out and gold was a distant memory), and down to Lone Pine. King had been geologizing in the West for a quarter of his life, eight of his twenty-nine years. He was born in Rhode Island and schooled in Connecticut—the mountains and deserts spoke to him in tongues he'd never heard at home. The crags, the colors, the dry winds and huge skies—these were the waking fulfillment of his youthful dreams of adventure.

With epic poetry on every horizon, King could never understand why Westerners squatted in such wretched camps and hovels. On the trail, King could live as rough as anyone—I found this out for myself, following his ghost around the Sierra with a wool blanket for shelter. But he thought a home should be different. If the body were going to be attached to a piece of ground, then a dignified mind should want to cultivate that space to reflect something of the soul. Never mind lace in the windows; I think King would have appreciated a bare shack if only it had a clean floor and some square corners. On the outskirts of Lone Pine, he found, at first, what he had come to expect. "The American residents," he wrote, "live in a homeless fashion. There is no attempt at grace, no memory of comfort, no suggested hope for improvement." They almost seemed to be making a statement through dilapidation, though what it meant King couldn't say.

Then King left the American shanties and entered what he called the Spanish part of town, though it was truly Old Mexican. There he found white adobe and cool shade and lattice fences with blooming hollyhock. Lettuce and pepper plants queued in the gardens, and more peppers hung drying under porch eaves. King greeted a "Castilian" matron sewing on her threshold, and she stirred up all his dormant domestic longings. He wrote about her white linens so passionately you'd think he'd had a saintly visitation.

Mary Austin called the Mexican half of Lone Pine El Pueblo de Las Uvas, "the town of the grapevines." There she befriended one Señora Josefa Maria de la Luz Ortiz y Romero, who mentored Austin in the intricacies of Spanish idiom and tamales. They held advanced practicums in chiles, until Austin could appreciate the flavors and uses of different peppers like a true connoisseur. Every September 16, Las Uvas celebrated Mexico's independence from Spain with meatball soup and chicken and enchiladas—all with different chiles—and a relish of chile *tepines* as a fiery digestive. They turned summer on the desert into an ingredient in their cooking. Even though they lived in California on the edge of the twentieth century, the land held them remote, allowing them to exist in another time and place. After the food came the flute and guitar and dancing, which was typical for the locals, who needed no excuse, except that on the sixteenth, everyone turned out with a new dress or new silver trim and the fever waxing in their blood. At midnight they'd lower the Mexican flag and refly the American. The musicians then played the "Star-Spangled Banner," and the hymn of Cuba, and the Chilean anthem for the two Chilean families, and "La Marseillaise" for the French shepherds who had come into town for the party.

Austin lived in Lone Pine for most of the 1890s. She used the town as the trailhead for *The Land of Little Rain* and *Lost Borders*, titles that have become synonymous with the country between Whitney and Death Valley. The meaning of the first is straightforward, and so is the book—until you read it over and catch the rasp of its jagged passages, all hidden in plain sight. I paged through it the first time with pleasant expectations on a pleasant afternoon under the overhang of a boulder up high in the eastern Sierra. When taken superficially, *The Land of Little Rain* fits a certain stereotype of a lady botanist writing about the desert. Afoot among the flowers, the springtime creeks, the general merriment of nature, one can easily pass over the butcher birds and pistol shots and madness. And disappointment. Which is the subject of *Lost Borders*.

The lost borders also have their physical reality. Where water flowed, Paiutes divided the land with well-nigh legal corners—a hilltop, a ridge, a spring. (The "Pah" syllable of their name, in fact, translates to "water.") But where the water ended, the borders trailed off into sand and rock. Laws of division became meaningless because no one bothered staking a claim to the waterless land. And this dissolution also happened to the laws of invading cultures and to the minds of individuals. The internal boundaries between soul and desert drifted. The land invaded men's minds, made them forget and yearn and wander. *Lost Borders* is a darker creature, impossible to mistake for an easygoing nature book. Mysteries, tales of cursed mines, tales of tragic love, ghost stories. Strange happenings occur outside the edges of law and conscience, though the desert has a way of extracting its pound (or more) of flesh from all of Austin's subjects in the end. Because it was the desert, coyote land, the designs of men usually failed. Mines failed miners, water abandoned the thirsty, fate turned against the needy, and men, above all, disappointed women.

Mary Austin moved to Lone Pine at the age of twenty-two, around the time of her first wedding anniversary. Her marriage had begun well enough. She and her husband Wallace didn't ex-change rings; instead, he gave her a pearl-handled pen, with the implicit message that she was to continue writing. At home, Mary had never received such encouragement from her mother. The one thing Susanna Hunter made clear was that she found her intense, dark-browed, iconoclastic daughter to be a difficult, alien presence. So when Mary moved away with her husband and her pen, she felt hopeful and free. In the community of writers in San Francisco, Mary thrived and quickly sold some of her first short stories.

A few months after they arrived in San Francisco, Wallace an-nounced that they would be moving to Lone Pine. Mary knew nothing about the place other than what a map could tell her, though she supposed she could write there as well as anywhere. Wallace's brother had come into an irrigation project. They would dig ditches out of the Owens River and turn the desert green with fruit trees and cash.

Wallace Austin always had a castle shimmering in his future. He was the kind of man who would have liked to build a salt tram or an aqueduct. The trouble was, he had no practical abilities and even less notion of how to acquire them. His ditches went nowhere,

Mary and Wallace Austin, wedding portrait.

and within months, the project died under his feet. During that time, his pregnant wife was tossed out of their hotel for the long-overdue bill. Wallace had been warned, and in an act of sheer spinelessness, he absented himself for the day and left Mary there on her own without telling her they were going to be evicted.

The Austins, now three in number, homesteaded in a cabin above the Alabama Hills, in the crook at the base of the Sierra wall. Wallace drifted the desert, looking for an enterprise on which to stake his future. Occasionally he taught at one of the local schools—he was educated and articulate—though he whined about how much he hated the work. No pot of gold ever waited at the end of a semester. Mary began walking the animal trails and studying the plants of the mesa. With her infant daughter on her back, she visited the nearby Paiute camp and the kitchen of Señora Josefa Maria de la Luz Ortiz y Romero.

Down in the white part of Lone Pine, Austin found repetitions of her own story, if not exactly kinship. The town was full of wives and children. It was a storehouse for families of men off on one errand of fortune or another. Austin discovered that white women in Inyo were always being left by their husbands: for a mine or a scheme or a Shoshone girl. After collecting enough of those stories, Austin came to believe that it wasn't the mine or girl the men were chasing, but the desert itself. White men found the desert irresistible. Lusting for its dangerousness, blinded by its come-hither beauty, they never woke to realize they were being lead on and ruined, while their families fossilized back in town. "Feckless men," she called them, "whom the desert sucks dry and keeps dangling like gourds on a string." She asked the women at the Paiute camp if they understood what happened to the minds of the men adventuring on their land. The Paiute women loved gossiping about the habits of white men, but they had no explanations. Those colors, those big skies, that sense of wide-open possibility—those were all the walls of the Paiutes' home. As far as they could make out, white men were mysterious lunatics.

There's no old Mexican adobe left in Lone Pine, nor wickiups by the seed fields. I've never seen a pepper garden there, and midnight on September 16 is pretty tame. When you get down to it, Los Angeles owns most of the town. On the way in, I walked past the Lone Pine Sports Complex—grassy ball fields for kids—and it had a sign at the entrance: LEASED FROM L.A. DEPT. WATER & POWER.

Austin saw the changes coming even before Los Angeles bought itself a shiny new watershed. She knew she lived in the gap between the old and new Americas. Miners' tales of lucky strikes, Paiute legends, stagecoach stories of bandits and strange midnight trails were all present on the land, but fading with the Jayhawkers' wagon tracks. The immigrant energy of Basque shepherds and bohunk miners still simmered with the remnant of Mexico, but the crust of ore and grass that made life on the land possible had been nearly consumed. Of course, the misogyny and racism and benighted parochialism of the time made her feel like a foreigner herself. Austin never fit in with the towns of the Owens Valley, even when she lived in a real house on a real street. She made folks too uneasy. She remembered a day when a squad of white ladies came trooping to her door in their Sunday best to tell her to stop dancing with the Paiutes and baking cakes for Chinamen.

I don't know where the Pizza Factory ("We toss 'em, they're awesome!") would rate on the Mary Austin spectrum of the sins of modernity. I silently begged her pardon and made a beeline for its swinging door, mindful of what had happened the last time I hit pavement and ended up eating pudding cups for dinner. I ordered a pie the size of a manhole cover and spent the next several hours slowly working it down, like a python swallowing a wildebeest.

The patchwork landscape of the Owens Valley.

I would have liked a Mary Austin or Shorty Harris to talk to. I had news to share, but I got the feeling it was the kind of news no one at the Factory was much interested in hearing. Laughing groups of local kids in skinny low-rider jeans and baggy shirts looked like grainy Xeroxes of Angelinos. Tourist families hurried through on their way to Mammoth or L.A. Eye contact was fleeting and disconcerting. I got a lot of careful avoidance. Austin warned me this would happen.

When I rolled myself out the door and back onto Lone Pine's main drag (which runs about ten blocks and includes one traffic light), it was early afternoon. Wizard Whitney still wrapped itself in impenetrable gray up in the storm. I'd come so far to see him, but he looked in no mood for visitors.

It was supposed to be a rest day. I couldn't get comfortable. My joints deserved the afternoon off. My mind was up in the Alabama Hills drumming its fingers and tapping its toes. And what was its rush? I asked around about the weather. Two inches, eight inches, or three feet of new snow today, depending on the prognosticator. New fronts would splash against the Sierra on and off as far as the weatherman's eye could see. A bedraggled dude with coke-bottle glasses followed me around, rolling his eyes and asking, first, if I were really going up there and, second, if he could come, too.

Evening slipped into the spaces in the sky and relieved my antsy brain. Fat, black clouds still hung low over Lone Pine. They looked brimful of rain. Austin called coyote the "lean hobo of the hills," and that's how I felt as I slipped behind a shed in a city park next to a Carl's Jr. I figured that no one would really mind if I used its eaves as an informal lean-to.

Austin saw the twentieth century coming to the Owens Valley like a rising tide. But she left the Owens (and Wallace) in 1906, before the aqueduct was even settled, while the landscape remained

more or less intact. Julian Steward, who interviewed Sam Newland in 1928 and Patsy Wilson of *Ko'o* in 1935, watched the full
fragmentation of culture and ecosystem. He arrived in the Owens
Valley in 1918, at the age of sixteen. Owens Lake—the huge sheet
of shallow brine at the end of the Owens River, just south of Lone
Pine—still had its colors and its ten million ducks, though it had
been five years since the aqueduct opened and its river got re-
routed. Steward had a fair artistic eye and painted the blue lake
and blue sky. A decade later, the lake had shriveled back, leaving
behind a hundred square miles of salt flats and dust.

The teenage Steward passed through the Owens Valley for the
first time on his way to an education. A new preparatory school
had opened the previous year in Deep Springs Valley, a remote
piece of open ground in the White Mountains. The school's
founder wanted a place where young men could train their minds
and hands together. He wanted the boys removed from urban and
materialistic distractions—and he couldn't have taken them much
farther away than Deep Springs. He would use the California wilderness to turn boys into self-reliant, freethinking leaders. His students spent mornings studying—social science, public speaking,
geology, language—and the rest of the day on the ranch, learning
to work, learning the land.

In May 1918, Steward left his childhood home in Washington,
D.C., rode the transcontinental to Carson, and then took the
narrow-gauge train down into the Owens Valley. Pure seren-
dipity brought him to the farthest edge of California. His parents'
broken marriage, the need for a scholarship, a loose connection
with the man who created the Deep Springs school—those were
the reasons Steward boarded the train. He had no idea he was
headed toward his lifework. He'd never been west before, though
like so many others, he had read enough Zane Grey to fill his

boyhood with horseback images of the desert. When he arrived, he didn't find any gunslingers, and working as a real ranch hand gave him an entirely different taste (and smell) of cowboy life. The land itself didn't disappoint. He climbed mountains in the Sierra, painted and photographed the open country, trekked through the White Mountains with his friends, just as Sam Newland had done. And even if Grey's characters suddenly seemed hokey and false, there *were* real adventurers in Eastern California. One of the nine other incoming students in 1918 was Frederick Coville's son Cabot, who brought stories to tell of his father's scientific odyssey through Death Valley when the times were peaceful and the land fierce.

Indians also inhabited Deep Springs alongside the students. A few Northern Paiutes worked around the ranch and lived in a wickiup of cast-off construction material. For the prior three thousand years, their people had gathered seeds and hunted there. Steward found petroglyphs and artifacts throughout the valley. In his first days and months in the West, he saw two sides of the desert, and these would stick with him for the rest of his life: the dying culture of the Paiutes and Shoshones, and the landscape of water. Water was central to the work of the boys; they wrestled it all around the ranch from the one source in the valley, the eponymous Deep Springs. When Steward looked at how the Paiutes and Shoshones lived prior to the white invasion, he realized that everything the original desert people did—from seeds to fish to their own migrations—also depended on water and its seasons.

Decades later, Steward would become one of the most widely read American anthropologists. His theory of cultural ecology fundamentally changed his field. Anthropologists had assumed that cultural traits diffused from one area to another, that tribes swapped basket designs or fishing methods the way diseases slip across geographical boundaries to colonize new hosts. Steward, instead, decided that culture emerged from the inhabited environment itself. Just like the boys at Deep Springs, the work, rituals, and games of a group came from the land on which they lived.

The notion that culture came out of the ground, that the land *made* the men and women who called it home, was no news to the Paiutes or Shoshones. They had been patiently repeating the idea in their foundational stories for centuries. And it wouldn't have been news to Mary Austin either, who, thirty years earlier, in *The Land of Little Rain*, wrote: "Not the law but the land sets the limit."

Carrying the seeds of those ideas, Steward left Deep Springs after three years to enroll at UC Berkeley. He started out in law, then switched to geology, then anthropology. He wanted, he wrote, "to go into work in exploration"—as if exploration were just another career path, like finance or plastics. The 1920s had started roaring, the frontier was three decades closed, and the American explorers of the previous age—Frémont, Muir, Powell—were all dead. Steward turned back to the desert and the fading Indian trails, searching for history and mystery in the wide-open spaces of the arid West.

Pavement has come. The water has been squeezed out of the ground. For all that, the land has kept its character. You can still track coyotes and elf owls on the mesa above the Alabama Hills. Deep Springs College, as remote as ever, still trains young men to get their minds into books and their hands in the ground. There's enough space between the mountains and deserts to make a boy want to get into exploration.

▲

Two days before I hopped the bus in L.A., I mailed myself tools for a snowy mountain: ice axe, crampons, backpacking stove, a floorless tent, and my much-anticipated snowshoes. You can send a box to yourself care of any post office in the country. It's one of the last surviving frontier practices, from a time when a stranger would stumble in from god-knows-where to check his mail. The goblin opened his crop on the post office steps, and I gorged him with the goods. I recycled all of my two-liter bottles. Behind a dumpster, I swapped my underwear for a clean pair, which wasn't exactly a hot shower but still felt awfully good.

I couldn't wait to get out of town. I had to *move*. West. I needed to get up on top of the tip of the rain shadow and have a look at what I'd done. Mount Whitney, white and sparkly, scattered sunlight in a pocket of blue sky. I kicked pavement just long enough to split the buildings and fences.

I passed over the aqueduct. The water of the entire region ran under my feet and sped south. Back when Mulholland first began minding ditches, he overheard a local man say: "*El agua es la sangre de la tierra.*" Water is the blood of the soil. The phrase stuck with Mulholland, and it stuck with me. The Owens Valley residents certainly felt the ground bleeding out from under them. In the 1920s, as the water table dropped and Owens Lake dried up and cropland became sagebrush, the farmers began dynamiting the aqueduct.

It became a local pastime. A midnight road, a case of dynamite. Local newspapers called it "shooting the duck." For a few days, Mulholland and his engineers would scramble to make emergency repairs, then the water would flow on again as always. Mulholland dismissed the explosions as a kind of native custom, like cannibals harassing missionaries in the hinterlands.

The faint echo of poetic justice seems to have gone unheard

Mount Whitney.

in the Owens Valley, which was suddenly full of hardy but belea-
guered pioneers and moral high dudgeon. In fact, the farmers and
ranchers were now renegades, pale Indians standing hopelessly
against power and the arrow of history. Their most serious up-
rising took place the same year as the first dynamiting. Instead of
stealing cows, they stole back the water. A hundred armed locals
seized the Alabama Gates just north of Lone Pine. They closed
the massive iron valves and turned the water into the riverbed.
The aqueduct went dry, and the insurrection turned into a kind
of holiday. The crowd swelled. Families brought picnics. Fires
burned day and night as rotating shifts of men maintained the occupation. Hollywood movie star Tom Mix, who happened to be
filming a Western nearby, lent an orchestra to keep the revolution
entertained.

During later rounds of duck shooting, Los Angeles sent police and Thompson machine guns to Lone Pine. To put down the revolution at the Alabama Gates, they used more insidious and effective countermeasures—bankers and lawyers. Reasonable-sounding voices offered sympathy and the dangling possibility of cash concessions (after all, it had worked before). If local property owners would only put their grievances in writing, they would be heard. Feeling like winners, the farmers and ranchers handed over their demands, along with the gates. The city's negotiator dutifully filed their papers into oblivion, while editorials in the city newspapers crowed about justice done and the dispersal of the mob. And the water flowed on.

There is one final irony to the Owens Valley land grab. Let's say that back in 1905, the farmers had tarred Fred Eaton and ridden him out of town. By the end of the century, the vastness,

Revolution at the Alabama Gates.

the sweeping curve from one mountain wall to the other, would have been filled with a monoculture grid of industrial agriculture and diesel machinery, just like California's Central Valley. Add a city, maybe the little sister of Fresno, only with dirtier air. Dam Lone Pine Creek, and flood Whitney Portal. All the creeks would have been stoppered in the name of late summer irrigation. Why not? Even peace-loving San Francisco dammed and flooded Hetch Hetchy, which was nothing less than a second Yosemite Valley. Why wouldn't the canyons of the eastern Sierra have become reservoirs, too?

By thieving the water, Los Angeles ended the economic potential of the Owens. The city made the ground worthless, but also saved the land's best quality—its wild openness. It's enough to make an environmentalist give up.

I left the pavement and stumped up into the Alabama Hills. Huge mounds of orange earth rolled above me. Clouds collected across the face of Whitney until the mountain disappeared again behind a wall of gray storm. Given the hubbub in the sky, I'd bought food for a week at Joseph's Bi-Rite, Lone Pine's one grocery store. Added to my winter mountaineering gear, the grub made a heavyweight of the goblin again. Before, I could at least drink away my freight of water.

The sand in the hills was deep, and my legs felt skinny. I floundered higher, fighting gravity, feeling more rusted than rested. Strange rocks, tens and hundreds of feet high, pushed out of the hills. I walked a labyrinth of orange quartz monzonite, which felt like navigating the folds of an old granite brain decomposing into the sand. The basin swept high above and far below me, up to the mountains and down to the sage floor. The monzonite and I were a knot in the equation, a few tangled stitches on the long, smooth curve into the storm. Wind spilled through spaces between the rocks. Off to my left, Lone Pine Creek tumbled down between polished stones and supplicant trees. Above me, the sky pressed low and dark.

My buddy Sisyphus walked beside me awhile, rolling his stone uphill. We joked about pleasure, which seemed in pretty short supply between us, what with our mountains and stones and deserts. I told him I thought innocent happiness might be something like sitting under a tree by a brook with a daydream in your head. Maybe if you sit long enough a fish will jump into your lap. Lone Pine Creek in blue early summer would be a good candidate, and the Paiutes may have come close on certain days when the seed harvest was in and the grinding stone quiet. Sometimes, one of Mary Austin's French shepherd friends would have hours or days of idyll by the creek when the grass was thick and the coyotes elsewhere.

What pulls a body away from the trout brook in the sky isn't fate or the gods but work. All of that toil and striving for some distant point on the horizon when you could be perfectly content in the shade by the creek. Your work will be undone in a year or ten or a hundred if you're lucky, but you cling tenaciously to it nevertheless. It's the life of Sisyphus the mountaineer. You pull yourself up to the summit, knowing you'll just have to turn your back to it and let it go once you get there. Sisyphus seemed kind of bummed that I blamed him for the end of innocence. I told him it was the other way around. He had his stone because of our aspirations. That perked him up. The idea of rolling all the collective dreams of humanity up his hill and watching them tumble back down clearly appealed to him.

The sky curdled. Wet, black boils dangled above me. The land seemed draped in a blanket of storm and approaching night. I found a sheltered trough of coarse sand and guyed out my tent, an orange triangle with a single pole in the center. The rain began just as I moved in. I watched it fall and pucker the sand, listened to a million drops run through the hills and over my little shelter. After crossing the land of little rain, I felt strangely hydrophobic in an old-fashioned soaking. So much water falling out of the sky seemed unnatural, a Martian landing. The mountain, buried under all that snow, had my sympathy.

▲

An odd fellow named Inyokel lived up here, where the land opens wide to the Sierra wall. In the 1930s, he kept a cabin among the rocks and walked the trails through the sage, tracking desert creatures, visiting ghost mines, even following Mary Austin's forty-year-old footprints. On one late fall day with snow on the Inyos, he decided to take down his old rifle and go hunting on the mesa above the Alabama Hills. He walked past the familiar stones and empty gaps of sage and sand. And then to his wondering eyes appeared, not a deer or an antelope, but four hooded hawks, an elephant, and a leopard. The menagerie had been trucked in by Paramount. On that day in 1934, Henry Hathaway was filming *The Lives of a Bengal Lancer*, with the Sierra standing in for the Himalaya.

Chances are you've seen the Alabama Hills yourself. If you caught *Iron Man*, you watched Robert Downey Jr. blow them up (virtually, thankfully). If you watched *Gladiator*, you saw Russell Crowe stumbling through his desert delirium with the Sierra as backdrop. These hills have been Afghanistan, India, the Pyrenees. Studios shot hundreds of Westerns here, from Tom Mix to the Lone Ranger. The far-out desolation of the rocks and sage stood for anywhere hard-bitten men with guns and cactus spines for souls might hang out. One look told audiences they'd traveled over the mountains and beyond the law. Half the businesses in Lone Pine seem to have a John Wayne autograph hung on one wall or another.

None of the tinsel sticks to this hard-baked ground. You'd never know Hollywood uses this patch of desert as a remote back lot, just as you'd never know you were seeing Eastern California while watching *The Lives of a Bengal Lancer*. For *Gunga Din*, another Himalayan epic of the 1930s, RKO built an entire tent city by the rocks for the cast and crew. Lone Pine about doubled in size overnight. Set designers drove narrow dirt tracks into the rocks to erect their temples, outposts, and miniature villages. When the shoot was done, the sets and actors and tent city disappeared on the wind, another mirage. Just like the miners and schemers, Hollywood found that it could project any fantasy it chose onto the desert.

Instead of hunting on that day in 1934, Inyokel spent the day watching local cowboys in turbans and spray-painted tans playing bit parts in the movie. Of course, Inyokel didn't really need the meat either. He was the fictional alter ego of a man named John Crowley, who created Inyokel to tell the stories of the sagebrush country. Two hundred short pieces featuring his "Inyo yokel" appeared in the *Central California Register* between 1934 and 1940.

John Crowley was a Catholic priest—*the* Catholic priest for all of Inyo County and parts of two others during the 1920s. On the first Sunday of each month, he'd hold Masses in Bishop and Big Pine; on the second Sunday, Independence, Lone Pine, Keeler, and Darwin; on the third Sunday, Randsburg and Trona; on the fourth Sunday, Barstow, Ludlow, and Death Valley. For a time, his parish covered thirty thousand square miles—about the same size as all of his native Ireland. Between Masses, he'd visit remote families and mines. Crowley drove the winding ruts that served as interconnecting roads in a Model T with the rear seat-back removed so that he could sleep in the car. He called himself an "ecclesiastical tramp."

Inyokel was also a tramp who traveled the mountains and deserts in between stints at his cabin in the Alabamas. In the Sage and Tumbleweed articles for the *Register*, Inyokel often had long talks with Crowley, whom he always called the Padre. Inyokel was the half of Crowley that lost his voice cheering at double-jack drilling contests and dug for lost mines with callused hands and sat on benches pumping old-timers for stories—the life Crowley might have lived if he hadn't felt called to be Father to all the desert's souls.

At a time when the mines had stepped down into their final decline and the spirit of the Owens Valley had been all but broken by Los Angeles, Crowley became the most outspoken booster of all things Eastern Californian, and the city became his opponent. Locals needed a good fight to revive them, Crowley decided, and the best scrap of all would be to challenge Los Angeles one more time for the Owens River. But he didn't seem to mind Hollywood's presence. Watching the commotion and sudden quiet of a set kept him enchanted for hours. He liked seeing the magic emerge out of actors and props. He had that Catholic love of pageantry.

Crowley even one-upped Hollywood for sheer spectacle when he orchestrated the most outsized celebration of the pairing of Death Valley and Mount Whitney the desert has ever seen. His Wedding of the Waters lasted three days in October 1937. It began with a Washoe runner bringing down a gourd of water from a high Sierra lake and passing it to a Pony Express rider at Whitney Portal. From there the gourd became a baton traveling along a relay of Western Americana: on the back of a mule led by a prospector; in two covered wagons, one each for the descendants of the Jayhawker and Donner parties; by twenty-mule team; in a stagecoach; by narrow-gauge rail; in a brand-new Zephyr driven by an Indy 500 champ; and, finally, to Badwater by airplane over the Panamint Mountains. Along the way were brass bands and parades and crowds wearing old-timey getups and waving flags. Sam Ball, the prospector whose headboard I had admired in the Mount Whitney Cemetery, had a turn toting the gourd. Frank Merriam, governor of California, drank a celebratory shot of the precious water at a dinner in Lone Pine and joined the festivities wielding an antique rifle. A captain and two sheriffs shot bullets through a blue ribbon to mark the opening of a new section of highway into Death Valley. Yahoo! Good times in the mythic West.

I crossed Lone Pine Creek and waded up through the last mile of open sage. On the basin floor, the immense white scab of Owens Lake smoldered and spat dust, dwarfing the blocks and threads of Lone Pine. From where I stood, I could see some of the places the revelers had congregated to watch the Wedding of the Waters, like the old rail intersection near Keeler. The rails were pulled for scrap during World War II; rabbitbrush has claimed the ground. It was hard to imagine a brass band assembling down there in the middle of nowhere. Crowley never got his chance to duke it out with Los Angeles. All that sleepless desert driving caught up with him. At three in the morning on March 17, 1940, on his way to the Death Valley Mass, he hit a steer on Highway 14 and swerved into the oncoming lane. A lumber truck hit him head-on. Since then, the remote edges of Inyo have only gotten quieter. And maybe that's a good thing.

The ghosts, the human trace on the land, dropped away below me. Fandangos. Dances. Race wars. Water wars. And the echoes: the whitewash of cowboys and Indians and hardy pioneers. The edges of the desert gone silent. Asphalt and speed down the middle. Stagecoach ruts plowed under to suit an Indy 500 champ. The slow sweat of tamales in El Pueblo de Las Uvas transformed into the Pizza Factory and Del Taco. But the asphalt ribbon is thin, and the desert is always right there, pressing in.

Above me, the granite levered straight up out of the sage, and the Sierra wall loomed gray and black and storm-shadowed. Though I couldn't see Mount Whitney, I knew where it stood, in the middle of the heavy weather and stone. John Crowley might have liked to think of himself as Father to the desert flock. But Mount Whitney is the true creator here, responsible for the desert and skies and all the crusty souls reared in between.

Chapter 9

MOUNT WHITNEY

For climbers there is a canyon which comes down from the north shoulder of the Whitney peak. Well-seasoned limbs will enjoy the climb of 9000 feet required for this direct route, but soft, succulent people should go the mule way.

—John Muir, *Century Magazine*, 1891

High summer on Mount Whitney looks like a medieval pilgrimage. Every year, thousands of the devoted travel from across the country to take part in the long walk up the mountain. A trail winds its way to the top through granite benches and climate zones. Once the snow clears by June or July, lines of head-bowed, penitent worshippers snake along the relentless switchbacks. The trekking poles and designer hiking shorts are distinctly American, but the rest of the vibe seems to come from an older, more dedicated culture. At the summit, people throw their hands in the air and prostrate themselves on the granite. Crowding on the trail has become so bad that an elaborate permit system has to be enforced by rangers with walkie-talkies.

Winter snow sets the clock back 120 years, erasing the trail. The hot, dusty switchbacks become long downward strokes of snow and ice, steep and quiet. Black and white, granite and snow, the mountain returns to its elemental state until the melt begins in May.

Ten days into April, with Whitney buried deep under its winter flood, I crossed the joint between mountain and sage eight thousand feet below the summit. I scrambled up steep, loose soil anchored by rocks and trees, and passed through the gate of Lone Pine Canyon. On the opposite canyon wall, a few cars beetled up the heavy grade of the paved road to Whitney Portal. The creek roared below me, turning white somersaults over itself. The clouds pressed down, thick and wet, looking like tarred cotton. Ankle deep in sandy alpine dirt, I plowed up the canyon-side, kicking steps, shaking off topsoil and rocks.

I was making a mess of it. In so many ways, the desert is fragile, but a person can walk through it without leaving a footprint. Here, I was leaving a lot more than footprints. The ground skin was soaked and soft. It held the canyon-side so lightly I cut a trench in it just by passing through. I had no idea how long my tracks would last, but they didn't look good. I knew of an old path nearby, not much used anymore because of the road. For a few miles, I followed it up into the trees and weather.

Snow began plopping down in wet, heavy clumps. It didn't fall so much as materialize out of the sodden air. I reached Whitney Portal, the end of the road, the beginning of most journeys to the mountain. A few families clomped around in the slush in plastic galoshes, looking more than a little lost. One woman asked me where they could go to see Whitney. I felt bad telling her their best bet was Lone Pine.

Massive walls and towers of pure mountain bone turned the space above the parking lot into an open-air palace. With the granite disappearing into the clouds, the walls seemed even taller. It looked as though the stone might just keep going up forever.

Just above the portal, the canyon of the north fork of Lone Pine Creek splits off from the main pilgrim path. In 1873, long before the trail, John Muir slipped into this canyon and pushed through a maze of interlocking willow, birch, pine, and rock. After gaining four thousand feet, peeling the layers of growth off the land until nothing remained but stone and snow, the canyon brought him directly to Whitney's feet. The steepest face of the mountain watched the little man approach, hopping from rock to rock across the glacial tailings below. It was the perfect kind of place for Muir, remote and difficult, with the granite skeleton of the Sierra laid bare for him to see. Muir followed a couloir, a chute of snow and rock, up around the shoulder of Mount Whitney, and then threaded a narrow passage through cliffs to the summit. Choosing the canyon and couloir as a means of reaching the top of the mountain was so far ahead of Muir's time that sixty years passed before other climbers rediscovered his route. I ducked past the brush and trees guarding the canyon entrance and followed Muir toward the mountain.

Bursts and chandeliers of ice hung from trees and cliffs. Little threads of ground plants froze inside heavy waxes of ice. The red-orange-purple of the desert seemed suddenly ridiculous, a tale for children about the other side of the world. I'd opened my eyes in a monochromatic land. I'd found all the desert's water.

I knew the canyon well enough. On climbing errands over the past decade, I'd been up and down it a lot. Each year, the many feet of Muir's distant descendants leave the canyon floor a little tamer, but snow is winter's big bottle of whiteout. With a few inches underfoot and more tumbling out of the sky, the canyon looked as wild as I'd ever seen it.

Three men with big packs, headed back down to the portal, appeared out of the whites and darks and falling snow. In thick Gore-Tex suits and beards, they looked like high-tech bears. We stopped for a few minutes by the creek to pass the news. Today was Saturday, I learned, and twenty or thirty other people were scattered around the canyon in small groups up higher. The three men took turns describing the past twenty-four hours for me. They'd charged up into the weather the day before. Around them, dark shapes moved in and out of view, other climbers struggling with the storm. At about eleven thousand feet, most everyone stopped. Tents had been slapped up in a full blizzard, fabric flying, snow pouring through open zippers. They'd spent a soggy night in the piling snow. The Friday forecast had been the worst I'd seen, so I asked why they hadn't waited a day or a week. They shrugged. "We'd been planning this trip two months," one said. Other climbers had attempted the summit today, but the guys describing the storm for me decided to charge right back downhill because a warm bed in Lone Pine sounded better than a cold avalanche in the couloir.

The men disappeared down the canyon, and I continued higher, chewing on their story and the weather, prescribing myself patience and altitude. I'd see what I'd see when I got there. Half an hour later, the snowfall petered out. Blue cracks broke through the clouds. I tunneled through brush bowed over with new snow, then climbed to ledges a hundred feet up the northern canyon wall to bypass a dense, white bunker of willow and talus on the canyon floor. Scrambling up short chimneys and walking along the ramps in the stone, I watched the clouds pull apart overhead. A subconscious bell rang. I stopped and looked around. I was standing on a flat bench, eight feet long, in the middle of the system of ledges. Some trick of wind or shade had kept snow from collecting here, maybe the last bit of bare ground I'd see on my way up the mountain. Deep drifts two hundred feet away on the opposite canyon-side showed the precise, four-dot tracks of phantom rabbits. A temporary creek spun down a nearby cliff. Keeler Needle jabbed up into the clouds ahead. The sun still had a ways to fall, but I had running water, flat dry ground, and a view. The spot looked an awful lot like home.

Talking to the three guys running away from the mountain, I'd sensed their haste. Down below were burgers, cars, and messages to check; the game was to get up to the summit and back to those things in as few hours as possible. Hearing about the commotion of the climbers above made me want to slow down. I had a different speed in mind—*glacial* sounded about right. The mountain would declare its intentions. The fish would jump into my lap, so to speak. I had food and a book and knew how to put the lid on impatience. I could wait out the weather as long as it took.

I unpacked the goblin and propped myself against a rock with my sleeping bag over my knees to fight off the cold. The cloud ceiling shattered and the gray shreds dissolved, like snow in water, into a dark blue sky. The break in the storm might not last the night, but the canyon and sky were too beautiful for tent walls. I'd sleep in the open and let the next blizzard wake me if it wanted. The sun sharpened Keeler's summit then sank below the canyon rim. Icicles shattered off the cliffs above me and jangled down the canyon walls, landing a few feet to my right and left. I never opened my book. I just watched.

Clarence King—the New Englander who tutted at the shacks of Lone Pine's whites—once spent an afternoon in the summer of 1873 in the sagebrush by Lone Pine, staring up at Mount Whitney.

He had climbed the mountain and returned to the desert, and he lay in the sand looking upward and inward, prodding his motivations, poking at the pressures that had driven him up there. A gray old Paiute came by and sat next to him. The man took out an arrow and sighted the summit along the shaft. Whitney, he said, in signs and shards of English, was an old man who watched over the Owens Valley and looked after the Indians and made earthquakes. For a moment, Whitney looked down at King, too. King saw the creature within the mountain. Then the Paiute walked away and his superstitions trailed off like a dust cloud behind him. The mirage collapsed. Mount Whitney became a glorious pile of weathered and levered granite, and King became a geologist again.

Knowing King, there probably was no Indian. That's the kind of figure he liked to use to portray his divided mind. And I don't believe King simply shrugged off the eyes of the Sierra and went forth a newly determined man, interested in rocks only for the sake of rocks and not for the ache the mountains put in his soul. King never shook his sense of wide-eyed wonderment. And why should he have? Superstition isn't the only alternative to geology. You don't have to turn a mountain into a god to feel its power. But King spent a lot of the second half of his life trying to convince himself he wasn't really a poet or mountaineer.

I watched the canyon shut down for the night. Backlit by the setting sun, the tip of Keeler burned out like a candle. Yellow, gold, orange, red, gray. Flat twilight settled in against the stone and brought the cold, which chased me deep into my sleeping bag. The icicles stopped rattling off the cliffs above me. The chatter of the creek dropped low. Shade by shade, the blue leaked out of the sky, but I never saw it turn black.

▲

I woke a few hours later. Some inner nag needed to check on the stars. There they were, packed thick. No clouds. The nag woke me every couple hours to look again, but the pattern for the night wasn't unpleasant. I'd open my eyes, see the Milky Way like a glittering fog just a few inches out of my reach, then slide right back down into the dark.

I woke up for good and watched the dawn for a moment while I braced for a cold jump into the day. I packed quickly, needing to move to get warm, but I could have just waited. The temperature spiked as soon as the sun came up. Mushy snow bombs whomped off trees. The falling glass of icicles was nonstop. The sky turned a shade of blue as deep as the sound of a two-ton bell.

Just past my sleeping ledge, the snow ruled. It was a white world with no bare spots. I put on my snowshoes and floated on top of a winter's worth of snowpack. A few months earlier, this had been Pacific saltwater. A year hence, it would be down an Angelino's toilet on its way back to the ocean again. Yesterday, the sun had run the water in the sky over the mountains like the ridges of a washboard, dropping fresh, clean new crystals in white billows over the land.

Three more guys with big packs came sliding on their backsides down an open bowl. I stopped them to ask how they'd done. I got the same story of the storm on Friday—the gung-ho rush out of the parking lot into the weather, blurry shapes wallowing through a hissy static of falling snow, flapping tents, wet and jumbled gear, a long night. The next morning, yesterday, fearing avalanches but going ahead because everyone else was, they'd pushed up to the top of the canyon, where the couloir dropped down the side of Whitney. They climbed to near the top of the chute, high up the mountain. Conditions were terrible. Loose snow, ice, wind. Most other groups had turned back lower in the couloir; a few were higher. Then one of the three of them fell a hundred feet. He'd tumbled through the snow and bounced off rocks and survived unharmed. He grinned bashfully at me, and I took an involuntary step back, maybe for fear of him getting struck by lightning out of the clear blue to balance his account.

I asked if anyone had actually made it to the summit. They hadn't seen anyone get to the top, though rumor was that one party had. In my head, it all looked like a Keystone Kops routine. Interchangeable climbers rushing up and down the mountain, wading through the storm, bumping into each other, falling. I thanked the three and snowshoed higher.

Temple mountains inspire fanaticism, and this was true for Mount Whitney from the start. In 1864, twenty-two-year-old Clarence King spent his first full summer in California—in the long tradition of new college graduates, he had wangled himself an unpaid internship with some of the best minds in his field. For a young geologist of his era, that also meant writing new maps, climbing unknown mountains, and sleeping through storms while wrapped in a horse blanket for shelter.

King first saw Mount Whitney from the shoulder of another mountain, miles away across the heart of the Sierra. Whitney had never been climbed, at least not by whites. (Knapping flakes and other signs have been found at tantalizing elevations, but at the time, no one bothered asking the Paiutes about their climbing past.) King and the mule packer for the geologists' little field party made a valiant effort to cross the intervening canyons and peaks, but the mountain was far, the wilderness deep, and their provisions amounted to a hunk of well-aged venison and some beans. They named the tallest mountains they saw, scattering an international cadre of scientists around the Sierra. Josiah Whitney, the chief of the statewide geological survey for which King worked, got the biggest prize—Mount Whitney was his namesake. At least half of this gesture probably came from genuine respect, with the rest amounting to some inspired flattery from his underlings.

When King returned to join the rest of the party camped high in the western Sierra, he begged the field director, William Brewer, for permission to ride round to the southern end of the Sierra and attempt Mount Whitney directly. Brewer acquiesced—possibly, I think, just to keep King from pestering him for the rest of the summer. Like an Ivy League Don Quixote, King quested up through the foothills and into the mountains, having courtly encounters with hunters, lumbermen, and itinerant pig herders along the way. He always seemed happiest as a romantic jack-of-all-trades, footloose in the wide world, writing love ballads and adventure tales and geologizing all at once. Alone, having left the horses and his escort of two soldiers and all the other people days behind, he made his second venture to the mountain, which ended in hail, snow, and cliffs five hundred feet below the summit. Mount Whitney grew larger in his mind as the years passed. As a young man, he didn't seem too disappointed. It was all part of the adventure.

By 1871, King had become one of those leading minds he had gone west to find, but each year, he spent less time vagabonding in the mountains and more time administrating fieldwork designed to dissect the western half of North America. That summer, King took a detour on his way back to his surveying work in Wyoming and trundled down the eastern Sierra. Whitney was still unclimbed, the mountain had its hook in him, and he craved a pure adventure like those of his first, revelatory days in the Sierra. He paid his respects to the gardens and snowy linens of Lone Pine's adobe district and made another attempt on the then-highest mountain in America. He reached the summit in dense clouds and a gathering storm and left a half dollar inscribed with his name under a rock on top. Trouble was, he'd climbed the wrong mountain. King received the embarrassing news two years later, while in New York. Not only had his half dollar been found on top of Sheep Peak (now Mount Langley), five miles south of Whitney, but three fishermen from Lone Pine—Albert Johnson, John Lucas, and Charles Begole—had already beaten him to the summit of the real Mount Whitney. King jumped on the transcontinental train and rushed back to California in time to become the ninth person to stand atop the mountain he'd named nine years earlier.

About this time, locals began to wonder why it should be that the mountain they looked up to every day from Lone Pine should be named Mount Whitney. Josiah Whitney had never climbed it, and his geologists couldn't even seem to *find* the right peak. So, briefly, the highest mountain in the United States became Fisherman's Peak. Such an unromantic title for a mountain of such stature horrified the geologists. They controlled the maps, and Fisherman's Peak soon became a relic.

I topped a little rise and came even with a familiar place of leaning boulders and dwarf trees and the last pocket meadows. The meadows were buried deep under the snow, but the mountaineering tents scattered around looked like neon mushrooms pushing out of white soil. Climbers slouched and blinked in the sun. It was Sunday, and most everyone was packing up to leave— under a sky filled with nothing but sunlight and sonic blue. No clouds had crashed the morning. People went into and out of their tents, pulling out wet sleeping bags, looking prickly and disgruntled, like snow moles expecting February and waking up in June.

The canyon broke down into short tributaries. I turned away from the tents and followed the highest branch. I floated along the edge of old moraines, titanic heaves and swells of glacial rubble frosted white. Then Whitney broke up out of the ground, suddenly very near and tall.

This is one of the edges of the earth. The granite climbs up out of the desert of its own creation, running up to cloud-land like a fairytale beanstalk. At the top of the mountain wall stands Whitney, the tallest in a row of gray and white towers, each with the same clean, vertical, eastern drop. They seem to prop up the sky, pillars cut by the tectonic mason to separate heaven and earth. Granite and sky above, the Sierra wall and the desert below—this place is a throne room, Olympus of the American West.

In 1897, twenty years after the dustup over Fisherman's Peak, climber and Stanford University art professor Bolton Brown pointed out the obvious, that *Whitney* was the least romantic, worst kind of name one could attach to a mountain. Particularly *this* mountain. Why, asked Brown, were we turning our mountains into humongous tombstones for a bunch of gray-haired men who would be forgotten in ten or a hundred years? Brown wanted names that captured something of a mountain's essence: Arrow Peak, Cloud's Rest. Or names that had some harmony, like Tuolumne or Tehama. Mary Austin also wrinkled her nose at the practice of embalming our corpses in lakes, mountains, and flowers. She preferred expressive names conceived by Indians and children, like the Shivering Dunes, or "evening snow" for the white gilia, or Oppapago—the weeper—for Lone Pine Peak. Few American Adams have followed Brown's plea for poetry, so even now, with our country only a few hundred years old, you must walk the land with a historical index just to make sense of the geography.

A man and a woman came slowly down through the snow above me. We talked briefly; they spoke with quiet, precise Austrian accents. They'd been the only ones to attempt the mountain today, and they'd turned back because the snow was too deep and they were moving too slow. The tracks of the previous day had all been wiped clean. They seemed a little spooked by this—the mountain shedding all human trace. Something up there was mobile, shifting. The two of them were the last people I saw above the snow-line.

With the sun straight overhead, I pulled up to the shore of Iceberg Lake—or at least, what would have been Iceberg Lake if it hadn't been shut under a thick lid of snow. A flat expanse with a slightly darker cast was the only sign of the lake below the surface. I stamped out a footprint for my tent and staked its corners in the snow, then crawled underneath to lock the center pole in place. Some shy away from floorless tents because they prefer to keep all of the outside out. I like the simplicity of sleeping in the snow with no fabric underfoot to tear or stain. Back outside, Whitney stood right there, on the same ground. I buried the hems of the tent with more snow to keep the wind from crawling in under the edges, and by the time I was done, it looked pretty snug. Nearby, a few rock islands—eight- and ten-foot boulders in summer—poked through the white flood. Their tops weren't exactly solar coals, but they felt better on my backside than the snow. I sat on one and stared up at the mountain. The sky hypnotized me. It backed Whitney with its radiant, motionless, opiate blue. I know I didn't fall asleep, but a slice of day wheeled by and I didn't notice it pass.

Another way to look at Mount Whitney and its towers is as the side view of a gigantic jawbone. Whitney is the big canine tooth at the end. Deep chutes separate the peaks, down to a gumline of stone. Muir ascended the chute just north of Whitney. What would he find where the couloir bent around the north face of the mountain and disappeared? Shuttered cliffs? Gates to the summit? The long bones of the planet? Muir had no idea. So he crawled through the teeth of the mountain to find out.

High camp in the snow.

It was October 1873, the same year the fishermen and Clarence King all reached the summit. Over the course of a month, Muir had horse-packed the length of the Sierra from Yosemite to Whitney, taking time in the high mountains, and among the Sequoias, and in the Kings and San Joaquin Canyons. He crossed over to the east side of the Sierra at Kearsarge Pass and traveled south along the joint between mountain and desert. He pushed back up into the mountains south of Lone Pine and nearly lost his horse in a bog. The next day, he left the animal in a meadow and climbed Mount Langley, the old Sheep Peak that had so badly fooled King.

Atop Langley, Muir saw the unmistakably higher mountain five miles to the north. A topographer's nightmare of canyons and granite saw blades filled the distance between the two summits. Muir had just climbed a 14,000-foot mountain, and he'd carried nothing but the clothes on his back and the bits in his pockets, and he decided the best time to set out for Whitney was immediately. People who think of Muir as a pen-and-paper naturalist should try following him on a starvation run through the mountains. He made it to the base of Whitney at sunset. He found no wood for a fire, he had no food, and the wind had taken his hat the night before. So he did the logical thing—he climbed through the night to stay warm. By midnight, he'd made it high up the shoulder of the mountain. There the starlight failed him. He couldn't see enough to climb higher. He spent the rest of the night dancing in the rocks, under the stars, so as not to freeze: a wide-eyed, bearded mountain druid. Dawn found him half out of his mind with cold, hunger, and weariness. He retreated back across the canyons and ridges and over the shoulder of Mount Langley to his horse and food and blanket, then limped back to Independence and spent a solid day eating and sleeping.

The route taken by the fishermen and King winds through a long meander to reach the southwest side of Whitney, and Muir also attempted that side of the mountain, though his cross-country approach was far rougher. Riding and walking back and forth through the sagebrush in the Owens Valley, Muir couldn't help but notice the east face of Mount Whitney, notched as through a gun-sight up the canyon of Lone Pine Creek. This is the famous face of Whitney—sheer, tall, proud. A backdrop for the desert, and paintings, and movies. In his era, Muir alone saw it as the right and proper route for mountaineers to take to the mountaintop.

Muir left his tired horse in Independence and set out on foot for the canyon. He slept a night in the sage, then a night at the tree line. In the journal he carried with him, he wrote as much about the willows, sedges, yellow pines, and lichens as the granite. Lone Pine Creek, settled into its autumn hush, kept him company. In the couloir in October, he would have found bare rock and pockets of withered alpine ice. The couloir narrowed and led him to a notch and the north face, where he picked his way through shadow and stone. He reached the summit with the sun still low in the east and spent the morning sketching mountains magnified through clear, cold air.

I heard a growl and watched a big pocket of snow avalanche off the face of the mountain, showering the ground with debris a quarter mile from my camp. I stirred off my rock and found my stove. The last liquid water I'd seen had been back at my ledge the night before. I lit the stove and began cooking pans of snow. I drank as much as I could hold, and filled the two metal bottles I'd carried with me.

For a day on which I'd seen plenty of people, my solitude felt deep. All the others were melting off the mountain like the new snow in the sun. And none of them had camped here. Nothing living tracked the snow around the lake, not even a rabbit or a finch. Rocks rolling down the steep bowl above the lake had left the only marks. The avalanches diving off the mountain made the only sounds.

I was bellied up to the mountain, sitting on a boulder in the snow and breathing thin, cold air—but the vanished clouds had uncovered the same sky and sun I'd walked under all through the desert. I knew them: the big, bright star, the river Lethe color. The sun has a different face for different places, and even at Whitney's feet, I found I hadn't ever left the desert. Wind slid past and nosed around the lake. Loose crystals levitated off the top layer of snow and stayed airborne. My shore filled with ghosts, translucent limbs curling around my rock and tent.

As far as anyone knows, John Muir was the first white to tres-pass here, and the next fifty-seven years went by with only a few stray human interlopers. During that time, a scientific research station reached the summit of Mount Whitney via the trail on the other side of the mountain. Pack trains hauled firewood to the top, pilgrims camped there, and the scientists studied the thermal output of the sun. Below them, two thousand feet straight down the east face, the little lake and the stone and snow remained secret, guarded by the canyon and the go-elsewhere face of granite above.

Norman Clyde rediscovered Muir's route up Whitney in 1930. Clyde came to California because he had read Muir's books and wanted to know the mountains Muir wrote into life. Up in the Sierra, Clyde became a force of nature. He was closer kin to the wind and snow than to other flesh-bound climbers. He weathered blizzards in his shirtsleeves and spent entire months in the summer climbing a new mountain each day. No one, not even Muir, climbed with Clyde's appetite. But Muir remained for Clyde the voice in the wilderness, the words in the trees and rocks, helping Clyde see beneath the granite skin. Like Muir, Clyde came to the eastern foot of Whitney alone, and he recognized the power of the place. In the couloir, Clyde found the biggest polemoniums he'd seen, purple flowers beloved by climbers for crawling out of the unlikeliest cracks on the tallest mountains. Looking at the polemoniums, Clyde imagined Muir doing the same. He could almost see Muir's tracks and sense the visionary climbing ahead of him, as if Whitney had purposefully held everyone else away so that Clyde could cross the eras and meet Muir on the highest Sierra peak.

Clyde called the couloir the Mountaineer's Route, a simple name that unpacks in interesting ways. As Muir hinted, the route is the essence of mountaineering: a little snow, a little rock, a guardian canyon, a hidden-in-plain-sight passage up into the wild vertical. The name carries pride of ownership. The couloir is for climber's—trail pilgrims need not apply. And the name is a tribute to Muir, the prototypical mountaineer. Muir understood that the roadways, mule-ways, and trail-ways weren't the best ways to elevate his soul. At a time when most were satisfied just to reach a summit, Muir looked for striking lines and difficult ground.

One last challenge to the Mount Whitney name came from the many men and women who, like Clyde, followed Muir as a guiding voice through the Sierra and who thought Muir's name belonged at the top of the range. After all, Muir had been the one to tell the mountains' stories most eloquently. He had saved the Sierra through his faith in the idea of national parks. And Muir, the scientist, was right about glaciers and mountain formation, about the basic architecture of the Sierra, while Josiah Whitney's notions of earthquake valleys and crustal spasms weren't much more than geological retreads of the Book of Revelations.

Muir probably wouldn't have cared for the renaming idea himself. He liked names with history and replaced modern labels when he could, like Tissiack—a crying woman from Indian legend—for Half Dome. Muir didn't see himself as a pioneer or an Adam—as an older man, he wrote that he'd never left his name "on any mountain, rock, or tree." For Mount Whitney, he seemed to favor the earthy anonymity of Fisherman's Peak, which is what he called the mountain in his journal. And Whitney had called Muir an ignorant shepherd for disagreeing with his interpretation of the birth of the Yosemite Valley, which couldn't have helped.

The movement came to nothing. Mount Whitney had too much historical inertia. In 1907, Muir's name ended up attached to the farthest tooth of the Whitney group. From one direction it is spectacular; from all others it is a nondescript, 300-foot bump.

Long shadows at sunset, Mount Whitney.

Maybe the best way to think of Mount Muir is as a thorn in Whitney's side.

The wind surged, dropped, and surged again, fingering my loose gear on the rock while I floundered through the snow after my hat. I turned off the stove and packed everything away in the tent. The sun slid down another inch, and the mountain seemed to step forward and catch it. The temperature dropped from skin deep to bone deep in seconds. I already had on all my clothes. There was nothing to do but pack myself away, too.

Inside, happy for the shelter, I lay on my back and listened to the wind. It rubbed against the mountain and the tent, sounding solid, raspy. Friction was in the air. Staring upward, seeing nothing, I thought I could sense the shape of the mountain by the way the wind moved around it. Whitney floated above me, stone made of air instead of light. I felt like a bat learning to fly. The towers emerged and swirled away.

▲

My eyes opened and it was black-dark and cold. Perfect. Snow is best climbed frozen stiff, when the pack hasn't woken up enough to avalanche. Bright, hard stars, thick as glowing snowfall. No moon. Black mountain. Pale snow silvered by starlight. The top layer had frozen to a crust that gave way under the least weight. I sank knee-deep into the powder below. I strapped on my snowshoes, then grabbed my ice axe, and plowed up toward the couloir.

The mountain ate the stars as I approached, turning the whole western sky into a dense void. I found the tracks of the last climbers I'd seen the day before, and we contoured together in the thin blue sphere cast by my headlamp. Beyond the radius of my light, depthless shapes loomed and overlapped. Somewhere below was the lake; somewhere above, the mountain. At the edge of the couloir, the tracks vanished into blank snow. That *was* eerie. Something shifting had been here and swallowed their steps. Even the historical tracks—Muir's, Clyde's, those of all the climbers who'd followed, including some of my own—were buried under the white flood that made the world new.

I kept my snowshoes on in the couloir and still nearly foundered. I'd rarely used them on such steep ground, but I couldn't find any resistance under my feet. While I huffed and puffed and hoarded vertical inches, the night warped my sense of time. It could have been one hour or three since I left my tent. The snow moved like a dry liquid, flowing around the snowshoe frames. I was treading water. Steep water.

Seven hundred feet up—an eternity of mucking for inches in the dark—the snow transformed. I crossed a divide, like the line from sand to stone at the edge of a dune. Instead of drowning in powder, my snowshoes skated. I stepped back and stamped out a perch. The long black slope below invited me to tip backward and down the chute. On my platform, I traded snowshoes for crampons, leaving the snowshoes stuck in the snow for my return.

The snow turned from brick to ice, pitched at an angle like a regular flight of stairs, only smooth as a frozen river. I kicked and scratched with the spikes on my feet, making about as much of an impression as fingernails on steel. Funky conditions for sure. One moment I was swimming in powder, the next bruising my feet against ice like granite. Where stone ribs breached the flood on either side of the chute, I climbed them instead because the rock was easier to handle than the ice.

The sun opened a thin blue line in the eastern sky. It thickened and cracked open, orange then pink. Clouds idled overhead, reminding me of turkey vultures waiting for a meal. I recognized the pattern, the same daily buildup to the storms of the past week. It made me want to hurry. Wind spun down the chute, sending snow ghosts tumbling past.

At the top of the couloir, I passed through a notch in the mountainside. I turned a corner and climbed up the edge of the north face in cold, dark shadow. The rock steepened and the snow turned back to powder. Two feet of loose white covered the stone. I pulled myself from ledge to ledge, digging like a badger for hard edges in the granite below the snow. I was climbing by Braille while wearing mittens. Doubly blind, I couldn't see or feel any of what I was holding on to.

Below me, the mountain fell away. Deep space gathered at my back. The other Sierra peaks dropped lower and lower. Sullen storm light filled the air. I seemed to be right up in the atmosphere, the place where stone met sky. The wind blew past me, scraping over the mountain, scouring itself on the rock, bound for the desert.

Holding on with one hand, I excavated with the other. I shoveled and groped, hunting under the powder cloak for something to wrap a hand around. Knees, elbows, shoulders—I used any kink of my body to stay wedged in the wrinkles of the mountain. Graceful climbing could wait for warm stone and a sunny day. This was a dirty bar fight, not kung fu. Finding nothing, I reached up with my ice axe and scraped it around until the pick hooked the lip of a block—that's what I surmised, anyway, since I couldn't see anything but my axe disappearing into the snow. I gave it a few tugs and then yanked myself higher in a flurry of scraping crampon spikes and knees and liquid powder, ready to do it all over again.

I reached a ledge just below the rim of the mountain. A wave of suddenly perfect snow, like hard Styrofoam, crested fifty feet over my head. I kicked in my front points and swung my axe, loving the solid *thunk* it made. The snow curved above me, steeper as I climbed higher, until I teetered on my front points, feeling gravity try to cartwheel me backward. One more *thunk*, one more kick, then I stabbed the shaft of my axe straight down through the top of the wave, stepped high, and rolled over onto the summit plateau.

Bury a brick in the sand. Pull up a side until one long corner surfaces. Cut slices from the corner until it's a jagged crest of peaks. That's the Sierra, carved into mountains by glaciers and weather. To climb Mount Whitney from the east is to know the tectonic nature of the range. A sheer east face, a sloping west. The whole 400-mile-long block of mountains is just one brick of the earth lifted and tilted.

I walked over to the highest edge of the plateau, the summit, where east and west join. The whitecapped mountain waves of the Sierra lined up north and south. The wind snapped and popped, forcing my back around like a weather vane. Clouds darkened above and below me. Drifting up behind them, the sun produced dangerous-looking reds and pinks and not an ounce of heat. The cold coiled around me like a snake.

No clouds crossed the black picket line of the Inyo Crest. On the desert, it was just another day in the furnace. Yellow heat shimmied up from between dark washboard ridges. I could hear

Summit view, Mount Whitney.

the salt creaking and the rocks moaning. The whole journey un-spooled: the salt, the sand, the snow. Ghosts walked the land, dreamers, schemers, and vagabonds. I saw my own past: a little figure in the distance bobbed up and down the purple-brown hills. And the deeper past: The People migrated with the sea-sons, up to the mountains and down into the mesquites, until the flood tide of whites arrived from the east. And the geologic past: cloudbursts opened canyon gates, mountains edged out of the earth. On top of a mountain, you can truly see. Blinders you didn't even know were there fall away. From Whitney's summit, the tallest for fifteen hundred miles in any direction, I could see everything.

THE FOOL ON THE HILL

Sage, because it covers most of Inyo; sage because it seems to this poor listener that there is a touch of the sage about you, Inyokel. In your apparently aimless knocking on the outcroppings you occasionally hit a paystreak. And to allow for the other and larger part of your nature, add the tumbleweed . . . That's you, Inyokel, sage and tumbleweed.

—John Crowley, August 12, 1934

On top of Mount Whitney, it occurred to me that old Sisyphus hoodwinked his god. Every day for eternity, he pushes his stone up his hill and drops it just when he arrives at the top. Which means that each and every day, his cares trundle away into the flatlands while he sits on the summit and looks around.

I tried to stuff my eyes full of the mountains, the desert, the storm light, the end of the journey. The cold squeezed me tighter. Avalanches ripened in the couloir. Storm clouds circled. I could only stay a few minutes—in fact, the sooner I left, the better. I asked Saint Sisyphus of the Mountaineers for safe passage, then hunched into the wind, ready to roll myself off the mountain.

It felt strange to turn away from the summit after chasing it so long. The first few steps seemed headed in the wrong direction. But then I felt a shove from behind, and all at once, I couldn't wait to be down.

I backed over the edge of the snow wave, feeling awkward as a cat trying to reverse out of a tree, then tiptoed down the nicks I'd left in the snow. I slithered down the grooves of powder and granite, blindly using the holds I'd already excavated, dismantling my ascent one move at a time. I was a loosed stone. My grip on the mountain seemed tenuous, slippery, but I couldn't convince myself to slow down. Too eager to care, I was suddenly sure that the mountain couldn't kill me. Gravity had a rope around my waist, and I picked up speed, climbing fast or falling slowly— sometimes I wasn't sure which.

At the top of the couloir, I put on the brakes. I forced myself to stand sideways and kick methodically down the hard ice. I kicked, kicked, set, waiting an extra half second to be sure my crampons bit and held, exaggerating each move, knowing I was more than a little summit-drunk and sloppy. Downdrafts barreled through the couloir, slinging frozen shot against my back. The rock above had been twice as steep, but the ice felt more dangerous. In the purr of the wind, I heard dark insinuations about falling climbers. If my spikes sheered out, I figured I'd have that same half second to stop myself, one shot at stabbing my axe into the stony snake-hide of the couloir, and if I missed, I'd accelerate into a luge match with the downdrafts. So I kicked and set, kicked and set, trying to hold urgency and carelessness at bay.

At the line between ice and powder snow, I tucked my snowshoes behind my back through the shoulder straps of my summit pack, left my crampons on my feet, and gave gravity back the reins, feeling grateful and free. An avalanche was the only danger left.

The faster I moved the less chance I had of getting caught. I galloped through the deep snow, frozen lips stretched by a happy grin, legs churning under me while little snowslides surfed by. I was already disappearing off the mountain. Whole blocks of my tracks had vanished under the broom of the wind. Where they hadn't, I covered four upward steps with each leap down. I turned the corner out of the bottom of the couloir and the last of my hurry boiled away. I put my snowshoes back on my feet and floated through the powder back to my tent under the mountain and the clouds, with the sun only a quarter of its way across the sky.

I'd been ready to live in the shadow of the mountain for a week waiting out the weather. Now that I'd been to the summit, I didn't know what to do next. I sat on my rock island, melting more pans of snow, staring up at myself across a wink of time and distance. The clouds tightened overhead, squeezing out the blue. The wind fidgeted around the lake, clapping me on the back and making me shiver. Even when the sun found my rock, the light felt cold. Time to go. For every two things I packed away, the wind pilfered another. I wallowed through drifts after stuff sacks and clothes and stove parts, muttering and cursing the air like a lunatic. By the time I'd herded all my runaways, the sun had disappeared above the clouds.

Time stretched. The tides—gravity, oxygen—came round in my favor. Places I'd watched creep by on the approach warped past me in minutes. I thought of birds swooping down off the crest. Just turn around and board the magic slide, easy as that. At the dwarf trees and buried meadows, all the neon mushrooms had been uprooted. I walked the ledge where I'd slept under the icicles—all the icicles had fallen and the creek I'd drunk from had dried up. I slipped through the forest of willow and pine. Before I was ready, I had gray pavement under my boots. The portal was

Mount Whitney under the next wave of storm.

soggy and deserted. A few cars and puddles and a lot of empty asphalt. I parked myself at the downhill end and waited to see who might come by.

I waved at a man and woman who drove past, and ten minutes later, they came back to pick me up. Their consciences had gotten the better of them, but they were noticeably wary—my beard would have suited a Dead Sea fisherman. They said they were painters, so I told them the story of John Muir leading a pair of painters deep into the Tuolumne wilderness to show them mountains unlike anything they'd ever seen. Muir was made particularly happy by one of the men who shouted and carried on like a madman at the sight of Mount Lyell rising out of its canyon. When I finished, the painters in the car seemed more at ease with me. They'd driven 150 miles to watch the clouds, which were indeed weird and beautiful. We stopped at one pullout and got out to gawk at lenticular clouds like UFOs rallying on the peaks. The woman showed me a picture of a cloud she'd taken earlier that morning, a floating hydrocephalic head with a huge brow and thin lips leaning down over Mount Langley. "Like it's going to kiss it," she said gleefully.

The painters dropped me at the side of the road a mile outside Lone Pine. I walked up into the outermost row of the Alabama Hills and had a seat against a rock. My hilltop overlooked Lone Pine and Owens Lake, and over my shoulder, I could look back up at the ruckus in the sky. It was Monday afternoon. The county bus south, my ride home, wouldn't run again until Wednesday.

▲

I spent two days in my holding tank on the hill, feeling hollowed out, as though I'd left bits of myself strung across the desert and had to wait for them to find me. I wondered how long I could stay right there, camped in the Alabamas, before I had my fill of staring at the mountains and sage. I saw half of myself sitting through the months like Inyokel, watching the blooms come up out of the ground and the sun rising over the Inyos and setting behind the Sierra. The other half went with the water to Los Angeles. I knew which half I'd follow, and that was all right. Ashley had a year of work to finish in the city. Afterward, with no strings left to keep us, we'd flee the concrete and exile ourselves away someplace where the population didn't exceed the elevation. Like the water, we'd return to the mountains. When the two of us watched it together, the light on the peaks would be that much sweeter.

Looking south along the aqueduct from my hill, I saw brown desert to the horizon. A vast metropolis rising just over the San Gabriels seemed like a phantasm. In terms of glitz and size, Los Angeles is the thing the desert men wanted and never achieved. All the appetites and fictions they brought to the desert, their craving to erect something huge out of nothing, became reality in the city. It's as if by building the city on the desert's water, Mulholland and the others drank the concentrated essence of all those desert dreams. Mary Austin felt unwell in the city, seeing the ideas of men like her husband made hugely real in asphalt and architecture. Wallace Austin's vague projects had been executed on a scale beyond the limits of his own imagination. "One recoiled from the evidences of planlessness," she wrote of Los Angeles, "the unimaginative economic greed, the idiot excitation of mere bigness."

I clearly wasn't right for civilization. But I had debts to repay my body, so I did go into town. I bought apples and a stack of pancakes that arrived like a cumulus cloud on a plate—a fit subject for the painters. And I found a book of Sherlock Holmes mysteries for a dollar on the surplus shelf at the Lone Pine library. Other than that, I sat on my hill and looked around.

Mountains surrounded me. White snowy mountains, black desert mountains, vapor mountains in the sky. The world's bones and breath. Below me, the fossilized track of the river wriggled through the sage. From my hill, the entire southern half of the Owens Valley was the blind old lake, a gigantic open wound eight miles wide. In Austin's time of ducks and phalaropes, evaporation prisms hovered over the water in morning and evening. She wrote of ladders of light descending from the sun. Paiutes told her that children of the Rainbow traveled back and forth on those paths.

A wind came up like the atmosphere itself had slipped its mooring. I watched rocks get lifted and tossed. Birds emptied out of the sky. There wasn't any shelter on the hilltop, and I didn't really want any. I let the air roar past me till my ears rang. Mile-high plumes of gray alkali dust climbed up off the dry lake bed. They looked mythic and angry and perfect for the modern desert: ancient spirits riding over the land in clouds of arsenic and cadmium. These wind storms are as old as this place—petroglyphs in the Owens Valley show shamans with spirals for heads. Flyers. Whirlwind travelers.

Wednesday morning broke calm and cold, and I woke up antsy. The tumbleweed had found me in the night. The missing fragments of myself I'd left scattered on the desert had finally reassembled. I wasn't ready to tuck my beard in my belt and put roots down with the sage—not yet, anyway. Time to begin again. Time to go find Ashley in our little box by the ocean and plan our next move.

I left Inyokel to sit on his hill in the Alabamas and watch the desert, the big, bare earth and the little human scribbles. Inyokel: sage and tumbleweed, wisdom and wanderlust. Son of the desert, grandson of the mountain. A vagabond prince in rags. And just another fiction, like all the others—only more to my taste. An ideal worth shooting for. I'd be back to talk with him again.

Down in town, with the sun barely peaking over the Inyos, the wind and I prowled around Lone Pine's empty blocks. You can't walk out a door or look out a window here without feeling the pressure of the land. The desert and the mountains squeezed in on the cracked streets, the dusty, sunburnt buildings. It felt as if the desert might just snuff Lone Pine out between its hands.

The sun lifted higher and warmed the day, luring people outside to tend to their affairs. The bus puttered up to its stop, and I got on and took a seat.

ACKNOWLEDGMENTS

I have great affection for big national parks and small libraries. Both are vital acts of preservation—acts generally undertaken by underpaid and under-appreciated librarians, archivists, and park rangers. This book could not exist without the work of the Inyo County Free Library, the Eastern California Museum, and the Death Valley National Park Research and Curatorial Facility.

My thanks go to Lauren Greene Martin for answering my questions about the geology of the Cottonwood Mountains, and to Craig London at the Rock Creek Pack Station for answering my questions about mules. David Whitley helped me to understand and interpret petroglyphs. Any factual errors in those respective sections of the text are, of course, my own.

I feel extremely lucky to be associated with Counterpoint Press. The entire staff—and particularly my editor, Roxanna Aliaga—have my thanks for their thoughtful approach to books and attention to detail. I am likewise lucky to have a close knit, endlessly supportive family made up of readers and writers. My two frontline readers, my wife, Ashley Laird, and my mom, Stephanie Arnold, are insightful and hard to please, qualities with value beyond measure. My wife and son make writing possible and a pleasure.

SOURCES

BACKGROUND

Bowers, Janice Emily, and Brian Wignan (illustrator). *Flowers and Shrubs of the Mojave Desert*. Tucson: Southwest Parks and Monuments Association, 1999.

Digonnet, Michel. *Hiking Death Valley*. Palo Alto: Quality Books, 1999. Indispensable guide to Death Valley with well-researched sections on natural history.

Lingenfelter, Richard E. *Death Valley and the Amargosa*. Berkeley: University of California Press, 1986. Extensive compilation of Death Valley history.

Mann, Bill. *Guide to the Remote and Mysterious Saline Valley*. Barstow, CA: Shortfuse Publishing, 2002.

Whitley, David S. *A Guide to Rock Art Sites, Southern California and Southern Nevada*. Missoula, MT: Mountain Press Publishing, 1996. Excellent field guide with valuable sections on theory and interpretation.

MARY AUSTIN

Austin, Mary. *Earth Horizons*. New York: The Literary Guild, 1932. Autobiography. Austin writes of the satisfaction of stagecoaches in book 3, chapter 4. She is thrown out of the hotel in book 4, chapter 2. The white ladies come and tell her not to bake cakes for Chinamen in book 4, chapter 7. She describes the children of the Rainbow in book 4, chapter 3, and Los Angeles in book 3, chapter 1.

————. *The Land of Little Rain*. Many editions. The Pocket Miner's adventure with the storm and sheep appears in "The Pocket Hunter." Coyote is called "the lean hobo of the hills" in "Water Trails of the Ceriso." Lone Pine's Mexican district has its own chapter: "El Pueblo de las Uvas."

————. *Lost Borders*. Many editions. The miner for whom houses in cities are always "bung up against" his eyes appears in "The Fakir." Austin describes the desert as a woman in "The Land." Feckless men are described as gourds on a string in "The Woman at the Eighteen-Mile."

Goodman, Susan, and Carl Dawson. *Mary Austin and the American West*. Berkeley and Los Angeles: University of California Press, 2008. The story of the wedding gift of a pen is related on page 19.

BEVERIDGE MINING DISTRICT

Swope, Karen K. *With Infinite Toil: Historical Archaeology in the Beveridge Mining District, Inyo County, California*. PhD dissertation. University of California, Riverside, 1993. Exhaustive investigation of the Beveridge Mining District.

BOLTON BROWN

"Notes and Correspondence." *Sierra Club Bulletin* 2 (1897). Features a letter from Brown about the naming of mountains.

NORMAN CLYDE

Clyde, Norman. *Norman Clyde of the Sierra: Rambles through the Range of Light*. San Francisco: Scrimshaw Press, 1971. "Up Mt. Whitney from the North" alludes to following Muir on the Mountaineer's Route.

"Mountaineering Notes." *Sierra Club Bulletin* 16 (1931). Includes Clyde's rediscovery (and naming) of Muir's route up Mount Whitney.

FREDERICK COVILLE

Coville, Frederick. *Botany of the Death Valley Expedition: Contributions from the U.S. National Herbarium, v. 4, U.S. Department of Agriculture, Division of Botany.* Washington, DC: Government Printing Office, 1893.

FRANK CRAMPTON

Crampton, Frank. *Deep Enough.* Norman, OK: University of Oklahoma Press, 1993.

JOHN CROWLEY

Brooks, Joan. *Desert Padre.* Desert Hot Springs, CA: Mesquite Press, 1997. Biography of John Crowley, including transcriptions of many Sage and Tumbleweed articles. Crowley describes his monthly desert route and calls himself an "ecclesiastical tramp" in chapter 2. Inyokel is the feature character of John Crowley's Sage and Tumbleweed articles, printed in the *Central California Register* from 1934 to 1940. The story of going hunting and finding the hawks, leopard, and elephant appeared in the October 7, 1934 issue. The story of the naming of Inyokel appeared August 12, 1934. Both articles are reprinted in *Desert Padre.*

CARL GLASSCOCK

Glasscock, C.B., and Curt Kunze. *The Death Valley Chuck-Walla.* Greenwater, CA, 1907. The promise to call a thief a thief appears in "The Theme of the Chuck-Walla," in vol. 1, no. 3, February 15, 1907.
———. *Here's Death Valley.* New York: Grosset and Dunlap, 1940. Glasscock acknowledges being ashamed of the *Chuck-Walla* in chapter 15, "Greenwater."

HARRY GOWER

Gower, Harry P. *50 Years in Death Valley: Memoirs of a Borax Man.* San Bernardino: The Death Valley '49ers, 1969. Gower criticizes Frank Crampton in chapter 12. He relates the origin of Stovepipe Wells in chapter 26.

ZANE GREY

Grey, Zane. *Tales of Lonely Trails.* New York: Harper & Brothers, 1928.
———. *Wanderer of the Wasteland.* Many editions. Dismukes describes the Imperial Valley in chapter 12; Magdalene looks at Telescope Peak in chapter 17; Adam talks of color in chapter 27.
Gruber, Frank. *Zane Grey: A Biography.* New York: World Publishing Company, 1970. Chapter 23 reproduces Grey's journal entries from the time during which he wrote *Wanderer of the Wasteland.* "Wonderful, beautiful, terrible" is from the entry dated March 1.

GEORGE HANSEN

Boyles, J.C. "He Witnessed the Death Valley Tragedy of '49," *Desert Magazine* 3 (February 1940): 3–6.

FRANK SHORTY HARRIS

Caruthers, William. *Loafing Along Death Valley Trails.* Ontario, CA: Death Valley Publishing, 1951. Caruthers relates his $10 million conversation with Shorty, as well as Shorty's opinion of his Ballarat schoolhouse, in chapter 17, "Shorty Frank Harris."
Coolidge, Dane. *Death Valley Prospectors.* New York: E.P. Dutton & Co., 1937.
Harris, Frank. "Half a Century Chasing Rainbows." *Touring Topics* 22 (October 1930): 12–20 (as told to Philip Johnston). Reprinted in Richard E. Lingenfelter and Richard A. Dwyer, eds., *Death Valley Lore* (Reno: University of Nevada Press, 1988).

CLARENCE KING

King, Clarence. *Mountaineering in the Sierra Nevada.* Many editions. The "Mount Whitney" chapter describes King's 1871 attempt and his appreciation for Lone Pine's adobe district. A postscript to the "Mount Whitney" chapter, included in some editions, describes King's musings in the sagebrush after his successful ascent of Mount Whitney. An excerpt of this postscript is included in chapter 11 of Thurman Wilkins's *Clarence King.*

Wilkins, Thurman. *Clarence King*. Albuquerque: University of New Mexico Press, 1988.

JOHN LᴇMOIGNE

Coolidge, Dane. *Death Valley Prospectors*. New York: E.P. Dutton & Co., 1937.

Crampton, Frank. "Legend of John Lamoigne." Pamphlet. In *Deep Enough* (Norman: University of Oklahoma Press, 1993). The pamphlet was originally published by Sage Books, Denver, in 1956.

WILLIAM LEWIS MANLY

Johnson, Leroy, and Jean Johnson, eds. *Escape from Death Valley: As Told by William Lewis Manly and Other '49ers*. Reno and Las Vegas: University of Nevada Press, 1987.

Manly, William. *Death Valley in '49*. Many editions available, but the best is edited by Leroy and Jean Johnson (Berkeley: Heyday Books, 2001). Manly builds his boat and leaves home in chapter 5, "Rather Catch Chipmunks in the Rocky Mountains than Live in Michigan." Manly imagines food on his father's table in chapter 9, "Off in Fine Style." He calls his mother the "best woman," Sarah Bennett calls him and Rogers "good boys," and Death Valley is named in chapter 10, "A Long, Narrow Valley."

CHARLES MANSON

Bugliosi, Vincent. *Helter Skelter*. New York: W.W. Norton, 1974.

Murphy, Bob. *Desert Shadows*. Morongo Valley, CA: Sagebrush Press, 1993.

JOHN MUIR

Mount Whitney Club Journal 1, 1902, includes a letter from John Muir to George Stewart, in which Muir writes that he never left his name "on any mountain, rock, or tree."

Muir, John. *The Mountains of California*. Many editions. Muir describes snow banners in chapter 3, "The Snow."

———. "A Rival of the Yosemite." *Century Magazine*, November 1891. Muir tells succulent people to go the mule way in this article.

Wolfe, Linnie Mae. *John of the Mountains*. Madison: University of Wisconsin Press, 1979. Wolfe transcribes excerpts of Muir's unpublished journals, including the one he kept for October 1873 describing his first ascent of Mount Whitney.

WILLIAM MULHOLLAND

Kahrl, William. *Water and Power*. Berkeley: University of California Press, 1983. Mulholland tells his friend not to go to Inyo County on page 70. Both *Water and Power* and Catherine Mulholland's *William Mulholland and the Rise of Los Angeles* describe (with decidedly different sympathies) the practice of "shooting the duck," as well as the insurrection at the Alabama Gates.

Mulholland, Catherine. *William Mulholland and the Rise of Los Angeles*. Berkeley: University of California Press, 2002. Biography of Mulholland. The *"el agua es la sangre de la tierra"* anecdote appears on page 221. Mulholland is called the "prime minister" of the water department on page 121 and the "biggest man" in Los Angeles on page 205. The story of him walking across Panama appears on page 12. Mulholland says: "There it is. Take it," on page 246. He predicts that the aqueduct will be one of the great engineering feats of history on page 118. Mulholland and Eaton's whisky drinking appears on page 348, note 13. Roosevelt gives priority to Los Angeles over the Owens Valley in a letter to the secretary of the interior, quoted on page 133.

SAM NEWLAND

DeDecker, Mary. "Owens Valley, Then and Now." In *Mountains to Desert: Selected Inyo Readings*. Independence, CA: Friends of the Eastern California Museum, 1988. Description of ecological change in the Owens Valley.

McGrath, Roger D. "No Goodee Cowman." In *Mountains to Desert: Selected Inyo Readings*. Independence, CA: Friends of the Eastern California Museum, 1988. Story of the conflict between Paiutes and ranchers in the Owens Valley.

Steward, Julian. "Irrigation Without Agriculture." *Papers of the Michigan Academy of Science, Arts and Letters* 12 (1929). Story of Paiute irrigation practices in the Owens Valley.

———. "Two Paiute Autobiographies." *University of California Publications in American Archaeology and Ethnology* 33, no. 5 (1934): 423–438. Spoken autobiography of Sam Newland.

EDNA BRUSH PERKINS

Perkins, Edna Brush. *The White Heart of Mojave*. Baltimore: Johns Hopkins University Press, 2001. Perkins outlines the human role in the natural universe in chapter 7, "The Burning Sands." She realizes that she hadn't really seen the outdoors before in chapter 12, "The End of the Adventure." She is tongue-tied in chapter 6, "The Strangest Farm in the World." She describes Joshua trees in chapter 2, "How We Found Mojave."

WHITE SMITH

DeDecker, Mary. *White Smith's Fabulous Salt Tram*. Morongo Valley, CA: Sagebrush Press, 1993.

JULIAN STEWARD

Kerns, Virginia. *Journeys West*. Lincoln: University of Nebraska Press, 2010. An account of Julian and Jane Steward's ethnographic expedition of 1935–1936. Jane Steward calls their desert time "Eden" at the end of the introduction, and calls Patsy Wilson's stories "really amusing" in chapter 3, "Valley of the Paiutes."

———. *Scenes from the High Desert*. Chicago: University of Illinois Press, 2003. Excellent Julian Steward biography, with careful attention to Steward's development as a theoretician. The details of Steward's childhood and move to California come from the "West to Deep Springs" chapter. Steward decides to "go into work in exploration" on page 67.

Steward, Julian. *Basin-Plateau Aboriginal Sociopolitical Groups*. Many editions. *Ko'o* is described under the *Saline Valley* heading of the *Western independent Shoshoni villages* section.

MOUNT WHITNEY

Farquhar, Francis. *The History of the Sierra Nevada*. Many editions. The "Mount Whitney" chapter is a fine summary of the climbing history of the mountain.

PATSY WILSON

Steward, Julian. *Some Western Shoshoni Myths*. Many editions. All of the Saline Valley myths in this collection are told by Patsy Wilson.